Of Bison and Man

Of Bison and Man

*From the annals of a bison yesterday
to a refreshing outcome from human involvement with
America's most valiant of beasts*

Harold P. Danz

UNIVERSITY PRESS OF COLORADO

Published by the University Press of Colorado
P.O. Box 849
Niwot, Colorado 80544
(303) 530-5337

The University Press of Colorado is a cooperative publishing enterprise supported, in part, by Adams State College, Colorado State University, Fort Lewis College, Mesa State College, Metropolitan State College of Denver, University of Colorado, University of Northern Colorado, University of Southern Colorado, and Western State College of Colorado.

The paper used in this publication meets the minimum requirements of the American National Standard for Information Sciences—Permanence of Paper for Printed Library Materials. ANSI Z39.48-1984.

Library of Congress Cataloging-in-Publication Data

Danz, Harold P.
    Of bison and man: from the annals of a bison yesterday to a refreshing outcome from human involvement with America's most valiant of beasts / Harold P. Danz.
      p.   cm.
    Includes bibliographical references (p.) and index.
    ISBN 0-87081-454-0 (casebound: alk. paper)
    1. American bison. 2. Wildlife conservation — United States. I. Title.
QL737.U53D35 1997
333.95'9643'0973 — dc21   97-15918
                                       CIP

10   9   8   7   6   5   4   3   2   1

To My Wife, Geri

Contents

Preface

Oh give me a home where the buffalo roam,
Where the deer and the antelope play.
Where seldom is heard a discouraging word
And the skies are not cloudy all day.

"Home on the Range"
From a poem written by Dr. Brewster Higley (1873),
and a folk song as written by John Lomax (1908)

Possibly the most popular American folk song of all time, "Home on the Range," has been acclaimed by a number of individuals as the cowboy national anthem, and we understand that it was also a personal favorite of former United States President Franklin Delano Roosevelt. The American West has changed somewhat since Dr. Higley crafted his wistful poem about an unsullied and uncomplicated way of life; skies are cloudy just about as often as they are sunny, buffalo have precious little opportunity to roam, and we certainly seem to hear more than our fair share of discouraging words.

This book is about buffalo, or more properly the American bison, which roamed the grasslands and prairies of the North American continent until approximately 1890, and now occupy a few limited acres of commercial pastures and public parklands. Although perhaps once considered a pariah by the United States government, no other North American mammal, or bird, has yet demonstrated that it has the ability, or capacity, to arouse the extraordinary level of public interest, support, and affection from an international community than has the American bison. In 1782, Congress made the bald eagle the United States national emblem because most people thought it was proud, strong, and free. Benjamin Franklin was displeased with this particular choice, noting that no bird with the habits of the eagle should represent the United States. It is unfortunate that Congress did not give greater consideration in its selection to the well-known attributes of the bison: strength, courage, and determination.

The American bison is a large animal, nearly twice the size of any other wild land mammal currently indigenous to North America. A bison will reach full growth maturity when it is about nine years old, at which time the male of the species will usually weigh somewhere between 1,500 and 2,100 pounds, and the female only approximately half as much. In the wild, adult bison could, and did, hold their own with nearly all predators, unless man created an artificial condition or personally intervened to stack the odds against them. Because the bison is a wild animal, and therefore more irascible than domestic cattle, it has not been fully accepted as yet by cattle ranchers and breeders as a viable substitute for their domestic cattle. The bison, however, does not require anywhere near the care, maintenance, and medical attention required by most, if not all, cattle breeds.

There are now more bison in the United States than there have been for more than twelve decades. The American plains bison is no longer endangered or even threatened as a specie at this time. However, there is a renewed popularity and interest in bison meat and bison by-products, and with this increasing demand we need to continue to focus our attention on what is still but a fragile supply of what was once an almost diminished resource. The Great American Bison is an irreplaceable national resource, a fundamental ingredient of American folklore and legend, cherished unlike any other animal or bird. However, the bison should not be placed on a preservative pedestal; or worse, revered in a fashion similar to the Hindu cow. To preserve bison as a specie, *the best thing we can do is eat them.* Animals that people eat and nurture do not become extinct. That's why we have so many more chickens than bald eagles in North America.

HPD
Lakewood, Colorado
August 15, 1995

Prologue

It was late September, and a bitter wind rushed through the grassy plains of Beringia. Without trees or even large shrubs to break the tedium of the landscape, the large herbivores grazing on the harsh steppe grasses stood in dark relief against a light grey sky. Mammoth, horse, and bison in abundance shared this expansive pasture along with an elite cadre of meat hunters, including dire wolves, lion, sabertooth cat, and short faced bear.

A sudden change of wind caused the large bull bison to stop his constant, but somewhat aimless, feeding and inspect the rolling hills to the west. His eyes were perhaps the weakest of his senses, and although he could not distinguish any perceived danger, the unknown scent left him somewhat apprehensive. He stood for a few moments listening for the betraying sounds of a familiar predator, but shortly resumed grazing. He was in his prime, heavy with fat after consuming summer grasses, and fully seven feet high at the shoulders. His horns were impressive even in comparison to other bull bison, extending to nearly four feet between horn tips. Few predators, even the lion, would seriously consider attacking a beast of his size without help.

The wind again carried the same strange scent to his nostrils and some nearby horses snorted their consternation, disturbing a solitary mammoth who promptly left at a brisk walk to rejoin others in his herd. The bison's ears detected the sounds of rapid movements that were unlike anything he had heard previously. His eyes detected a series of small shapes approaching in a slow but determined fashion. He now was able to savor the full scent of the approaching creatures but he could not associate it with any known predator. The horses began to drift away in obvious concern about the approach of these new beasts. The bison resumed grazing but kept a wary eye on the strangers. The creatures moved on only two legs, were basically hairless, but exuded a confidence and assurance that seemingly surpassed even that of a resolute pack of dire wolves.

The bison sensed that he was surrounded, his tail arched, and he began to defecate. The intruders moved in closer, his tail rose to a vertical position, and he slowly began walking toward the nearest of the group. Suddenly he felt pain as these creatures began to jab his body with pointed spears. He became overcome with rage and his strength and fury were such that some of his tormentors attempted to flee. His horns caught one of the creatures and with singular dispatch easily killed it. The bison gave no thought to flight, and he continued to pursue his attack on this new, but rather elusive and stubborn enemy. Again and again he charged, and occasionally he was successful in reaching his quarry, but eventually the sheer number of attackers and his loss of blood weakened him and he could no longer stand. He fell to the ground, and after his death his flesh and hide were claimed by the strangers.

Of Bison and Man

1

Introduction

The American bison, although commonly referred to as buffalo, occupies a special place in American history and in the hearts of the American people. No other animal has been so closely associated with the western plains, prairies, and wilderness empire as the bison, and this magnificent beast is still one of the most well liked and respected of all North American wild animals.

Although primarily thought of as an animal of the Great Plains, the range of the historical bison had extended into Canada, Mexico, Alaska, and nearly every state in the contiguous United States, with the possible exception of the extreme New England states and California. Bison numbers were once countless, possibly exceeding sixty million. Travelling in enormous herds, bison were the principal herbivore ingredient of a wildlife display that was more numerous and perhaps even more spectacular than that to be found on the fabled Serengeti plains of Africa.

Prior to the arrival of the white man on the North American continent, more than fifty families of American Indians, comprising one or more tribes or confederations of tribes, occupied the land. These tribes subsisted through a near constant process of hunting, fishing, and gathering and raising of crops. However, for the tribes that lived on the Great Plains of America, the availability of bison was the dominant concern. From the bison came almost everything that was essential for their way of life: meat, clothing, housing, and even certain religious beliefs and convictions. In the pursuit of western expansion and the establishment of resultant land conversion policies, the nomadic practices of the Indian and the bison quickly became unacceptable. The Indians were eventually banished to reservations and the unprotected bison were virtually exterminated by a remorseless cadre of meat and hide hunters. By 1887, it was estimated that there were fewer than 600 bison remaining in the United States.

This is a book about the American bison: its arrival in North America, its evolution, its demise, and its eventual recovery. In the course of natural as well as manufactured events, conditions and circumstances can change; and for the bison it has been a change for the better. Long considered by many to be perhaps an endangered or threatened species (although never officially declared as such), the bison is now the catalyst for a whole new industry. Previous literature on the American bison has concentrated on what once was; the purpose of my writing this book is to portray not only what once was, but what is now and what can yet be. In the ensuing chapters I have described the path followed by bison and their pursuers, the Paleoindians, to the North American continent, and how the paths of the Indian and the bison were still seemingly joined toward what could have been their potential oblivion as a result of western expansion of the United States. The near annihilation of the vast bison herds is a well-known but still pathetic aspect of the bison story, but what has not been described previously, with sufficient emphasis, is the possible existence of an unofficial policy to remove the bison in order to more thoroughly subrogate the Indian.

The resurgence of the bison as a species is a tribute not only to the remarkable physiology of the bison, but also to that special group of bison conservationists and entrepreneurs who were responsible for preserving the remnants of the once vast herds that covered the western plains. Building from this modest collection of animals that were contained in the foundation herds, a new generation of Americans has begun the task of restoring the bison to its former position of prominence. This book recounts the efforts of individuals who were involved in those very crucial early preservation activities and the subsequent surge of public and private sector interest and support that has led to the establishment of viable bison herds in all fifty of the United States.

2

In the Beginning

When we were all a lot younger, and still busily experiencing the unabashed wonder and thrill of life that is characteristic of youth, we perhaps rarely heard anyone use the word "bison," unless we had a relative who happened to be a zoologist. But we all were quite familiar with the American buffalo and the American Indian. Our history teachers used textbooks in their classes that usually conveyed the image of a splendidly productive United States that responsibly evolved from a somewhat crude frontier beginning featuring raw land, Indians, and wild animals.

From these three exquisite and irreplaceable natural resources, the first to face assault from profiteers and speculators was America's raw public land. From the original 1.8 billion acres of public domain land that became available between 1781 and 1966, 813 million acres eventually ended up in private hands, and 228 million acres were granted to various states for a myriad of governmental purposes (Clawson 1971, 14). In addition to those who were simply barefaced speculators, legislators and the general public all connived to secure for themselves whatever advantage they could from governmental land disposals. Even members of Congress, such as Daniel Webster and Thomas H. Benson, were not reluctant to sponsor legislation that would further enhance the value of public lands that they had previously acquired, nor at that time did anyone perceive that these actions could represent a conflict of interest. Public land and the future of the Indian had also become inevitably intertwined as Indian land had politically become part of the total redistribution process. An example of this is the comments of Henry Stuart Foote, who was a noted attorney and a U.S. senator from the state of Mississippi; Senator Foote was quoted as follows in the *Congressional Globe* of March 3, 1849, regarding public land and Indians:

> What two things can be mentioned more closely connected than our Indian policy and the policy of the public lands? We claim the fee simple title to all the lands on the continent possessed by the various Indian tribes; we only recognize them as having a usufructuary interest, and some immense span of territory is every year or two falling into our hands by some treaty effected with them. Children of the forest, which speedily become subject to all our general regulations for the disposition of the public domain.

The original meaning of the word "reservation" was that certain lands of the public domain were to be set aside, or reserved, for Indian tribes to reside on in presumed perpetuity. However, as soon as all other free public lands were distributed, the Indian lands were subsequently coveted. Under duress and pressure, between 1853 and 1857 (the peak period of acquisitions), 174 million acres of Indian lands were either sold or redistributed. Without sufficient land to accommodate their culture and lifestyle, reservations became little more than Indian concentration camps.

Whereas United States public land and Indian policies of the 1800s often reflected an insensitive and occasionally unscrupulous approach to the resources they addressed, at least there were a General Land Office (1812–1946) and a Bureau of Indian Affairs (1824–1849 in the War Department and after 1849 in the Department of Interior) to administer and moderate these resource dissipations. However, there was no governmental agency or effective advocate for the wild animal population. The American bison, which formerly served as the staff of life for the Plains Indian, was not generally considered to be a public asset, but rather an impedance to the subjugation of the Indian and continued western development. Only when the slaughter process reached the point of near extermination for the bison was protective legislation considered by Congress. Between 1871 and 1876, bill after bill was introduced and argued. In 1874, a bill to protect the buffalo (bison) was passed by the House, reported to the Senate, passed the Senate and went to President Grant for signature, and expired with the adjournment of Congress. In 1876, another bison protective bill passed the House, was reported to the Senate, and subsequently referred to the Committee of Territories. The bill was never returned.

Without protection, the bison herds were subject to continual harassment and devastation. There were no hunting regulations to abide by, no penalty for taking just the hide of the bison or its tongue, or for simply shooting the animal and then leaving it. By 1900 there was no reason to believe that, outside of the less than fifty that were sheltered within Yellowstone National Park, a single wild bison remained in the United States from the former gigantic herds that had earlier totalled over 60 million animals. Private sector bison owners and zoological gardens provided sanctuary for all of the other remaining bison in the United States, estimated at that time to be not more than 350 animals. Unable to adequately protect the bison when remnants of a vast northern herd still flourished (Hornaday 1889, 519), the United States government eventually commemorated the bison by issuing over 1.1 billion Indian head or buffalo type nickels between 1913 and 1938, and the Department of the Interior adopted the image of the bison on its Interior seal in 1917. (An eagle was the first Interior insignia in 1849, and the eagle was again chosen in 1923 to replace the bison. In 1929, the bison returned only to be replaced in 1968 by an abstraction that purportedly symbolized the sun, mountains, and waters. The bison image was returned to the Interior seal and flag in 1969.)

After the massive slaughter of the bison herds was over, the bison was more with us in spirit than in body. The American people rarely saw one of the captive beasts, and most were convinced that the animal had become extinct. Most people were not too troubled by this. After all, didn't we have a treasured five cent piece bearing the bison's likeness that could be used to purchase a bottle of soda or other such necessities? Outside of that "buffalo" nickel, very few of us were lucky enough to have seen a real live bison, but we all may have vicariously dreamed of a bygone time when the plains were covered with these magnificent beasts and adventure could just be right outside our door. Because a few thoughtful individuals took control of what was a most regrettable situation, we still have the buffalo, or more properly, bison, with us, but it is unlikely that the nickel will ever again buy what it once did.

The bison is not a buffalo. There has never been a "buffalo" in America. While scientists have given a name to and categorized nearly everything, they have not elected to include that humpbacked mammal that populated most of North America in the same genus with buffalo because (1) it is anatomically different from that of the true buffalo, and (2) the buffalo is indigenous only to Africa and Asia. The buffalo and bison are both in the same family, Bovidae (which they do have in common); each, however, has a different genus and species label. There has been any number of explanations offered over the years as to how these particular animals came to be called "buffalo," but only one salient observation can be made after all word discovery processes have been exhausted: the assigned common name, "buffalo," is obviously a derivative from other assigned names given by early discoverers of this yet unnamed and unknown (by Europeans) beast. The terms *cibola, bisonte,* and *armenta* were used as descriptive names for the bison by the early Spaniards, along with the English translations of kine, Mexican bull, and oxe or oxen. It was not until later that some of the more depictive names such as *bufs, buffes, boeuf, bufflo, buffelo, buffilo, buffles,* and *buffaloe* came to be used. These were depictive terms in the sense that *bufle* and *buffe* were actually words in common usage that applied equally to any animal thought to provide good buffe (hide) for buff leather.

Although most bison historians and breeders were, and are, aware that the proper name is bison and not buffalo, many still stubbornly persist in using the name "buffalo" for the extant species — but they find no difficulty in referring to its ancestors as bison. Although a not necessarily persuasive, but clearly a poignant, reason given in support of this practice was espoused by Colonel Richard Irving Dodge in 1877 (Dodge 1959, 119):

> I suppose I ought to call this animal the "bison;" but, though naturalists may insist that "bison" is his true name, I, as a plainsman, also insist that his name is buffalo.
>
> As buffalo he is known everywhere, not only on the plains but throughout the sporting world; as buffalo "he lives and moves and has being;" as buffalo he will die; and when, as must soon happen, his race has vanished from earth, as buffalo he will live in tradition and story.

Most scientific authorities recognize the existence of two extant species of bison, *Bison bison* and *Bison bonasus*. *Bison bison* is the American species of bison and *Bison bonasus* is the European. Within species, circumstances and conditions occasionally provide for the evolution of these organisms to the degree that some groups eventually possess certain continuing distinctive characteristics. These characteristics, or features, are visible, structural, and thus set this subspecies apart from others within the species. However, in order for subspecies to develop, the area occupied must have geographical boundaries that inhibit or prevent a generalized species breeding process. For the bison, geographical conditions as well as other circumstances related to habitat led to the evolution of two subspecies for both *Bison bison* and *Bison bonasus.*

Our plains animal, the American bison, is genus *Bison*, species *bison*, subspecies *bison.* We should also note, at this time, that *Bison bison bison* is not a threatened or endangered species. A threatened species is designated as such if its population is on the decline and there is ample evidence that it may become endangered. An endangered species is one where the numbers and conditions of existence are such that extinction is a distinct possibility. The second identified subspecies of *B. bison* is the woodland variety or wood bison *(Bison bison athabascae).* The wood bison tends to be a little taller and longer-legged than the plains bison. Its coat is much darker and its head is carried lower. The wood bison has a more angular than rounded hump, the highest point tending to be farther forward, the back slopes less, and the horns are more prominent above the hair cover on the skull. Because of its limited numbers, the wood bison is counted among the threatened species.

During historic times there were also two subspecies of bison that existed on the European continent, *Bison bonasus bonasus* and *Bison bonasus caucasicus.* *B. b. bonasus*, or wisent, was found in forests of central Europe, and *B. b. caucasicus* on the highland steppes of the Caucasus border region between the Black and Caspian Seas. Although there are now a modest number of living specimens of *B. b. bonasus* it is still listed as a threatened species. Interbreeding with *B. b. bonasus,* hybridized *B. b. caucasicus* and its existence as a subspecies are no longer recognized. The wisent is a more svelte version of the bison, its hair shorter but basically more curly, with a less pronounced hump, a longer tail, and heavier hindquarters. The wisent's horns are longer, more curved, and not as thick at the base as those of the plains bison. Its beard is rather short, and its head and forequarters are less impressive in size when compared to either *B. b. bison* or *B. b. athabascae.*

Over the years the relationship between bison and man has been dynamic. In prehistoric America the bison had evolved from a belligerent brute estimated to be at least ten or eleven feet high (Allen 1876, 10), to

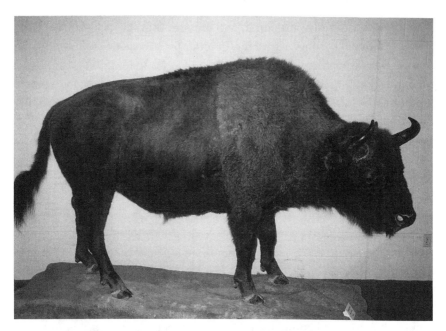

Wisent specimen, as mounted and displayed at the International Wildlife Museum, Tucson, Arizona.

that of an animal slightly more than half its previous size but with far greater agility. Although the larger bison were more capable of defending themselves against the four-footed predators who followed them to North America, they found that their strength and bulk were largely ineffective against the Paleoindian immigrants. Much as they do today, animal predators studied herd animals carefully, and would first cull from the herds the easy targets, that is, the sick or injured, the very young or the very old; and thus, in this manner, indirectly strengthening the species. Human predators, however, did not necessarily seek out the infirm, and with their continually improving hunting techniques would quickly dispatch all animals that were otherwise unable to escape. By the time that the bison were all but exterminated, it was claimed (Grinnell 1892, 282) that another evolutionary bison prototype had appeared: a bison with longer legs and a lighter body, formed for running. It is also possible that, through the near-domestication process associated with human ownership of bison, an entirely new strain of bison will eventually be developed, a bison that is more docile and has more meat on its hindquarters.

From the standpoint of the bison, this dynamic relationship has not proven to be a favorable one. Humans, however, have definitely benefitted. The western expansion of the United States would have been a more difficult experience for pioneers and settlers without the abundant bison herds that emigrants could depend upon for food on their trek westward. For many North American Indians, the bison represented much more than just meat; bison were clothing, housing, tools and utensils, weapons, and a way of life. The Indians of the Plains tribes held the bison in esteem above all other animals. In mythology and legend the bison (buffalo) was spoken of with great reverence and was endowed with great wisdom and understanding, even with an ability to assume human form. An old Cheyenne legend, as told to Alice Marriott and Carol Rachlin by Mary Little Bear Inkanish in 1960 (1968, 21–26), describes how the world was made. This myth tells us that in the beginning there was nothing, and Maheo, the All Spirit, created the waters, the land, the peoples, and the animals to feed and care for the people. It was then that Maheo called upon his awesome power, and created one animal that could take the place of all of the others put together, and he made the buffalo. Other similar Indian legends identify the consistent belief that bison were created primarily for the comfort of people.

Bison have existed on this planet, in one transitory form or another, for over two million years. Exclusive of any "near" human life-forms, anthropologists conclude that the zoological subfamily Hominidae, which includes fossil and modern human life-forms, may have been around for about half that time. Based upon fossil collections, *Homo sapiens* specimens began to appear approximately 300,000 years ago, with the rugged Neanderthal type developing not more than 125,000 years ago and anatomically modern humans only about 30,000 years ago. It is this latter form of human life that is the catalyst exacting the greater tribute from other mammalian species, and, in addition, has effected evolutionary and environmental changes upon a total earthly ecosystem.

Through the more than four billion years of earth history, there have been at least three major "ice ages" to consider as well as a continuing geological phenomenon associated with plate tectonics, more commonly referred to as "continental drift." All of these events provide a basis and reason for the existence of fossil similarities on different continents as well as expanding the potential for movement of mammals between continents now separated by oceans and seas. The Pleistocene Epoch, or most recent ice age, was not a time of constant glaciation, but was represented by a series of advances (glacials) and retreats (interglacials). It was during the glacial periods that ice sheets absorbed much of the earth's water, oceans receded, continents expanded, and a land connection, which was up to one thousand miles in width, existed between Siberia and Alaska. This land bridge, and the lands immediately to the east and west of it, scientists have named *Beringia*.

In order for Beringia to attract from Asia the large resident herds of herbivores that it did, ordinary tundra vegetation, as existing today, would not have been adequate to provide a continuing and sufficient nutritional diet as needed for such large mammals as bison, wooly mammoth, American mastodon, camel, musk ox, and horse. Thus, scientists believe that a long and coarse grass covered much of Beringia's plains. The climate was predominately cool and dry, without extensive winter snow cover, and all of this would have been thoroughly to the liking of the aforementioned mammals during the Pleistocene Epoch.

The extant mammal that many people now routinely refer to (albeit incorrectly) as "buffalo," the North American bison, is the descendant of a species of bison that first appeared in fossil records during the late Pliocene geological epoch (perhaps two million years ago) in Asia. During the middle Pleistocene, which began about 1.5 million years ago and ended about 10,000 years ago, bison were, at times, indigenous to many areas within the European continent and throughout northern Asia. Herds of bison found their way into Beringia, and when conditions permitted, they achieved access to the North American continent. Migrations were influenced by both the glacial and interglacial periods. When the glaciations were in effect, the land connection from Asia into eastern Beringia was open, but passage to the interior of the North American continent was blocked by massive ice flows. During interglacial periods the land connection was submerged but the ice flows blocking eastern Beringia from inner continental North America were gone.

It is believed that *Bison priscus,* or the steppe bison, was the first bison species to occupy Beringia and eventually cross into Alaska. It is further thought that these early bison travelers eventually evolved into three other distinct bison species, *B. latifrons, B. antiquus,* and *B. occidentalis*, who had by now extended the range of the bison into the middle and lower portions of North America. *Latifrons* was the largest of all bison species, perhaps twice the size of our current-day largest bison, with inwardly curving horns that may have measured more than eleven feet between horn tips. It is believed that *latifrons* became extinct sometime during the mid- to early Wisconsin glaciation period, or approximately 20,000 to 28,000 years ago. *Antiquus* was much smaller than *latifrons*, and was, in all probability, the most widely distributed of all known bison species; paleontological specimens have been found in a variety of locations from Alaska to Central America. When *antiquus* actually became extinct is not quite clear, but it is presumed that sometime during the late Wisconsin glacial period or early Holocene, because of environmental and other factors, the *antiquus* population evolved into two subspecies, *B. a. antiquus* and *B. a. occidentalis,* and eventually was fused into just one species, *B. a. occidentalis*, from which the smaller plains bison *(B. bison bison)* and wood bison *(B. bison athabascae)* descended.

Based upon past results of paleontological and archaeological discovery, bison were common, at one time or another, to much of the North American continent. Considering these historical dispersal patterns and the suggested length of North American bison habitat (>160,000 BP), the potential undeniably existed for bison to demonstrate certain minor evolutionary adaptations within their different climatic and geographic domains. Accordingly, it is not unexpected that hairsplitting over zoological classification has occurred, and this has resulted in the purported identification of other bison species and/or subspecies. The scientific community, however, has not generally sanctioned these variations as being new species or subspecies. Thus, only the two North American subspecies, *Bison bison bison* and *Bison bison athabascae,* and the European species, *Bison bonasus,* are universally accepted.

During their time on this planet, bison have faced and overcome numerous adversaries: massive ice sheets, powerful and tenacious predators, fire, flood, drought, and competition from other herbivores. For unknown reasons, disease seemingly has never been an issue or impediment to their existence. Many of the diseases that bison now experience were previously endemic to other Bovidae and acquired only after domestic cattle spread throughout the North American continent. An excellent example of this is brucellosis or Bang's Disease, caused by the bacteria *Brucella abortus*. This disease is distinguished by the female aborting her fetus in approximately the fifth month of her pregnancy (the gestation period for bison is about 275 days). Although bison are seemingly quite susceptible, they can, and often do, build resistance to this illness and seldom abort twice from it. Bison herds in Yellowstone National Park are known to have experienced brucellosis as early as 1917, and even though Yellowstone bison do not receive vaccination, herd size or general health of the park bison has not been adversely affected.

The large bison herds that had formerly populated the Great Plains of America were predominately the plains bison (*B. b. bison*). The bison and its remarkable road to recovery are what this book is all about. However, the other two extant bison subspecies, the wood bison and the European bison or wisent, have not seemingly fared as well — but then they were never as populous as the plains bison.

The wood bison (*B. b. athabascae*) is believed by a number of scientists and historians to have prehistorically ranged from northern Alaska to as far south as Texas and even northeastern Mexico, and easterly to Pennsylvania and North Carolina. Then, in more recent times, they occupied a geographical domain that encompassed the Colorado, Idaho, Montana, and Wyoming segments of the Rocky Mountains as well as western Canada. Currently wood bison are only found in Canada. In identifying subspecies of the bison there is understandably some confusion that will arise unless there are some rather distinct differences that can be readily observed. Meagher (*The Bison of Yellowstone National Park*, 1973, 1) suggests that the bison that originally inhabited Yellowstone and surrounding country were the "mountain or wood bison (*Bison bison athabascae* Rhoads)," although early explorers and writers have suggested the existence of three different variations: a plains bison, a wood bison, and a mountain bison. The mountain bison was said to be smaller than the wood bison (Roe 1972, 35) and practically the same size as the plains bison, but more vicious and of a wilder nature (Garretson 1938, 5). Allowing that possible local environmental conditions may have influenced size and behavior, the existence of other distinctively different subspecies, such as a mountain bison or a Pennsylvania wood bison (*Bison americanus pennsylvanicus* as suggested by Henry W. Shoemaker, 1919, 65), has not been totally received or accepted, suggesting that perhaps these animals were ecotypes or ecospecies rather than a valid taxon.

The wood bison was designated as an endangered subspecies by the United States Fish and Wildlife Service and the Committee on the Status of Endangered Wildlife in Canada (COSEWIC) in 1978, and downlisted to threatened in 1988. The population of the wood bison as of April 1991 was projected to be 2,897 (Gates, Chowns, and Reynolds 1992, 151).

The years have also not been kind to the European bison (*B. bonasus*) or wisent. The European bison were originally animals of the open forest, able to survive on leaves, grass, twigs, and even bark. Traveling in small family groups rather than the large herds common to the plains, they were well adapted to their environment; when threatened they would retreat further into the forests. Never found in the numbers of the American bison, their demise was primarily due to a loss of habitat. A few *B. bonasus* can still be found in a few protected areas in a wild state, but the captive animals (currently estimated to total about fifteen hundred) may still be enough to ensure the continued existence of this threatened subspecies.

George Orwell's comment in *Animal Farm* that "all animals are equal, but some animals are more equal than others" could arguably apply to the bison. Of all wild animals in North America none has had a more profound impact upon the peoples of the continent than the bison. Assuredly the bear, the coyote, the wolf, and the deer contribute much to the life and excitement of wilderness or untamed land, but the bison does not slink into shadows and darkness; the bison courageously occupies the land! The timeless connection between man and bison was driven by the need of man for the bison. It satisfied needs for food, clothing, and shelter for the Paleoindian as well as those later human societies that occupied the Great Plains. The bison was respected and even revered by these societies and the vast herds continued to prosper. With the introduction into North America from Europe of a dominant culture exhibiting differing needs, the values associated with native cultures, including those relating to the bison, were diminished. Exercising uniform contempt for both land resources and the wildlife thereon, the invading white man nearly eliminated a species from the plains that had formerly been the sustenance of many preceding human cultures.

3

How Many Bison
Were There?

Eminent zoologist Dr. William T. Hornaday once observed: "It would have been as easy to count or to estimate the leaves in a forest as to calculate the number of buffaloes living at any given time during the history of the species, previous to 1870" (1889, 387). The Great Plains and grasslands of the North American continent formed an absolutely ideal environment and habitat for the bison. A gregarious animal, it was accustomed to roaming in vast herds throughout its domain. Prior to the coming of the white man, its only impediments to continued herd growth were the unforgiving vagaries of nature and a limited number of predators, including the American Indian.

It would be futile to even speculate who may have been the first white man to see the American bison; some people have suggested that it may have been the explorer Hernando Cortez and/or members of his party who perhaps viewed bison in the zoological collection of the Aztec emperor Montezuma in 1519. Others submit that since most of the earlier explorers to the North American continent landed at, or visited, areas where bison only infrequently or never habituated, it is possible that Francisco Coronado and his army, who explored the lands that now form the southwestern states of the United States, were the first white men to see a wild bison. Whatever the case may be, the first sight of a wild bison and the immense herds that were commonly found over four hundred years ago in America stirred the excitement of early chroniclers who took the time to comment on the appearance, behavior, and seeming unlimited numbers of these strange

beasts. The following observation was provided by a member of
Coronado's army in 1541:

> These Oxen are of the bignesse of our Bulls, but their hornes lesse,
> with a great bunch on their foreshoulders, and more haire on their
> fore-parts than behind, which is like wool; a mane like a horses on
> their back-bone, and long hair from the Knees downward, with store
> of long haire at the chinne and throat, a long flocke also at the end
> of the males tailes. The Horses fled from them, of which they slue
> some, being enraged. . . . (Purchas his Pilgrimes, XVIII. 64-5;
> "Anonymous Document," Traslado de las Nuevas in *Journey of
> Coronado,* ed. Winship, 194; "Relacion del Suceso." Quotation
> used as found in *The North American Buffalo,* F. G. Roe,1972, 210–
> 211)

As more European explorers and missionaries found their way into
America's heartland they were uniformly astonished by the numbers of
bison that they saw:

> . . . The country was one robe . . . The plains were black and appeared
> as if in motion . . . (Observations from early journals reported on by
> Joel A. Allen. *The American Bisons, Living and Extinct.* Memoirs
> of the Geological Survey of Kentucky. 1876)

> Buffalo are exceedingly numerous — from the summit of a hill
> which afforded an extensive prospect, we observed the face of the
> Country entirely covered by them, in short they are numerous as the
> locusts of Egypt . . . (Duncan McGillivray. *The Journal of Duncan
> McGillivray,* ed. A. S. Morton. Toronto, 1929. An account of
> experiences with the North West Company, Fort George, North
> Saskatchewan River, 1794–1795. Quotation used as found in *The
> North American Buffalo,* F. G. Roe, 136–137. 1972)

A variety of eyewitness accounts attempted to describe herds of
bison the numbers of which were almost inconceivable to the viewers:

> twenty miles in width and sixty miles in length . . . (William D.
> Street, "The Victory of the Plow," Kansas Historical Collections,
> No. IX, 42–44, 1905–1906)

The whole plain, as far as the eye could discern, was covered by one enormous mass of buffalo. (John K. Townsend, Journey Across the Rocky Mountains to the Columbia River. Vol 21, 161, *Townsend's Narrative 1833–1834*, R. G. Twaites, 1966)

. . . was about five days passing a given point, or not less than fifty miles deep . . . This whole vast space was covered with buffalo. (Col. Richard Irving Dodge in letter to W. T. Hornaday dated September 21, 1887, as reprinted by Hornaday in *The Extermination of the American Bison,* 1887, 390)

The panorama of plains animals perhaps seemed even more spectacular to western explorers and pioneers since, in numbers and variety, it differed so dramatically from wildlife conditions that existed in the more easterly environs of what is now the contiguous United States. The original range of bison reached to most eastern and southeastern locations, but this was only in limited numbers. By the time that President Thomas Jefferson completed the Louisiana Purchase in 1803, only isolated herds existed. In order to obtain reliable information about the acquired Louisiana lands, Lt. Zebulon Montgomery Pike led two expeditions into this still largely unknown and unexplored addition to the United States. During the years of 1805 to 1807, his travels took him from St. Louis, Missouri, to Minnesota and, later, to Colorado and the Spanish border areas. Living off the land, his journals almost exclusively mention their acquiring for provisions deer (venison), pigeons, elk, and other lesser species of wildlife while along the Mississippi, and only when the expedition turns westward into Kansas does bison seemingly become a major food source. It was not until November 6, 1806, when Pike's expedition was following the Arkansas River and approaching what is now the Kansas-Colorado border, that Pike felt compelled to include something in his journal about the impressive size of the bison herds that they had been seeing (1966, 161):

Marched early, but was detained two or three hours by the cows, which we killed. The cow buffalo, was equal to any meat I ever saw, and we feasted sumptuously on the choice morsels. I will not attempt to describe the droves of animals we now saw on our route; suffice it to say, that the face of the prairie was covered by them, on each side of the river; their numbers exceeded imagination.

Historical Range of North American Bison

John Dunn Hunter, who claimed to have been a captive of a number of Indian tribes for more than ten years, reported, after his release in 1816, that he had once accompanied his captors on a hunting trip into what is now Kansas, and upon entering the hunting grounds of the Osages he found (1973, 22): "The buffalo herds were here more numerous than I had ever before witnessed." Some years later, after personally viewing scenes of natural devastation and oppressive hunting that affected large numbers of bison, Hunter was of the belief (1973, 138) that: "notwithstanding the great extent of this sweeping destruction, there is no apparent diminution of their number, the increase being, at least, equal to the waste. Such are the opinions of the old Indians, who have had good opportunities to judge, and such, I have no doubt, is the fact, from the existence of so many circumstances favorable to their propagation."

Merrill J. Mattes, former historian for the National Park Service, in completing research for *The Great Platte River Road*, provides the source for a number of similar such observations (1969, 254–255):

We saw them in frightful droves, as far as the eye could reach, appearing at a distance as if the ground itself was moving like the sea. Such large armies of them have no fear of man. They will travel over him and make nothing of him. (John Wyeth, 1832)

Buffalo abounds along the Platte River in such vast numbers, that it is impossible for mortal man to number them. . . . Sometimes we would see the Plain black with them for ten miles in width . . . [north side]. (John Pulsipher, 1848)

The buffalo resemble forests of cedar, and present a low, black, and undefined appearance, but occasionally shifting to and fro like the dark shadows of a cloud. . . . the road appeared like a wellstocked cattle yard, covered with manure. (J. McBride, 1850)

Buffalo extended the whole length of our afternoon's travel, not in hundreds but in solid phalanx . . . thick as sheep in a pasture. . . . I estimated two million . . . [north side]. (William Kilgore, 1850)

I am perfectly safe in saying I have seen in one herd many millions. . . . When the buffalo stampede, it is like the continuous roll of distant thunder. (Henry Davis, 1850)

"Buffalo on the March: A Drawing from Eye-Witness Accounts." A drawing by M. S. Garretson, last president of the American Bison Society. A spectacular but totally exaggerated representation of how the vast herds of bison in 1860 travelled and filled the landscape. Courtesy Denver Public Library, Western History Department.

As we were entering the buffalo country every one was on the alert to catch a view of that celebrated animal. . . . finally the huge animals, in very deed, burst upon our vision. Since then we have seen thousands upon thousands. . . . They first appeared in small scattered squads and gave the impression of cattle grazing in their pastures. (Mrs. Ferris, 1852)

We saw one black, living, moving mass spread out far and wide over the bottom. Yes, all the buffalo from the four quarters of the globe seem to be congregated there. (Charles Teeter, 1862)

The whole country . . . presented a mass of buffaloes on a stampede, coming towards us. . . . It was estimated that this army of buffaloes was at least two hours in passing. . . . (Samuel Hancock, 1845)

Estimates offered of the numbers of bison that were contained in these extremely large herds ranged from 125,000 to over a million animals. It was totally inconceivable to those who had viewed these herds prior to

1880 that bison did not truly represent a virtual inexhaustible supply of animals.

These remarkable and massive herds constituted the bulk of the population of American bison and they were primarily located in the Great Plains area of the United States. With their nucleus situated in what was the approximate center of the country, bison were beginning to spread to both the Atlantic and Pacific Oceans when the Europeans began to settle within the eastern coastal areas. The actual climax range for the bison is still a matter of some dispute; however, it is generally accepted that herds of *B. b. bison* and *B. b. athabascae,* at their maximum range, extended north into Canada as far as the Great Slave Lake, southward to mid-Mexico, perhaps to the Tropic of Cancer, east over the Allegheny Mountains and approaching the eastern seaboard and into Florida, and west to the Sierra Nevada and Cascade Mountains. Since bison tend to move as the whim may suit them, or as feeding and climatic conditions suggest, their presence in any given location on a continual basis could not be certain. Because of their nomadic habits and patterns of movement, bison may not have been in residence on a year-round, or even a yearly, basis in all areas of the suggested maximum range.

During most months of the year bison travelled in small groups, but because of the large number of such groups or "clans," it sometimes appeared as if there were just one large group or herd. During other times of the year, groupings of cows or cows, calves, and yearlings could be found, with solitary bulls and groupings of bulls moving within a somewhat loose herd structure. During the rut period, larger herds became common along with an increased herd activity. Although it had been earlier believed that bison were animals subject to extensive periods and distances of migration, it is now generally accepted that migrations were seasonal reactions to grass and weather conditions and the distances of movement was probably limited, that is, more often less than four hundred miles.

How many bison were there? This provocative question has become a matter simply of pure conjecture. Understandably, those who based their estimate on only the numbers of bison that they may have personally seen would be offering nothing more than their restricted opinion — which is basically all that they were qualified to offer at that moment. In addition, the point in time that the estimate was delivered would also have considerable bearing upon the total number. Bison were never very populous east of the Mississippi River, and by the early 1830s none were left. Most scientists agree that the peak number must have occurred prior to the bison being driven westward and/or eliminated from its eastern range, which would mean that the maximum herd size would probably have occurred earlier than A.D. 1700.

The most often quoted figure is sixty million, an amount that is close to the seventy-five million estimated by naturalist Ernest Thompson Seton (1927, 655) and the estimates of several other knowledgeable individuals. Since no effort was deemed necessary or warranted to conduct a scientific survey or census of bison when the great herds roamed the prairies and plains, there really isn't any reasonably accurate way to construct what the total may have been at this earlier time. Biologist Tom McHugh, however, did attempt to undertake this task in *The Time of the Buffalo* (1972, 16–17). McHugh was of the belief that the earlier figures were somewhat excessive, and using the principle of grazing capacity and magnitude of grass and woodlands used by bison, he estimated that there were perhaps not more than thirty million bison that could have been supported by the available range. His calculations were based on the grazing of cattle "since the two species are roughly the same size and can be expected to exert about the same amount of grazing pressure." Dan Flores (1991, 470–471), working with a 1910 agricultural census and considering cattle-equivalent grazers, suggested that the Great Plains could have only supported twenty-eight to thirty million bison, even allowing for bison use of native grasses. These comparability claims, I believe, are subject to some question as bison will eat and obtain nourishment from much vegetation that cattle will normally overlook, and, as further advanced by Tom Deliberto's Utah State University report (Ph.D. dissertation), *Comparative Digestive Physiology of American Bison and Hereford Cattle*, bison are more efficient in processing low-protein, poor-quality forage than are cattle.

Speculation as to the probable number of bison during the zenith period for the former seemingly measureless herds, without having greater points of reference than we now have in our possession, presents a perplexing problem and virtually unsolvable question. Even if we would consider how our American countryside would appear if all fenced cattle were permitted to run free, it seems rather doubtful that we would be that much impressed by the extent of this singular mammalian display even though there are now over 102 million cattle in the United States. Although we have no exact number to recite with respect to bison at their maximum, we do know that the plains bison was found in such abundance that the sheer numbers of animals contained in the former large herds were, more often than not, found to be beyond the comprehension of the always fascinated, but basically unsophisticated, bison observers of days that have long since passed.

Early Spanish explorers of the North American continent had fundamentally limited their geographical investigations to the southern and warmer environs. These were areas that were not known to be particularly favorable for, or had ever been heavily populated with, our extant species of bison. That these explorers had encountered bison is a matter of historical fact as abundant evidence has been left through the writings of members of the Alvar Nuñez Cabeza de Vaca, Francisco Vasquez Coronado, and Hernando Cortez expeditions. Unfortunately, however, the chronicles of these early writers only gave but token mention of the existence of vast herds of these animals, and left no lasting impression as to what were the possible number of bison that may have occupied the southern plains of the United States.

The journals and writings of Sieur Robert (René) Cavelier de La Salle, Jacques Marquette, and Louis Hennepin, for example, offered only narrow accounts of bison and other wildlife that they encountered, but these writers did devote considerable depth to relationships and confrontations with Indian tribes. Another complication surrounding use of these journals is the continuing controversy as to exact source of authorship.

The first effort of de La Salle to explore the "Ohio" seemingly ended in disarray in 1669, and his second and extensive effort (1679–1687), following Louis Jolliet and Father Jacques Marquette's exploration of the Mississippi River, yielded but very little in the way of personal wildlife observations. The presumed writings of Father Louis Hennepin, who accompanied de La Salle in 1679 and, after becoming a captive of Indians in 1680, explored much of the future state of Minnesota, however, did provide a little more documented information regarding the bison. In December 1679, near the present city of South Bend, Indiana, Father Hennepin first took note of the presence of large numbers of bison and recorded the following: "We found there a number of buffalo horns and the carcasses of those animals, and some canoes that the Indians had made, of buffalo skins to cross the river with their load of meat." Hennepin then went on to describe in great detail how the Miami tribe hunted the bison and the uses and purposes that the Indian made from the bison. Because of the historical and depictive values that were expressed in Hennepin's observation regarding bison, the following quotation, although lengthy, is provided (Hennepin 1880, 143–149):

> These animals are ordinarily in great numbers there, as it is easy to judge by the bones, the horns and skulls that we saw on all sides. The Miamis hunt them at the end of autumn in the following manner:
>
> When they see a herd, they gather in great numbers, and set fire to the grass every where around these animals, except some passage which they leave on purpose, and where they take post with their bows and arrows. The buffalo, seeking to escape the fire, are thus compelled to pass near these Indians, who sometimes kill as many as a hundred and twenty in a day, all which they distribute according to the wants of the families; and these Indians all triumphant over the massacre of so many animals, come to notify their women, who at once proceed to bring in the meat. Some of them at times take on their backs three hundred pounds weight, and also throw their children on top of their load which does not seem to burden them more than a soldier's sword at his side.
>
> These cattle have very fine wool instead of hair, and the females have it longer than the males. Their horns are almost all black, much thicker than those of cattle in Europe, but not quite so long. Their head is of monstrous size; the neck is very short, but very thick, and sometimes six hands broad. They have a hump or slight elevation between the two shoulders. Their legs are very thick and short, covered with a very long wool. On the head and between the horns they have long black hair which falls over their eyes and gives them a fearful look. The meat of these animals is very succulent. They are very fat in autumn, because all the summer they are up to their necks in the grass. These vast countries are so full of prairies, that it seems this is the element and the country of the buffalo. There are at near intervals some woods where these animals retire to ruminate, and to get out of the heat of the sun.
>
> These wild cattle or bulls change country according to the season and the diversity of climate. When they approach the northern lands and begin to feel the beginning of winter, they pass to the southern

lands. They follow one another on the way sometimes for a league. They all lie down in the same place, and their restingground is often full of wild purslain, which we have sometimes eaten. The paths by which they have passed are beaten like our great roads in Europe, and no grass grows there. They cross rivers and streams. The wild cows go to the islands to prevent the wolves from eating their calves; and even when the calves can run, the wolves would not venture to approach them as the cows would exterminate them. The Indians have this forecast not to drive these animals entirely from their countries, to pursue only those who are wounded by arrows, and the others that escape, they suffer to go at liberty without pursuing them further, in order not to alarm them too much. And although these Indians of these vast continents are naturally given to destroy the animals, they have never been able to exterminate these wild cattle, for however much they hunt them these beasts multiply so that they return in still greater numbers the following year.

The Indian women spin on the distaff the wool of these cattle, out of which they make bags to carry the meat, boucanned and sometimes dried in the sun, which these women keep frequently for three or four months of the year, and although they have no salt, they dry it so well that the meat undergoes no corruption, four months after they have thus dressed this meat, one would say on eating it that the animals had just been killed, and we drank the broth with them instead of water which is the ordinary drink of all the nations of America, who have no intercourse with Europeans.

The ordinary skins of these wild cattle weigh from one hundred to a hundred and twenty pounds. The Indians cut off the back and the neck part which is the thickest part of the skin, and they take only the thinnest part of the belly, which they dress very neatly with the brains of all kinds of animals, by means of which they render it as supple as our chamois skins dressed with oil. They paint it with different colors, trim it with white and red porcupine quills, and make robes of it to parade in their feasts. In winter they use them to cover themselves especially at night. Their robes which are full of curly wool have a very pleasing appearance.

When the Indians have killed any cows, the little calves follow the hunters, and go lick their hands or fingers, these Indians sometimes take them to their children and after they have played with them, they knock them on the head to eat them. They preserve the hoofs of all these little animals, dry them and fasten them to rods, and in their dances they shake and rattle them, according to the various postures and motions of the singers and dancers. This machine somewhat resembles a tambour.

These little animals might easily be domesticated and used to plough the land.

These wild cattle subsist in all seasons of the year. When they are surprised by winter and cannot reach in time the southern land and the warm country, and the ground is all covered with snow, they have the tact to turn up and throw aside the snow, to crop the grass hidden beneath. They are heard lowing, but not as commonly as in Europe.

These wild cattle are much larger in body than ours in Europe especially in the forepart. This great bulk however does not prevent their moving very fast, so that there are very few Indians who can run them down. These bulls often kill those who have wounded them. In the season you see herds of two and even four hundred.

For business reasons, de La Salle was obliged to return to Fort Frontenac (located at the eastern tip of Lake Ontario), but not until he had instructed Hennepin to follow the Illinois River to the Mississippi, and then go upstream on the Mississippi. Reluctantly following de La Salle's instructions, Hennepin left in either late February or early March of 1680. His journals mentioned meeting a variety of Indian tribes, observing moderate numbers of bison, and learning of the immense plains to the west and northwest "abounding in buffalo and peltries, where they [tribes] are obliged to make fires with buffalo dung, for want of wood" (Hennepin 1880, 236–237). Hennepin and his small party were later made prisoners in February 1680 by a large band of Sioux, and it was nearly six months later before he was released through the intercession of Sieur de Luth (Duluth).

Henri Joutel, through his journals, offers his version of de La Salle's final excursion to find the mouth of the Mississippi; in these journals he refers to the surrounding country as having many resources: "These Bullocks are very like ours, there are thousands of them, but instead of Hair, they have a very long curl'd Sort of Wool" (Joutel 1966, 55). In February of 1686, in describing this area of Texas along the Gulf near the current town of Port Lavaca, Joutel notes: "We were in about the 27th Degree of North Latitude, two Leagues up the Country, near the Bay of St. Lewis

[Matagorda Bay] and the Bank of the River *aux Baufs,* on a little Hillock, whence we discover'd vast and beautiful Plains, extending very far to the Westward, all level and full of Greens, which afford Pasture to an infinite Number of Beeves and other Creatures." Throughout the remainder of his journals, Joutel instilled the impression that bison were rather common and inland they could be found in great numbers along the Gulf from Texas to Louisiana.

The notes of Louis Jolliet and Father Jacques Marquette, taken during their five-month expedition to explore the Mississippi River, also had some controversial aspects. Leaving in May 1673 from St. Ignace, this expedition followed the Fox and Wisconsin Rivers to where the Wisconsin joins the Mississippi near the current city of Prairie du Chien, Wisconsin. Jolliet and Marquette explored south along the Mississippi until the Mississippi was joined by the Arkansas. Not wishing to risk arrest for trespass into Spanish territory, they returned to St. Ignace by an alternate route, which is presumed to include the Illinois River. Using their notes and personal recollections, Marquette's Jesuit superior, Claude Dablon, obtained a copy of the journal, apparently edited it, and this edited work was later inserted in *Recueil de voyages* in 1681 and, accordingly, was then read by the general public for the first time. Dablon did frequently refer to the wildlife that Marquette and Jolliet observed on their southward journey upon the Mississippi, including reference to several large herds of "oxen." On their return trip, Dablon recorded that Jolliet was quite impressed with the Illinois River valley, and that "oxen, cows, stags, does and turkeys are found there in greater number than elsewhere," but no further comments were offered regarding the extent of bison herds or the number of animals.

The journal, published as *Voyages of Marquette in the Jesuit Relations* (Marquette 1966), contained one particular entry that I consider to be quite interesting and therefore have quoted in full:

> We call them "wild cattle," because they are very similar to our domestic cattle. They are not longer, but are nearly as large again, and more Corpulent. When our people killed one, three persons had much difficulty in moving it. The head is very large; The forehead is flat, and a foot and a half Wide between the Horns, which are exactly like Those of our oxen, but black and much larger. Under the Neck They have a Sort of large dewlap, which hangs down; and on the back is a rather high hump. The whole of the head, the Neck,

and a portion of the Shoulders, are Covered with a thick Mane Like That of horses; It forms a crest a foot long, which makes them hideous, and falling over their eyes, Prevents them from seeing what is before Them. The remainder of the Body is covered with a heavy coat of curly hair, almost Like That of our sheep, but much stronger and Thicker. It falls off in Summer, and the skin becomes soft As Velvet. At that season, the savages Use the hides for making Robes, which they paint in various Colors. The flesh and the fat of the pisikious are Excellent, and constitute the best dish at feasts. Moreover, they are very fierce; and not a year passes without their killing some savages. When attacked, they catch a man on their Horns, if they can, toss Him in the air, and then throw him on the ground, after which they trample him under foot, and kill him. If a person fire at Them from a distance, with either a bow or a gun, he must, immediately after the Shot, throw himself down and hide in the grass; For if they perceive Him who has fired, they Run at him, and attack him. As their legs are thick and rather Short, they do not run very fast, As a rule, except when angry. They are scattered about the prairie in herds; I have seen one of 400.

The journals of Meriwether Lewis and William Clark were not necessarily meticulously pedantic in nature, but they were thorough and did go into considerable depth over a number of minor events that transpired during their 1804–1806 expedition. These daily notes of Lewis and Clark, as well as others of their party, were placed in the hands of Nicholas Biddle who transcribed the journal. Both Lewis and Clark made numerous spelling errors that Biddle later corrected. Among the instructions and objectives for the expedition, as given to Captain Lewis by President Jefferson, was the guidance to observe "the animals of the country generally, and especially those not known in the United States [that area designated in 1804 as the United States]."

Departing from the eastern side of the Mississippi near St. Louis on May 14, 1804, the expedition set sail up the Missouri, and the first mention of bison occurred over three weeks later when they were southwest of the current city of Columbia, Missouri; it was stated that they "had seen some indication of buffalo" on June 7. However, since this was thus far basically a voyage upon the Missouri River, it could have been entirely possible that there were bison in the vicinity but not necessarily along the river. The expedition continued their voyage up the Missouri and on October 27, 1804, Lewis and Clark decided to winter in a Mandan village, which would have been near the current town of Stanton, North Dakota.

The journals, covering the time of their departure until the winter encampment, made but limited reference to the sighting of bison, but several entries suggest the possibility of a wide distribution and that there may have been a number of rather large herds that had been observed:

> June 28 — This nation [Kansas Indians] is now hunting in the plains for the buffalo which our hunters have seen for the first time.

> September 8 — we here saw herds of buffalo, and some elk, deer, turkies, beaver, a squirrel, and a prairie dog [along the Nebraska/ South Dakota border near the present town of Greenwood, South, Dakota].

> September 9 — In the plains, to the south, are great numbers of buffalo in herds of nearly five hundred; all the copses of timber appear to contain elk or deer.

> September 10 — The elk and buffalo are in great abundance, but the deer have become scarce.

> September 15 — The timber consisted chiefly of elm; they saw pine burrs, and sticks of birch were seen floating down the river; they had also met with goats, such as we have heretofore seen; great quantities of buffalo, near to which were wolves, some deer, and villages of barking-squirrels [a description of the country surrounding the confluence of the White and Missouri Rivers near the current city of Chamberlain, South Dakota].

> September 17 — all around the country had been recently burnt, and a young green grass about four inches high covered the ground, which was enlivened by herds of antelopes and buffalo; the last of which were in such multitudes, that we cannot exaggerate in saying that at a single glance we saw three thousand of them before us.

> September 20 — Great numbers of buffalo, elk, and goats are wandering over these plains, accompanied by grouse and larks

[within the bend of the Missouri between Chamberlain and Pierre, South Dakota].

October 17 — We also saw buffalo, elk and deer, and a number of snakes; a beaver house too was seen, and we caught a whip-poor-will of a small and uncommon kind [approximately thirty-five miles south of Bismarck, North Dakota].

October 18 — we also saw a herd of buffalo and of elk.

October 19 — In walking along the shore we counted fifty-two herds of buffalo, and three of elk, at a single view.

October 21 — It is situated on the north at the foot of a hill in a beautiful and extensive plain, which is now covered with herds of buffalo [referring to the ruin of a Mandan village that was probably located near the current city of Mandan, North Dakota].

The Lewis and Clark expedition departed on April 7, 1805, from the winter encampment. The winter journals made only brief mention of bison, and this was primarily limited to a few comments from time to time regarding the hunting of animals in the vicinity of their winter camp. Continuing their westward journey, the journals continued to note the numbers of bison observed:

April 21 — We saw immense quantities of buffalo, elk, deer, antelopes, geese, and some swans and ducks, out of which we procured three deer, four buffalo calves, which last are equal in flavour to the most delicious veal [near the mouth of the White Earth River, about forty miles east of the current city of Williston, North Dakota].

April 22 — There are large herds of deer, elk, buffalo, and antelopes in view of us: the buffalo are not so shy as the rest, for they suffer us to approach within one hundred yards before they run, and then stop and resume their pasture at a very short distance.

April 26 — On leaving us yesterday [Captain Lewis] he pursued his route along the foot of the hills, which he ascended at a distance of eight miles; from these the wide plains watered by the Missouri and the Yellowstone spread themselves before the eye, occasionally varied with the wood of the banks, enlivened by the irregular windings of the two rivers, and animated by vast herds of buffalo, deer, elk, and antelope.

April 29 — We are surrounded with deer, elk, buffalo, antelopes, and their companions the wolves, who have become more numerous and make great ravages among them.

May 8 — As usual we are surrounded by buffalo, elk, common and blacktailed deer, beaver, antelopes and wolves [near the current Peck Dam, Montana].

May 9 — The game is now in great quantities, particularly the elk and buffalo, which last is so gentle that the men are obliged to drive them out of the way with sticks and stones.

May 17 — The game is in great quantities, but the buffalo are not as numerous as they were some days ago [within the current Devil's Creek Recreation Area].

June 3 — While they were gone [two reconnoitering groups] we ascended together the high grounds in the fork of these two rivers, whence we had a very extensive prospect of the surrounding country: on every side it was spread into one vast plain covered with verdure, in which innumerable herds of buffalo were roaming, attended by their enemies the wolves [near the current town of Loma, Montana].

June 12 — Here they saw great numbers of the burrowing squirrel, also some wolves, antelopes, mule-deer, and vast herds of buffalo.

June 13 — At the extremity of this course they overlooked a most beautiful plain, where were infinitely more buffalo than we had ever before seen at a single view [near the present city of Great Falls, Montana].

June 14 — [Captain Lewis undertakes a personal examination of the area near the Great Falls of the Missouri] Captain Lewis then descended the hill, and directed his course toward the river falling in from the west. He soon met a herd of at least a thousand buffalo, and being desirous of providing supper shot one of them.

June 17 — There are vast quantities of buffalo feeding on the plains or watering in the river, which is also strewed with the floating carcasses and limbs of these animals. They go in large herds to water about the falls, and as all the passages to the river near that place are narrow and steep, the foremost are pressed into the river by the impatience of those behind. In this way we have seen ten or a dozen disappear over the falls in a few minutes. They afford excellent food for the wolves, bears, and birds of prey.

June 22 — We saw in the plains vast quantities of buffalo, a number of small birds, and the large brown curlew, which is now sitting, and lays its eggs, which are of a pale blue with black specks, on the ground without any nest.

Upon following the course of the Missouri southward, the Lewis and Clark expedition reached the three-fork area, the confluence of the Jefferson, Madison, and Gallatin (source of the Missouri River), on July 25, 1805. With the exception of earlier reporting of large herds of bison grazing on the plains immediately south of the Great Falls area, no other reports of bison sightings were recorded. After ascending the Jefferson, the expedition crossed the Continental Divide and reached the Columbia River where they wintered on the Netul River near the mouth of the Columbia. The journals carefully gave note to all manner of quadrupeds encountered, and bison were not mentioned. The expedition began their return to St. Louis on March 23, 1806, and when they reached the summit of the Bitter Root Mountains in Montana on July 3, the expedition split up and Captain Lewis, along with nine men, pursued a direct route to the falls of the Missouri. Captain Clark, and the rest of the expedition, followed a more southerly course toward the head of the Jefferson River. Throughout this return trip, the Lewis and Clark journals frequently cited the expedition's lack of quality meat, and the resultant dependence on dog and horsemeat. It was not until July 7, 1806, when Lewis's group crossed the Divide and were near the current city of Missoula, that they "saw some signs and tracks of buffalo, from which it seems those animals do sometimes penetrate to a short distance within the mountains."

While Meriwether Lewis's group was in the vicinity of Great Falls on their return trip, the Lewis journals once again give mention to the numbers of bison in the surrounding area:

> July 10 — We saw vast numbers of buffalo below us, which kept up a dreadful bellowing during the night.

> July 11 — They had seen elk [hunters sent out by Lewis]; but in this neighbourhood the buffalo are in such numbers, that on a moderate computation, there could not have been fewer than ten thousand within a circuit of two miles. At this season, they are bellowing in every direction, so as to form an almost continued roar, which at first alarmed our horses, who being from the west of the mountains, are unused to the noise and appearance of these animals.

Moving up the Missouri, the Lewis group explored the Maria River upstream, and then returned to the Missouri where they note on July 29: "The buffalo continue to be very numerous, but the elk are few." They later observed large herds of bison at the confluence of the Milk River and the Missouri and yet still further east where the Little Dry joins the Missouri.

Captain Clark and his party followed the Bitter Root and the Big Horn Rivers until the Big Horn joined the Jefferson. They followed the Jefferson until it reached the Missouri, and then went up the Gallatin, crossing over by land to the Yellowstone and northeast to the Missouri where they rejoined Captain Lewis and his group on August 12, 1806. It was apparently not until July 20, approximately three weeks before they rejoined with Lewis, that the Clark group encountered bison. An entry was made to this effect when they were camped on the Yellowstone, about thirty miles southwest of the junction of the Bighorn and Yellowstone Rivers: "The rest of the party were occupied in dressing skins for clothes, or in hunting, in which they were so fortunate as to procure a deer, two buffalo, and an elk." Immense herds of bison were recorded while they were travelling along the Yellowstone, and at one campsite it was recorded that "during the whole night the buffalo were prowling about the camp, and excited much alarm, lest in crossing the river they should tread on the boats and split them to pieces."

Once again a united expedition, Lewis and Clark continued to descend the Missouri, and on August 20 passed the present town of Cannonball, North Dakota; the journal commented: "We have seen great numbers of wolves to-day, and some buffalo and elk, though these are by no means so abundant as on the Yellowstone." Continuing their journey, they reached the junction of the Cheyenne and Missouri Rivers on August 25, and after making camp on August 27 (probably near the present city of Fort Pierre, South Dakota), the following was recorded: "But after a hunt of three hours, they reported that no game was to be found in the bottoms, the grass having been laid flat by the immense number of buffaloes which had recently passed over it; and that they saw only a few buffalo bulls, which they did not kill as they were quite unfit for use." Two days later, August 29, the expedition reached the White River and it was then noted: "The day was spent in hunting along the river, so that we did not advance more than twenty miles, but with all our efforts we were unable to kill either a mule-deer or an antelope, though we procured the common deer, a porcupine, and some buffalo. These last animals are so numerous that from an eminence we discovered more than we had ever seen before, at one time; and if it be not impossible to calculate the moving multitude, which darkened the whole plains, we are convinced that twenty thousand would be no exaggeration number." The journals did not make further mention of any other encounters with bison. Lewis and Clark returned to St. Louis on September 23, 1806.

John Bradbury, a botanist who travelled extensively throughout the plains in the years 1809–1811, often commented, in his memoirs of that journey, about the high quality of the prairie grasses that he had seen and the numbers of bison occupying the lands. On June 8, 1811, Bradbury, along with fellow botanist Thomas Nuttall and a group of hunters from Manuel Lisa's fur company, was near the junction of the Cheyenne and Missouri Rivers in central South Dakota. For many days he and his companions had seen a great number of bison herds "consisting of from fifty to a hundred in each." According to Bradbury (1966, 106), the hunters were not astonished at the number of bison and recalled seeing such large herds that "they were able to distinguish where the herds were beyond the bounds of the visible horizon, by the vapor which arose from their bodies."

They also claimed to have seen herds "extending many miles in length." By June 22, 1811, they had reached the junction of the Heart and Missouri Rivers in south-central North Dakota. Bradbury, who was completely taken by the quality and extent of the grasses of the American prairies, observed (1966, 135) that: "the whole of the plain was perfectly level, and, like the rest of the country, without a single shrub. It was covered with the finest verdure and in every part herds of buffaloe were feeding. I counted seventeen herds, but the aggregate number of the animals it was difficult even to guess at; some thought upwards of 10,000."

Although Bradbury and Nuttall were primarily interested in collecting and examining plants, many of Bradbury's journal comments, especially those covering bison sightings and herd activities, yielded some rather fascinating insights as to what these immense herds were like and how they may have appeared to western travelers. One particularly informative observation was that recorded by Bradbury in late May 1810, while he was travelling south on the Missouri River near the South Dakota–Nebraska border. From their riverboat, those onboard could hear the sounds of what seemed to be the bellowing of bison. After landing and securing the boat, most of the party elected to follow the bellowing sounds. Skirting some shrubs and trees, they then came upon an extensive plain. Bradbury describes what they saw in the following manner (1966, 182):

> On gaining a view of it, such a scene opened as will fall to the lot of few travellers to witness. This plain was literally covered with buffaloes as far as we could see, and we soon discovered that it consisted in part of females. The males were fighting in every direction, with a fury which I have never seen paralleled, each having singled out his antagonist. We judged that the number must have amounted to some thousands, and that there were many hundreds of these battles going on at the same time, some not eighty yards from us. It will be recollected that at this season the females would naturally admit the society of the males. From attentively observing some of the combats nearest to us, I am persuaded that our domestic bull would almost invariably be worsted in a contest with this animal, as he is inferior to him both in strength and ferocity. A shot was fired amongst them, which they seemed not to notice. Mr. Brackenridge joined me in preventing a volley being fired, as it would have been useless, and therefore wanton; for if we had

killed one, I am certain the weight of his carcass in gold would not
have bribed us to fetch him.

Another very helpful observation was by Colonel Richard Irving
Dodge. Dodge's comment appeared in *The Hunting Grounds of the Great
West: A Description of the Great American Desert* (Chatto and Windus,
London, 1877), and also in a later publication (*The Plains of the Great West
and Their Inhabitants*, 1959, 120–121).

In May 1871 I drove in a light waggon from Old Fort Zara [northeast
of Larned and near the present city of Great Bend, Kansas] to Fort
Larned, on the Arkansas, thirty-four miles. At least twenty-five
miles of this distance was through one immense herd, composed of
countless smaller herds, of buffalo then on their journey north. The
road ran along the broad level "bottom," or valley, of the river.
    Some few miles from Zara a low line of hills rise from the plain
on the right, gradually increasing in height, and approaching the
road and river, until they culminate in Pawnee Rock, when they
again recede.
    The whole country appeared one mass of buffalo, moving slowly
to the northward; and it was only when actually among them that it
could be ascertained that the apparently solid mass was an
agglomeration on innumerable small herds, of from fifty to two
hundred animals, separated from the surrounding herds by greater
or less space, but still separated. The herds in the valley sullenly got
out of my way, and, turning, stared stupidly at me, sometimes at
only a few yards distance. When I had reached a point where the
hills were no longer more than a mile from the road, the buffalo on
the hills, seeing an unusual object in their rear, turned, stared an
instant, then started at full speed directly toward me, stampeding
and bringing with them the numberless herds through which they
passed, and pouring down upon me all the herds, no longer
separated, but one immense compact mass of plunging animals, mad
with fright, and as irresistible as an avalanche. The situation was by
no means pleasant. Reining up my horse (which was fortunately a
quiet old beast that had been in at the death of many a buffalo, so
that their wildest, maddest rush only caused him to cock his ears in
wonder at their unnecessary excitement), I waited until the front of
the mass was within fifty yards, when a few well-directed shots from

my rifle split the herd, and sent it poring off in two streams, to my
right and left.

In reading the foregoing, William T. Hornaday was so taken by Col.
Dodge's report of his encounter with this large herd that he wrote to Dodge
and asked him for an estimate upon which a calculation of the number of
bison in that great herd could be based. Col. Dodge wrote back to Hornaday
on September 21, 1887, and provided the following information:

> The great herd on the Arkansas through which I passed could not
> have averaged, *at rest*, over fifteen or twenty individuals to the acre,
> but was, from my own observation, not less than 25 miles wide, and
> from reports of hunters and others it was about five days in passing
> a given point, or not less than 50 miles deep. From the top of Pawnee
> Rock I could see from 6 to 10 miles in almost every direction. This
> whole space was covered with buffalo, looking at a distance like one
> compact mass, the visual angle not permitting the ground to be seen.
> I have seen such a sight a number of times, but never on so large a
> scale.

Dodge had arrived on the plains in 1849 and spent the next thirty
years on a variety of military assignments. He was a skilled writer and
extremely knowledgeable observer of Indian and animal life on the western
plains. Hence, there was really no reason for Hornaday to doubt the veracity
of Dodge's observations. With the level of detail supplied by Dodge,
Hornaday used the more conservative parameters in his computations, and
estimated that there were not less than five hundred thousand bison in this
herd, and he further postulated (Hornaday 1889, 391):

> If the advancing multitude had been at all points 50 miles in length
> (as it was known to have been in some places at least) by 25 miles
> in width, and still averaged fifteen head to the acre of ground, it
> would have contained the enormous number of 12,000,000 head.
> But judging from the general principles governing such migrations,
> it is almost certain that the moving mass advanced in the shape of a
> wedge, which would make it necessary to deduct about two-thirds
> from the grand total, which would leave 4,000,000 as our estimate
> of the actual number of buffaloes in this great herd, which I believe
> is more likely to be below the truth than above it.

Another sighting of a large bison herd occurred in either late April or early May 1875, by John R. Cook, a bison hunter who lived on the Great Plains from 1874 until 1880. In his reminiscences (Cook [1907] 1967, 180–181), Cook described a bison herd he encountered while moving along the Brazos River near Fort Griffin in Texas [during 1867–1881, Fort Griffin and the surrounding town was a supply and shipping center for bison hide hunters]:

I had not gone five miles until I saw the great mass of moving creatures, on the annual northern swing. Looking to the east and south as far as the eye could reach, it seemed to me that I saw nothing but a solid mass of bison; and I had to either turn back or go through them. The wind was from the north, and they were heading it and were moving in a quick-step gait. I was supposed to be at this time ten miles from Goff's [John Goff was operating a bison hide camp in the vicinity and Cook wanted to acquire some flour which he understood was plentiful in the Goff camp].

I had heard of stampedes where they ran over everything in their way, and I thought "now should I get out into that big field of animals and they should make a run, there would be annihilation." Then I thought, "to go back to camp with word that I was turned back by the main herd would be construed as weakness."

Looking to the southwest and west, I saw a moving sea of that one countless host. I decided that it was just as safe going ahead as turning back. So, taking the landmark in view that I was to go to, I started on, and was soon among them. Of course there were intervals of bare ground; but they were small in comparison to the ground actually covered by the buffaloes. As I drove on, they would veer to my right in front and to my left in rear; the others following on behind them, would hardly seem to vary their course.

I had gone perhaps five miles in this way, when all fear from them seemingly disappeared; and, looking that day at that most wonderful sight, I thought it would take the standing army of the United States years to exterminate them. In fact, it was the opinion of conservative hunters as late as the new year of 1877 that the present army of hunters were not killing the original herds, but only the natural increase.

The large bison herds had already disappeared from eastern Kansas by June 1847, when fifteen-year-old William F. Drannan, accompanying Kit Carson, passed through Fort Scott. The first bison herd that Drannan ever saw was near Pawnee Rock along the Arkansas River in mid-state Kansas. After killing his first bison, and visiting in his first Indian camp, they travelled along the Santa Fe Trail and he subsequently reported (Drannan 1909, 43):

> We took the Santa Fe trail and the buffalo were so numerous along the way that we had to take some pains to avoid them, as when they were traveling or on a stampede, nothing could turn or stop them and we would be in danger of being ground to atoms beneath their thousands of hoofs.

As the herds began to decline in size and number after 1830, it would seem that it would have been much easier to offer estimates or assumptions regarding the remaining animals, as they were not observed in as many diverse locations. This, however, was not the case. The number of bison occupying mid-America remained largely unknown, although it was presumed by most people that bison herds were still basically robust. Seton estimated that in 1830 there remained but forty million bison (1927, 656), one half of which he suggested were cows, or females of the species, a view that Frank Gilbert Roe (1972, 505) did not apparently elect to dispute in 1951 — although he certainly took issue with a goodly number of other scholarly assertions by Seton and others.

It might be well at this point to consider the possibility that a fifty-fifty herd split between wild male and female bison in 1830 may not be altogether appropriate. If we assume that spring calving resulted in an equal amount of young bulls and young heifers, then herd replenishment would, at that point, serve to maintain an existing balanced sex distribution. However, prior to 1830, the emphasis on taking of bison by the Indian and white hunter was driven more by the perceived quality of the meat, and thus hunting was directed more toward younger bison and cows. What is important regarding this observation is that except for the advantages to be found in (1) a larger gene pool, and (2) less opportunity for inbreeding, a ratio of one bull to five, or even eight, cows could still result in 90 percent bred cows and two-year-old heifers. The number of cows will always dictate potential herd size, not the number of bulls.

As late as the early 1870s a number of large herds were still reported. The number of bison represented in one herd located in the Arkansas valley in 1871, between Fort Dodge and Fort Supply in Kansas, was estimated to be in the millions by General Philip Sheridan. This figure is certainly open to some question of veracity as Sheridan and his staff initially suggested that this particular herd, said to be one hundred miles in width and of unknown length, must have represented not fewer than ten billion bison. Sheridan and his staff again made an effort to estimate bison on a march between the Cimarron and Canadian Rivers in northern Oklahoma, and from daybreak until 4:00 p.m., the average number, as reported by Sheridan's eleven staff officers (one of whom was "Buffalo Bill" Cody), was 243,000. In spite of reports of large herds, it was estimated that the total number of free-ranging bison remaining in the United States by 1870 was fifteen million.

William Blackmore, who wrote the introduction to Col. Richard Irving Dodge's book, *The Plains of the Great West and Their Inhabitants*, was one of a very select few who had spent some time on the western plains and had also detected a lessening in the numbers of bison from the late 1860s to the early 1870s. Blackmore explains in his introduction:

> In the autumn of 1868, whilst crossing the Plains on the Kansas Pacific Railroad — for a distance of upwards to 120 miles, between Ellsworth and Sheridan, we passed through an almost unbroken herd of buffalo. The Plains were blackened with them, and more than once the train had to stop to allow unusually large herds to pass. A few years afterward, when travelling over the same line of railroad, it was a rare sight to see a few herds from ten to twenty buffalo. A like result took place still further southwards, between the Arkansas and Cimarron Rivers. In 1872, whilst on a scout for about a hundred miles south of Fort Dodge to the Indian territory [Oklahoma], we were never out of sight of buffalo. In the following autumn, on travelling over the same district, whilst the whole country was whitened with bleached and bleaching bones, we did not meet with buffalo until we were well into the Indian territory, and then only in scanty bands. During this autumn, when riding some thirty to forty miles along the north bank of the Arkansas River to the East of Fort Dodge, there was a continuous line of putrescent carcases, so that the air was rendered pestilential and offensive to the last degree. The

hunters had formed a line of camps along the banks of the river, and had shot down the buffalo, night and morning, as they came to drink. In order to give an idea of the number of these carcases, it is only necessary to mention that I counted sixty-seven on one spot not covering four acres.

Perhaps it is not really important for us to know precisely how many bison there were in the United States prior to those regrettable days of wanton and wasteful slaughter. Although the methods may have been cruel and the outcome for the bison and the Indian pathetic, we also need to consider that at that time the United States was an emerging nation, much like those innumerable young but undeveloped African nations that are now struggling to strengthen their future. While we may now lament the loss of these large bison herds, I think we can agree that this nation could not have acquired its current wealth, international eminence, and recognition of the need for human rights and freedom for individual expression, without having experienced the expansion and growth that occurred in the 1800s. It is easy to criticize the bison hunters, the hide men, and other opportunists of those times, but they were a part of a whole that was inevitably in the process of evolving. Or, perhaps we could view them in a manner as Tolstoy suggests in the epilogue, part II, chapter VII, to *War and Peace:*

> They remove moral responsibility from those men who produce the events. At the time they do the work of brooms, that go in front to clear the rails for the train: they clear the path of men's moral responsibility.

Counting bison is still not any easier today than it was 150 years ago. Unlike this nation's cattle, hogs, and sheep, the United States Department of Agriculture takes little interest in maintaining records on bison or other animals labeled in the wild category regardless of their actual or potential agricultural utility. Without a neutral or objective agency to seek and maintain this information, current bison counts are haphazard and actual individual herd totals are known only to the over fifteen hundred private and public sector owners and managers — who may or may not be willing to divulge their precise herd totals.

4

The Indian

Thomas E. Mails, in his outstanding book on the Plains Indian, *The Mystic Warriors of the Plains,* stated that "those who would know the Indian must study the buffalo intensely . . ." Perhaps the same thing could also be said about the buffalo (bison); if you want to know and understand the bison's impact upon America you must also know the Indian.

According to some rather carefully prepared estimates (Wissler, 1947), there were approximately 846,000 Indians residing in the United States in 1492 upon the arrival of Columbus. Thomas E. Mails claims that at their population peak, around A.D. 1800 (1972, 12), "all of the Plains tribes together numbered no more than two hundred thousand people. . . ." Indian tribal communities rarely exceeded one hundred people from all age groupings. At times a small number of these communities or bands would find it useful, for one reason or another, to live with other communities in a village or camp, but each community still felt free to come and go at will or perhaps even join other communities that were banded together at another village or camp. Now and then, aggressive activities of other tribes forced villages to combine their resources and take defensive measures, or perhaps even take some significant retaliatory steps, but normally the establishment of large encampments was the exception rather than the rule. Conceivably these community living practices served the Indians well in reducing the spread of disease and avoiding possible environmental contamination. When the various Indian tribes were forced from areas of natural habitation and placed on reservations, the confinement proved to be simply devastating for all of the tribes that became involved in the reservation process. Disease, coupled with the lack of adequate health care, significantly reduced their numbers.

If we elect to overlook a variety of theological explanations offered as to the origin of the American Indian, we would have to assume that the ancestors of the myriad tribes found in the United States migrated across the Bering land bridge from Asia over 40,000 years ago, in much the same fashion as did the mammals they sought. In addition, the possibility exists that some of these new Americans may have come by sea, and landed countless years ago on the eastern and western coasts. Indian legends, folktales, and even certain anthropologists suggest that some tribes may have always been here, or, in other words, they did not have to come from somewhere else; they were already here. However, the significant differences in physical characteristics and culture would seem to support the common contention of multiplicity in ancestral source. Whatever the circumstances may have been, the early immigrants were primarily itinerant hunters; they pursued the animals, found the hunting good, perhaps returned with others, but eventually stayed on this new continent.

As more immigration took place, these early peoples moved south, through the open grasslands of Alaska, into the Great Plains of the North American continent and further southward into the South American continent. They spread through lands that were overflowing with horses, camels, ground sloth, mammoths and mastodons, bison, and many other smaller mammals. They faced competition from a variety of powerful animal predators, but left only little archaeological evidence of their culture except for the bones of their quarry and the chipped stones from their weapons. It is interesting to speculate as to why Indian tribes were so impressed and even astonished by the horses brought to America by the Spaniards when their ancestors had often hunted and relished the meat of the wild horse. The same is true with other mammals that had later become extinct, such as the camel, mastodon, mammoth, and giant sloth. Indian mythology is silent with respect to all of these animals, formerly common to North America, except for the bison.

In the prologue to this book, an imaginary tale is told of an encounter between an early bison *(Bison priscus)* and a hunting party within the Bering land bridge perhaps 20,000 to 30,000 years ago. Evidence of human presence south of the North American glaciated regions dates from about 11,500 years before the present time (B.P.), and, according to Paul Martin *(Discovery of America,* 1973), the human population subsequently advanced through North and South America at an extremely rapid pace, arriving at the tip of South America by 10,500 years B.P. The Paleoindians were apparently a very vigorous group who flourished in this new land. For much of their early life in North America, they faced a climate that was considerably different from that of today. The massive ice sheets had retreated, leaving many rivers and large lakes. Areas that are now deserts were swamps or grasslands. This was indeed a fabulous land for the large herbivores — and also for the carnivores who preyed upon them. However, the discovery and inhabitation of America by the new immigrants, the Paleoindians, may have led to the extinction of a number of late Pleistocene mammals as a result of overhunting. Gone by 9,000 years B.P. were various horses, the giant ground sloth, the giant beaver, the mastodon, the camel, the wooly mammoth, the long-nosed and flat-headed peccaries, the four-horned pronghorn antelope, and a number of lesser herbivores as well as certain carnivores who depended upon these now extinct species for their existence.

Russell Dale Guthrie (*Frozen Fauna of the Mammoth Steppe,* 1990) is of the belief that late and post-Pleistocene climate changes were sufficient to have caused the widespread extinctions of many of these land mammals. There is the distinct possibility that these climatic changes could have come about quite suddenly, and perhaps many of the species did not have the time to adapt or evolve; but there is also the rather obvious impact of the *Homo sapiens*, those of the Clovis, Plano, and Folsom cultures, who emerged from the ice age with hunting technologies that the naive mammals had not previously experienced, and thus they would have been particularly vulnerable to these newly arrived predators. Paleontological and archaeological discoveries have well documented the fact that there is a definite association between the findings of large groupings of skeletons of extinct animals and the cultural debris left by early North American man, the Paleoindian.

When all the mastodons and mammoths were gone, the Paleoindians concentrated their meat foraging efforts on bison. Methods became more sophisticated, and some of the techniques that were adopted proved to be so successful that many of their hunting practices remained virtually unchanged for thousands of years. For example, they would drive a bison herd into a gully, a canyon, or some other natural trap having inescapable sides, where the bison could be killed off. Some of these kills were immense, resulting in the slaying of over one hundred animals — most of which were females and the young. At one kill site located near Casper, Wyoming, scientists recovered fifty-nine bison skulls, only three of which belonged to adult males. However, the same method of capture had been employed in Europe. Great piles of animal bones were found when these beasts had been stampeded over steep riverbanks or cliffs. After analysis of bones discovered at all located North American Paleoindian kill sites, evidence suggests that bison were by far their most common quarry. However, because the reproductive rate for bison apparently far exceeded all predator takings — including man — there is no evidence to suggest that the bison's existence at that time was endangered or threatened.

A gradual climatic warming offered an abundance of other foods. Streams, rivers, lakes, and oceans provided a whole host of marine life. Through use of boats and canoes, of one kind or another, people were able to add variety to their diets and were not necessarily required to maintain their former nomadic existence. Eventually at least three different Paleoindian cultures could be identified in what is now referred to as the contiguous United States: (1) those that followed the herds for survival — when the herds moved, they moved too; (2) those that occupied heavily forested areas offering a stable population of smaller game animals; and (3) those who hunted on an opportunity basis but also foraged for various seeds, nuts, and other plants. Anthropologists found that the concept of culture was very helpful to them in their efforts to classify these early Americans. Scientists ultimately suggested the existence of ten major cultural areas in North America: Arctic, Subarctic, Northwest Coast, California, Plateau, Great Basin, Southwest, Plains, Southeast, and Northeast–Great Lakes. Although bison offered an occasional feast for peoples located in many of the other nine cultural areas identified, it was the Plains culture that placed the greatest dependence upon the bison for its existence.

A number of anthropologists have suggested that certain Indian tribes "always" lived on the plains, that is, Apache, Arapaho, Blackfoot, and Kiowa. In taking a more conservative view with respect to the term "always," it is submitted that these tribes have resided on the plains throughout historical times. As a few of the Eastern Woodland tribes grew in strength, the less powerful tribes were forced further west, moving other tribes before them. The same circumstance occurred with respect to western tribes, and based upon either intertribal conflicts, encroachment of the

Europeans, or the lure of the bison, by the mid- to late 1700s approximately twenty-five tribes resided in the Great Plains area. Like separate nations, each tribe had its own language and customs; however, because of certain similarities in speech, all tribes can be conveniently arranged into "families" that would basically represent for the various tribes genealogical family trees. The principal Indian families at the time of Columbus were the Algonkin, Iroquois, Muskhogean, Caddoan, Siouan, Dene, Uto-Aztecan, and Penutain. Although most, if not all, tribes in the continental United States hunted bison at one time or another — and some on a regular basis — no tribes have been more closely associated and identified with bison and the Great Plains than the Siouan family.

The name Sioux is reportedly an abbreviation of *Nadowessioux*, a French corruption of a name once applied to an enemy tribe by the Ojibway (Algonkin), which meant snake or adder. To many people today, the name Sioux suggests a vision of horses, bison, and wars between soldiers and Indians. The Dakota Sioux, or Dakota, the most powerful member of the Siouan family, were the principal Indian representatives of the original "Wild West" shows. The Dakota is generally the artist's rendition of what a Plains Indian looked like: tall, slender, strong features, high cheekbones, beaked nose — the Indian on the nickel. We have come to expect that all Indians dress like the Dakotas. A number of paintings, such as that depicting the Pilgrims landing at Plymouth Rock and being greeted by Indians wearing Dakota clothing and feathers, have also contributed to this misconception.

The Sioux tribes, along with the Blackfoot, Arapaho and Cheyenne (Algonkin); Arikara, Pawnee, and Wichita (Caddo); and Kiowa and Comanche (Uto-Aztecan), all shared the Great Plains area and had their own generally accepted tribal boundaries. However, even though they may share common boundaries and belong to the same family language grouping, tribes were not always on good terms with one another. Confrontations were, for the most part, limited, but were often exacerbated by (1) territorial disputes, (2) an imbalance of resources such as horses, and (3) problems occasioned by the migrating and decreasing bison. All-out wars never really took place, but raids and minor skirmishes seemingly became part of their normal way of life. In spite of these differences, all of the Plains tribes were nonetheless bound together in their dependence upon the bison for their very existence.

The obvious first need that the bison satisfied was that of food. The Plains Indians were not known to be planters or gatherers. Some tribes may have collected berries and grew corn, squash, beans, and other minor vegetables, but their staple food was meat — predominately bison meat. On some of their occasional forays into higher elevations, they may have secured elk, deer, and perhaps even antelope and mountain sheep, but bison was always the primary objective. Most Plains tribes did not really care for fish, although in times of tribal hunger they would eat most anything readily available, even dogs or horses. It was not only Indians who considered bison meat the best of all possible foods. The early fur trappers, the mountain men, all attested that bison meat, an incredibly rich, tender, fiberless, and less gamey meat, was the greatest meal a human had ever tasted. The mountain man boiled some cuts, more than likely from the hump, seared some over their campfires, but more frequently the meat was slow-roasted on a skewer. Implausible as it may seem, eight pounds of bison meat was the standard daily ration for Hudson's Bay Company employees, but it was claimed that when bison meat was plentiful a man might eat eight pounds for dinner, sleep for a couple of hours, wake and build up his fire, and eat more. Although the diet of the Plains Indians and the mountain men consisted almost exclusively of bison meat, there is little doubt that there never existed a more hardy and healthful group of people. Disease, particularly heart disease and cancer, was virtually unknown within the tribes until some rather devastating viruses, such as smallpox, measles, and diphtheria, were introduced by the white man.

The bison was not a single-purpose animal as far as the Indians were concerned. Meat was, of course, the first consideration, but other parts of the bison had their own functions and uses. The hide of the bison served to satisfy the more utilitarian purposes — housing, clothing and bedding — but the bones, organs, and even its dried feces (buffalo chips) were used as fuel and as markers in the absence of rocks. While temporarily encamped with a tribe of Arikara Indians on the Missouri River and near what is now the boundary of the states of North and South Dakota, John Bradbury (1966, 165) observed several Indian squaws hoeing their corn with the blade bone of a bison that was "ingeniously fixed in a stick for that purpose." Apparently the Arikara also supplemented their meat diet with vegetables, as Bradbury elected to comment on the fine appearance of the Indian corn, squashes, beans, and small species of tobacco. Unfortunately, it was eventually the market demand for the hide of the bison that was perhaps the deciding factor in the decline of the large herds. Although our Native Americans were assuredly participants in what was an overall reduction process, the eventual role of the Indian and the thrust of tribal actions with respect to the bison were more those of obstructionists to an indiscriminate and wasteful slaughter.

In spite of a few examples that would suggest otherwise, Indians were, more often than not, careful custodians of the resources that nature placed at their disposal. They did not unnecessarily waste but basically only trimmed the excess from the bison herds. The Indians also provided fresh and juicy grasses for the bison and other herbivores by burning sections of prairie and thereby promoting new growth. Although a few individuals found it convenient to include Indian tribes when they busied themselves with leveling blame for the demise of the bison, there is no evidence to support this contention. There were no evidential reductions in the number of bison or bison herds prior to the intervention of the white hunters and the subsequent development of the hide markets. Although some Native Americans may have been passive participants in the latter decades of bison slaughter (in order that they may obtain money or goods that would not otherwise have been available to them), most eschewed the waste and resented the unjustified squander of the herds.

Indian tribes hunted the bison based upon conditions of need and want. Slaughter without purpose, or killing without intention of making full use of the animal, was unthinkable. Prior to the hunt, there were a number of prehunt ceremonies that normally took place. These ritualistic preparations were performed not only for the purpose of petitioning from the unseen and eternal the success of the hunt, but also to pay reverence and respect to the animal they were to hunt.

For the Plains Indians, the mobility that they achieved through use of the horse significantly enhanced their skill as hunters. Prior to their use of the horse, Indians employed a number of methods to secure bison. Two of these methods, the jump and impoundment, were old and proven hunting practices that were used even by the Paleoindian. The hunting concept of the impoundment is rather simple: the bison are driven into a natural or constructed pen or corral, and after their escape is blocked, the trapped animals are slaughtered using whatever weapons or means the hunters have at their disposal. The bison "jump," should perhaps be considered as another form of impoundment. In the "jump," bison are driven toward a cliff or precipice, and unable to stop their forward momentum, animals at the front of the herd are consequently pushed off by the herd mass and fall to their death. The "jump" may also involve the use of one of the more active and fleet tribal members who will disguise himself with a bison robe and headpiece and lure the harassed herd to a precipice and then attempt to secure a preselected shelter to avoid being caught up with the herd.

Indian use of the "jump" was vividly depicted in the journals of Lewis and Clark. On May 29, 1805, when the expedition was on its way west and passed the Judith River, the following entry was made:

> On the north we passed a precipice about one hundred and twenty feet high, under which lay scattered the fragments of at least one hundred carcases of buffaloes, although the water which had washed away the lower part of the hill must have carried off many of the dead. These buffaloes had been chased down the precipice in a way very common on the Missouri, and by which vast herds are destroyed in a moment. The mode of hunting is to select one of the most active and fleet young men, who is disguised by a buffalo skin around his body; the skin of the head with the ears and horns fastened on his own head in such a way as to deceive the buffalo: thus dressed, he fixes himself at a convenient distance between a herd of buffalo and any of the river precipices, which sometimes extends for miles. His companions in the meantime get in the rear and side of the herd, and at a given signal show themselves, and advance towards the buffalo: they instantly take the alarm, and finding the hunters beside them, they run towards the disguised Indian or decoy, who leads them on at full speed towards the river, when suddenly securing himself in some crevice of the cliff which he had previously fixed on, the herd is left on the brink of the precipice: it is then in vain for the foremost to retreat or even stop; they are pressed on by the hindmost rank, who, seeing no danger but from the hunters, goad on those before them till the whole are precipitated and the shore is strewn with their dead bodies. Sometimes in this perilous seduction the Indian is himself either trodden underfoot by the rapid movements of the buffalo, or missing his footing in the cliff is urged down the precipice by the falling herd. The Indians then select as much meat as they wish, and the rest is abandoned to the wolves, and creates a most dreadful stench. The wolves who had been

feasting on these carcases were very fat, and so gentle that one of them was killed with a spontoon [a short pike carried by infantry officers].

Another method frequently used was the "surround." In this hunting technique the bison are surrounded, and the bison, thus encircled, mill about and are dispatched in the same manner as an impoundment except that occasionally determined animals will break free from the surround and, particularly if the Indians are on foot, afflict punishment if not death upon their tormentors in making their escape. Frank Collinson described one surround he saw in Texas in the 1870s in his book *Life in the Saddle* in the following manner (1963, 63): "On one occasion I saw hundreds of Comanche Indians on a buffalo 'surround.' They were escorted by the United States Cavalry and killed about two thousand buffalo with guns, pistols, and arrows. It was a colorful sight, but did not compare with the art of the *cibolero* and his lance." Use of fire by various Indian tribes in encircling a bison herd and to inhibit the bison from fleeing also proved to be quite effective.

The hunting system used by the Mexican *ciboleros* (Chapter 6), and depicted in movies featuring bison chase scenes, such as *Dances with Wolves*, has been referred to as "running" the bison. In this the bison are chased and their pursuers use whatever weapons they have at their disposal to kill the animals. The most undesirable outcome from running bison, as far as the hunter is concerned, is that (1) kill percentages are lower, and (2) dead animals are often strewn over the countryside rather than centralized all in one spot.

One such chase is described by William Thomas Hamilton *(My Sixty Years on the Plains)*. Accompanied by a group of hunters and trappers, Hamilton visited a Cheyenne camp, and on March 24, 1842, he elected to join the Cheyenne on a bison hunt. He describes the hunt and chase as follows (1982, 29–30):

> There was yelling and shooting in every direction; and many riderless ponies were mixed in with the buffalo, with Indians after them, reckless if they in turn were dismounted as their friends had been, by the ponies stepping into prairie-dog or badger holes. Many an Indian has come to grief by having an arm or leg broken in this way. Ponies are sure-footed, but in a run such as this one, where

over a thousand buffalo are tearing at full speed over the prairie, a
dust is created which makes it impossible for the ponies to see the
holes, hence the mishaps, which are very common.

All the meat required lay in an area of three quarters of a mile.
I had brought down four and received great praise from the Indians.
I could have done much better, but boy-like, I wanted to see the
Indians shoot their arrows, which many of them used. One arrow
was sufficient to bring the buffalo to its knees. They shot behind the
shoulder, sending the arrow deep enough to strike the lungs. One
shot there is enough for any animal in the United States.

Now came the butchering, which was completed in two hours,
and each pony was packed with three hundred pounds of the choicest
of meats.

The various methods employed by Indians to hunt bison had been
often mentioned by the early chroniclers. Father Louis Hennepin gave
meticulous attention in his journals to the customs of the various Indian
tribes he encountered. He was taken captive by the Sioux on April 11, 1680,
and after travelling with them for nineteen days, he began to describe some
of their hunting customs (Hennepin 1880, 217–218): "These Indians at
times sent their best runners by land to chase the herds of wild cattle on the
water side; as these animals crossed the river, they sometimes killed forty
or fifty, merely to take the tongue, and the most delicate morsels, leaving
the rest with which they would not burden themselves, so as to travel more
rapidly. We sometimes indeed eat good pieces, but without bread, wine, or
salt, and without spice or other seasoning." Hennepin's description of
another bison slaughter inferred the use of terrain or similarity to practices
used in "impounding." After locating a herd of bison, the tribe offered
suitable prayers for the animals they were about to slaughter and then
Hennepin went on to recount the method of hunt: "a hundred men went
behind the mountains on one side, and a hundred on the other to shut in the
buffalo whom they killed in great confusion. The women boucanned the
meat in the sun, eating only the poorest, in order to carry the best to their
villages, more than two hundred leagues from this great butchery." On
another occasion he recalled that when he was with another large hunting
party that "we again went down the river Colbert [Mississippi] about eighty
leagues way to hunt with this multitude of canoes; from time to time the
Indians hid their canoes on the banks of the river and in the islands; then

struck into the prairies seven or eight leagues beyond the mountains, where they killed, at different times, as many as a hundred and twenty buffaloes."

Father Hennepin, as perhaps were all other missionary explorers, was primarily interested in bringing the Christian religion to the Indians, and perhaps because of this his journal and/or memoirs appear to be more the observations of a rigid social witness than that of an objective historian. After being held captive by the Sioux for nearly six months, he had subsequently acquired some rather harsh opinions of Indian behavior. His summation of Indian culture, behavior, and appearance (Hennepin 1980, 277–339) draws heavily upon his observations of the Sioux, and describes a vigorous and simple people who frequently exhibit conduct that is both rude and cruel. He indicated that he found them to be generally unclean, both morally and physically, and that they "follow simply the animals." This form of generalization, at that time, was really not unique and it was a rather common thought that Indians are Indians, but Indians are also savages, and thus there is but little difference between tribes with respect to beliefs and behaviors.

Bernard DeVoto, in his book *Across the Wide Missouri,* suggests that when bison were plentiful, Indians were perhaps as discriminating as the later-day white hunters, collecting only the cuts they liked most. George Catlin, the artist, described the results of an Indian "surround" of bison near the Teton River in the spring of 1832, as reported in Wayne Gard's *The Great Buffalo Hunt.* Gard describes a time when a party of five or six hundred Sioux on horseback attacked an immense herd of bison at midday, and after spending a few hours among them, they approached a nearby fort with fourteen hundred fresh buffalo tongues, "which were thrown into a heap for a few gallons of whisky. Not a skin or a pound of meat except the tongues, was brought in" (1960, 30). However, it is questionable that this particular event would ever have taken place if the Indians were not aware that the bison tongue was considered to be a delicacy, and the one item that could be exchanged with the soldiers to satisfy their acquired affinity for whisky.

For many reasons, perhaps too many to even attempt to understand or classify, the white man never acquired the ability to understand the Indian thought process. The divergence between the two cultures was gigantic, and, unfortunately for the Indian, the white man had little patience or appreciation for many of the Indian beliefs and values. The culture and day-to-day lives of the Plains Indians were perhaps even more steeped in religious mystique and tradition than were the more eastern and western tribes. A number of Plains Indian religious ceremonies are dependent upon the availability of bison meat. Until bison recently became more plentiful, these ceremonies were limited not only because of supply, but also because the cost of obtaining bison was prohibitive.

There is one encouraging corollary that has resulted from the current increase in the availability of bison in the United States and Canada: the Native American has now begun to progressively develop bison herds of their own. Through individual tribal initiative, as well as cooperative action with other tribes, nearly thirty-six hundred bison are currently owned and managed by Indian tribes, along with a number of small herds that are individually owned by Native Americans.

Within Indian culture, mythology, and religion, animals and animal spirits are iconic figures of the first magnitude — and this is not perhaps without considerable justification. With the advent of the horse, the Indian could easily capture animals that were previously too elusive; it was not necessary to depend solely upon patience and guile. The Indian no longer needed to wait for bison herds to come to them, or to dart out in semi-nomadic bands to hunt bison at jumps or pin them in arroyos. They could now move whole villages and follow the bison herds. Each of the native animals demonstrated considerable powers that, if emulated by a tribal member, would certainly lead to a better life or social outcome. The Bear Cult is a prime example of this. In nearly every Plains tribe there were a small number of men who believed that they had obtained supernatural bear powers through dreams. They painted bear symbols on their tipis (tepees) and personal items, and when they died their power went with them — it was not an inherited characteristic or honor. The bull elk, as another illustration of animal symbolism, was considered an effective helper in love since he had shown them his ability to call females. But above all others, it was the bison that dominated this strongly anthropomorphic society.

Plains Indians did not necessarily hunt bison to the exclusion of all other animals. Deer, antelope, and elk were also taken whenever possible, but the bison offered the greater opportunity for hunting success. Josiah Gregg's travels throughout the West placed him in contact with most of the Plains tribes from time to time. From his observations of their hunting practices, he concluded that the bison was more susceptible than any other animal to the methods of stalking and pursuit that these tribes employed. Since guns were not as yet common to many of the tribes at the time of Gregg's visits (1839–1843), he had undoubtedly based his assumptions on the use of more primitive weapons. In *Commerce of the Prairies* (1966, vol. 2, 285) Gregg suggested that:

> The antelope is too wild and fleet for their mode of hunting, and is only occasionally taken by stratagem; while the deer, as difficult to take in the chase, is less easily entrapped. But mounted upon their trained steeds, and with the arrow or lance, they are not to be excelled in the chase. A few of them, let loose among a herd of buffalo, will soon have the plain strewed with their carcasses.

Tribal legends addressed all parts of the natural world, but the Plains Indians daily shared their habitation with the animals and birds and expressed a closer kinship to them rather than the mysterious workings of celestial and climatic phenomena.

The bison was a central figure in many of their folktales. One Cheyenne legend was so sacred that the storyteller, most often the medicine man, felt obliged to offer a prayer asking for forgiveness before he began. It relates the gift of the buffalo (bison) to the people by a mythical individual who was called Yellow Haired Woman. The tale recounts a time when the tribe had no large food animals and had to be content with fish, geese, and ducks. At one point the tribe was so hungry that the chiefs sent two young men out to search for food. Not finding any food after eight days, they tried to cross a stream in their weakened condition. They were seized by a great water serpent, and would have perished if an old man carrying a large knife and wearing a coyote skin had not leaped into the water and cut off the serpent's head. The old man and his wife took the two young men to their home, cured them of their weakness, and fed them. The old couple had a fair-haired daughter, Yellow Haired Woman, and they urged the young men to take their daughter for a sister or wife. One of the young men agreed to marry her. The girl then went with the young men and brought with her some gifts, including the knowledge of corn planting and the use of the buffalo for food. Before leaving, however, the father cautioned his daughter never to express pity or sorrow over any suffering animal. The Cheyennes were overjoyed when the two young men and new bride arrived in their camp, because shortly afterward they were surrounded by many buffalo and were able to get their fill of meat. But later, some boys dragged a buffalo calf into camp, threw dust into its eyes, and killed it. Yellow Haired Woman indicated her sorrow over the death of the calf, and by doing so she had broken the taboo imposed by her father. That day all the buffalo disappeared. Yellow Haired Woman knew she had to go back to her mother and father. Her husband and the other young man went with her, and all three were never seen again. The legend goes on to say that much later, other mythical figures restored the buffalo to the tribe.

There are literally uncountable numbers of bison myths and fables that are still being told, or perhaps by now have been forgotten, by Indian tribes that attempt to express in their own unique way the true meaning and purpose of the bison.

Legend and mythology only further serve to underscore the sacred and unique place that the white bison has held over the years with respect to Native American culture. Among animal species it is not unusual to find variation in size as well as range of coloration throughout their populations. Although these variations are primarily inherited characteristics or derivations from parents or ancestors, the occasional event of interbreeding between species can result in progeny that exhibit selected characteristics of both parents. Deliberate crossbreeding, for example, has produced a number of remarkable hybrids, such as "ligers" or "tigons" (product of a male lion and female tiger, or a male tiger and a lioness), and "leoponds" (male leopard and lioness) along with a number of less exotic offspring. These hybrids, however, are generally found to be sterile. Another oddity is a condition called albinism, where there is an absence of the normal brown/black pigmentation values of melanin. This absence results in white, colorless hair, skin, eyes, etc., and is always an inherited characteristic. However, when true albinism does actually occur, it serves as conclusive evidence of the existence of a recessive gene that had been passed on from generation to generation within that species.

Unusually large or unusually small representatives of any of the species of plant or animal tend to be the recipient of greater human attention than those considered to be normal sized because they visibly stand out from their peers. The same situation is true with respect to color variation: the greater the contrast, the greater the interest. The albino of an animal species is thus thrust into a position of extreme visibility, subsequent notoriety, and, all too often, an early death.

From historical times we know that the prairies and plains of North America once teemed with a variety of animal life. Predominate among all of these animals were the herds of brownish black bison that were the staple of life for the Plains Indian. Although some of the bison were occasionally lighter or darker than the bulk of their dusky peers, these differences became a matter of trivial interest when an albino, pied, or light cream–colored bison suddenly materialized in the herd. For many of the Plains Indians, particularly those from the northern tribes, the arrival of a white bison was indeed something very extraordinary, and an event that nearly always resulted in the eventual killing, or sacrifice, of the animal, followed by ritualistic and religious ceremonies demonstrating the deep reverence that the Native American held for the white bison.

Although not all Indian tribes placed religious importance or attached mystical symbolism to the white bison, those Indians who were nonbelievers did recognize the white bison's remarkable value as an item of barter or trade. For many Native American religious ceremonies or to make "medicine," the robe of the white bison was considered essential. The Mandan, Minatari, and Hidatsa tribes, for example, had White Buffalo Cow Societies, which contained primarily the older, and perhaps their more venerated, women. These women were asked by their tribal leaders to perform spiritual dances that would serve to attract the bison herds. A key ingredient to this ceremonial process was the possession of a white bison robe that the society leader could cloak herself in. Of the many Indian legends and myths that exist involving bison, one example of such, related by Black Elk, an acclaimed spiritual leader of the Oglala Sioux, is quite revealing in its meaning and substance. This legend describes how Black Elk's people received the gift of the Sacred Pipe Ceremony from White Buffalo (bison) Woman. In his story, a very holy and beautiful woman, wearing a white buckskin dress, suddenly appeared to a tribal chief and indicated that soon she would return and that a large tepee should be built for her in the center of the nation. She began to sing and exuded from her mouth at the same time a white cloud that was good to smell. After giving the chief a pipe with a bison calf carved on one side and eagle feathers attached to the stem, she said that with that pipe in their possession, the tribe would multiply and become a great nation. She then left the chief's tepee, and all that could be seen was a departing white bison that shortly disappeared from sight.

Possession of a white bison robe is considered to be powerful medicine, and its very presence was said to cure illnesses or even ward off injury if it were carried into battle. Other beliefs of Native Americans surrounding the white bison, such as those associated with the Hunkpapa (Sioux) White Buffalo (bison) Festival, attempt to respond to and address the full meaning of human life and the renewal of total spiritual being.

Although a white bison robe was eminently prized, any unusually colored robe was also extremely desirable and often held in equally high esteem. Dary (1974, 208) described an incident, recorded by Edwin James, whereby a trader visiting an Indian village was unable to purchase a bison head with a white star on its forehead because its owner believed that the bison kept returning to the area to "seek their white faced companion."

There is no record of a wild white bison surviving long enough to experience full maturity or old age. Its presence in a herd was so remarkable and so visibly evident that it was not possible for the white bison to avoid human attention and interest for very long. Discovery, unfortunately, was soon followed by slaughter and ceremonial and ritualistic dressing of the white robe. With this in mind, it is quite unlikely that many white bison were able to reach normal breeding age, a condition that would further limit the near negligible potential for birth of a white bison calf. Hornaday indicated (1889, 414) that even with the vast number of bison that formerly inhabited the plains and prairies of North America, it was his belief that not over ten or eleven white bison, or white bison skins, were ever seen by white men.

While I was still involved with the former American Bison Association, our Denver headquarters office would occasionally receive information regarding the recent birth of a white bison calf. However, none of these reports later proved to be legitimate. From time to time an animal appearing to be a white bison can be produced by crossbreeding a bison cow with a Charolais bull. The Charolais bull calf, along with several young bison heifers, are raised together, and when they reach breeding age, with a great deal of luck, any offspring that results could be white. The white females are normally fertile, but any male progeny will be sterile.

Another less idiosyncratic means of obtaining bison-like animals is the so-called beefalo or cattalo livestock concept that could assemble some rather interesting-looking progeny in a variety of shapes and colors. The same phenomenon may have naturally occurred in the past from

"Big Medicine on the range, Montana." This legendary white bison was born in 1933 at the National Bison Range and died in 1959. He sired an albino calf through his mother, but the calf was blind at birth and was later exhibited at the National Zoo in Washington, D.C., where he died in 1949 at twelve years of age. Courtesy Montana Historical Society, Helena, Montana.

interbreeding between bison and light-colored cattle that joined wild bison herds. It is interesting to note that Roe (1951, 726), who was somewhat cynical in his critique of many of the reported sightings of white bison in the wild, seemingly supports the suggestion of Charles Jesse (Buffalo) Jones that many of the white bison observed in wild herds were actually cattalo.

Possibly the most celebrated of all white bison was "Big Medicine," who was born in May 1933, at the National Bison Range, Moiese, Montana. Normal in nearly every respect except for color, Big Medicine grew to become a magnificent bull and ultimately a top competitor for leadership of the range herd. However, because of his popularity as a visitor attraction, and to avoid the potential of an unwanted injury from other bulls and winter discomfort, he was eventually restricted to an exhibition pasture. Not a true albino, Big Medicine had bluish gray eyes and boasted a clump of brown fur between his horns. Matings between him and other cows at the refuge

"Sam Gilluly and Big Medicine." After his death, the remains of Big Medicine were given to a Montana taxidermist who worked on the mounting for almost two years. Still on display at the Montana State Historical Society Museum, Big Medicine is one of museum's more popular attractions. Sam Gilluly was director of the Museum from 1967 to 1974. Courtesy Montana Historical Society, Helena, Montana.

produced normal-colored calves except for an albino bull calf born in 1937 as the result of a mating between Big Medicine and his mother. Blind at birth, the white calf was shipped to the National Zoo in Washington, D.C., where he died in 1949. Big Medicine passed on ten years later, and after his death his remains were mounted and displayed at the Montana State Historical Museum in Helena.

There have been limited records of other white bison that were born in this century, but all these occurred within the Big Delta herd in Alaska. Their lineage can be traced to the same National Bison Range herd that produced Big Medicine.

Most bison calves are born in May, but they can sporadically show up anytime between April and June. Late-year calves are uncommon and those few that are born in July, or even after, often do not fare as well as those that have had an earlier start in the year. Thus, the August 20, 1994, birth of a bison calf in Wisconsin within the small herd of David and Valerie

Heider was somewhat unique because of the date of its birth, but the event became even more remarkable when it was discovered that the heifer calf was white. With brown eyes and nose, the calf was not a true albino, but its striking appearance certainly must have presented a breathtaking sight to the Heiders. In recognition of this unique event they named the calf "Miracle." Without any known possibility, to his knowledge, of cross-breeding taking place, Dave Heider contacted the American Bison Association (now National Bison Association) to determine if birth of a white bison calf was really considered to be a rare occurrence. When they were advised that it indeed was, and the Heiders further indicated their willingness to submit the white calf to blood tests along with the calf's mother and the herd bull, the association's executive director was convinced of the legitimacy of the claim.

When news of the birth of Miracle received national press interest, the Heiders were deluged with visitors. In addition to media representatives and a curious public, Native Americans quickly responded to express their particular interest in the little white bison heifer and its welfare. Scholarly attention to this event was well represented by the early visit of Dr. Robert Pickering, Department of Anthropology, Denver Museum of Natural History, who then subsequently provided three excellent articles that were published in the American/National Bison Association's *Bison World*. Although all of the overwhelming national inquisitiveness has disrupted the normal activities of the Heiders, they have still maintained considerable sensitivity and appreciation for the significance of this event to the Native American and also for the American public. Dave Heider related to me a rather touching story regarding an early morning visit he received from a young couple whose child was awaiting surgery in a local hospital for an aneurysm. Although not Native Americans, they asked permission to see the white calf, and upon viewing the calf they asked Dave if he would join them in prayer. This event obviously still carried considerable emotional influence on Mr. Heider as he was unable to complete the story but gave a "thumbs up" sign when I asked if the operation was successful.

At the time of my visit to the Heider farm on June 17, 1995, the number of visitors had declined to fewer than one hundred per day, and the Heiders had restricted visitation to Saturdays and Sundays, from 12 noon until 5 p.m. "Miracle," the former white calf, was now nearly as dusky brown in color as its three yearling peers. The fences surrounding the designated viewing area were symbolically decorated with numerous articles left by visiting Native Americans expressing the religious significance of the birth event. Red, yellow, black, and white prayer cloths were carefully placed, or affixed, to the fences, along with knives, coins, feathers, tobacco, and ornamented medicine pouches. Tribal members who were present at that time were of the belief that Miracle's former white color would return.

Dan and Jean Shirek own and operate a medium-sized bison ranch near Michigan, North Dakota. In June of 1996 an albino calf was born within their herd, but it died about a month after birth. However, in July a second albino bison calf was born. This little female calf, which the Shireks have named "White Cloud," was still alive as of January 1997, and if it can be proven to be an animal that has pure bison lineage, the Shireks and their albino bison may have an interesting future.

Color has always held a position of vital significance and fulfilled an unmistakably profound and often mystical role within Native American expression. While the Indian visionary would often relate dream visions in black and white, other colors have also appeared, especially yellow, green, and red. When these other colors appeared, they extended particular impact and symbolism to the vision. Of all colors, red is the most exalted and sacred. Associated with the quality of either beauty or power, or perhaps both, red is frequently identified in dream visions as being the color of symbolic feather tips, face paintings, tepee markings, and even issues from the dream vision subject's body.

The bison was, and still is, an integral part of Indian culture. Strongly featured in a number of rituals and tribal religious ceremonies and dances, it was seen as a protector of their people. Unfortunately, many of these very wonderful traditions and ceremonies have become lost because their passage from generation to generation depended only upon the spoken word.

Over the years, a number of efforts have been made by certain organizations and individuals to explicitly record some of the more culturally meaningful Native American religious ceremonies, legends, and dances. One of the better examples was an effort that was made in 1928 by the Smithsonian to document for posterity an extremely intricate ceremonial dance. The Smithsonian Institution published, through its Bureau of American Ethnology Bulletin 87, *Notes on the Buffalo-Head*

Dance of the Thunderhead Gens of the Fox Indians. This bulletin very meticulously describes, in ninety-four pages, how this ceremonial dance is conducted and the story behind the dance, that is, how one young man was blessed by a bison a long time ago and, after becoming blessed, what he later accomplished. Through exquisite detail each aspect of the ritual is explained, and particular attention is given to the preciseness of each individual facet of the ceremony, including the number of times certain phrases must be repeated in song. The Indians, however, did not have historians to provide written accounts of their accomplishments or instruction on how certain religious ceremonies or other procedures should be conducted. Each tribe had to depend upon oral passage of this knowledge from generation to generation. Indian history seemingly only begins with the arrival of the white people upon the North American continent. This history speaks mainly to the relationship of the Indians to the white people, and little attention was given to the unbiased recording of tribal activities and events. It was seemingly only infrequently, such as was the case with regard to the above-cited Bulletin 87, that tribal religious ceremonies were accurately recorded. The Indians' first impression of the white man was not very favorable, and the continued attempt by the white man to exact unfair trade agreements and seek religious conversion did not improve relationships.

As the great herds of bison on the open plains were being rapidly depleted, the meat and hide hunters then began to look enviously at Indian lands where bison were still to be found in large numbers. Since the Europeans first arrived on the North American continent, the relationship between the white man and the Indian reflected mutual distrust, was frequently contentious and often hostile, and was burdened by written agreements and treaties that were seemingly only enforced when it was to hold the Indian accountable. In retrospect, it seems abundantly clear that the many treaties that were negotiated between the two factions were motivated primarily by the desire of the federal government to gradually assume possession of all Indian lands. George Dewey Harmon, who had completed a study of Indian affairs between 1789 and 1850, submitted that in order to make room for the advancing frontier, a drastic change in government policy had to be taken. Harmon went on further to suggest that "the year of 1825 might be regarded as the year terminating the old Indian policy of peaceful persuasion and negotiation and beginning the new coercive policy" (Harmon 1941, 169). This new policy was never any more evident than through quick passage of the 1830 Indian removal bill. Forced to give way to the pressures of a more powerful society, many eastern Indians were subsequently relocated to less desired western locations. Even this, however, would not prove to be the final and conclusive action, and in 1854 the Senate Committee on Indian Affairs then theorized as to what would be an eventual outcome (*Senate Document,* 33rd Congress, 1st Session No. 379, p. 6):

> Over and over again, in the most solemn manner, we have guaranteed to nation after nation [Indian] such of its lands as remained to it, after we had cajoled or forced it into a cession; and as often, after a lapse of a few short years, has the wave of white population again overtaken the hapless people, forcing it ever westward, and by new negotiations, new appliances of money and presents to corrupt greedy chiefs, and new threats of leaving them to the tender mercies of state sovereignty, another and another cession of land has been extorted, until the last grave of their fathers was included in the field of a stranger.

Although many of the buffalo and hide hunters had expressed but little remorse over the eventual outcome from their actions, it is interesting to note the comment of one buffalo hunter who had remarked: "And to-day, 1907, it is a pleasing thought to the few surviving hunters of the old Southwest to know that the then vast unsettled region is now dotted over with thousands of peaceful prosperous homes." This same hunter, however, had earlier observed: "And at times I asked myself 'What would you do, John R. Cook, if you had been a child of this wonderfully prolific game region, your ancestors, back through countless ages, according to traditional history, having roamed these vast solitudes as free as the air they breathed? What would you do if some outside interloper should come in and start a ruthless slaughter upon the very soil you had grown from childhood upon, and that you believed you alone had all the rights by occupancy that could possibly be given one?' Yes, what would you do?" (Cook [1907] 1967, 410, 166).

5

Predators and
Natural Adversities

Carefully crafted by nature and perfectly suited to a grassland and plains environment, the bison was seemingly assured of a near eternal survival in its North American domain. Endowed with great strength and agility, quickness of movement, keen hearing, sense of smell, and resistance to disease, this large horned mammal's only perceived weakness was less than average eyesight. It endured through evolutionary processes that extracted major changes from most species and/or eliminated those that could not or did not evolve. Because it is instinctively social, as far as members of its own species are concerned, the bison is also the recipient of levels of security offered only to herd animals.

Economist Kenneth E. Boulding *(The World as a Total System)* suggested that the aggregate of all living organisms, spread over the surface of the globe, has always represented a total system. Each living species had a specific habitat to live within, and other species that interacted with one another observed these habitat boundaries. However, with the arrival of the human race, the system found it necessary to adjust to a species that had the whole world for its habitat — thus, this led to a series of catastrophic extinctions in the more isolated environments. Boulding also suggested the existence of three different relationships between species: *competition, mutual cooperation,* and *predation* or *parasitism.* In predation, if there were more of A, there would be less of B, but if there were more of B, there would be more of A (that is, the more predators, the less bison; the more bison, the more predators). This he sees as being surprisingly very stable for all species involved, unless it should get out of hand — a circumstance that did occur with respect to the bison.

When the ancestors of the current-day bison crossed into Beringia (the name given by scientists to the Bering land bridge), they were accompanied by a number of predators: the short faced bear, the American lion, the sabertooth cat, and the dire wolf. As climatical changes permitted the bison to migrate into the body of the North American continent, predators also followed these herds. Pleistocene carnivores were formidable adversaries for even the large bison of ice age times, *Bison priscus*. Except for the short faced bear, other predators customarily travelled in packs or prides, since it was unlikely that just one of these intrepid hunters could single-handedly overcome a healthy and mature bison. Russell Guthrie, who conducted research on a mummified carcass of a steppe bison found in Alaska in 1979, suggested that this adult of the species was killed approximately 36,000 years ago, but it was not killed by a single predator but by two or more Alaskan lions.

The first humans likely crossed into Beringia more than 40,000 years ago. Their weapons were rudimentary and could not have offered to their owners much assurance that they possessed an offensive capability that was greatly superior to that of the animals they hunted. Because of their lack of individual offensive capability, humans had to hunt in large groups, much like the animal predators that hunted in packs or prides, so that by their sheer numbers they could overcome the large herbivores. Analogous to all predators of those times, kills were made simply to obtain a necessary food supply, and as the climax of a hunt might also extract a penalty from the hunter as well as the hunted, it was far from being considered a sport. Since the larger animals provided the most meat, it was preferable, if the opportunity presented itself, to kill one of the larger animals and thus reduce the number of hunts. If this was not possible or practical, the more defenseless, and usually smaller, animals were then typically selected.

According to Jon Erickson *(Ice Ages-Past and Future)* and Paul Martin *(Quaternary Extinctions)*, the human hunters advanced southward and reached the southern end of the South American continent more than 11,000 years ago, thereby reaching a critical density. With the exception of a few ungulates, more notably the bison, this led to the extinction of many species of large animals. These vanished animals were believed to have been destroyed by heavy and efficient predation by a rapidly growing population of hunters, such as is suggested by Martin's overkill-by-blitzkrieg hypothesis. Even though the bison was one of their favorite prey (manifested by the extent of cultural debris found with discarded bison bones), there is no evidence to suggest that this predation served to significantly diminish the numbers of bisons or that it did other than perhaps mitigate the rate of growth of the herds.

When *Bison bison* and *Bison athabascae* eventually evolved from *Bison antiquus occidentalis*, *B. bison* were found in nearly all the plains and grassland areas in North America, and *B. athabascae* generally in the more forested areas of the north-central interior plains of Canada. The wild North American bison had but only two serious animal predators: the wolf *(Canis lupus)* and the grizzly bear *(Ursus arctos horribilis)*. However, the more relentless of all bison predators were the humans *(Homo sapiens),* the only life-form that has clearly demonstrated its unique ability and willingness to obliterate other species.

There were perhaps more than one million Great Plains wolves *(Canis lupus nubilus)* when the bison herds were at their peak. Barry Lopez (1978, 174) claims that Meriwether Lewis had once referred to the wolf in his journals as "the shepherd of the buffalo," because of its propensity to constantly follow the herds. Wolves would normally take the very young, the old, the injured, or the sick, individuals that the bison populations could easily do without. Even under conditions of extreme hunger, wolves may hesitate to attack a healthy, vigorous, adult bison whose horns and hoofs could create havoc and death within a wolf pack. Dr. Edwin James (1966, 474) vol. I, who travelled from Pittsburgh to the Rockies with Major Steven Long, stated: "In whatever direction they [bison] move, their parasites and dependents fail not to follow. Large herds are invariably attended by gangs of meagre, famine-pinched wolves, and flights of obscene and ravenous birds." Early trappers and frontiersmen also observed that in winter, wolves would drive elk, and occasionally bison, out on the frozen surface of a lake, where the hoofed animals would subsequently lose their footing and become easy prey for the wolf pack. Wolves prowled around nearly all bison herds and were always alert for the opportunity to make a kill. Wayne Gard (1960, 19) commented upon an incident that George Catlin observed when he was travelling through the West in the 1830s. An old bull, isolated from the herd, was the focus of a concentrated attack by a pack of wolves: the bull "had made desperate resistance. His eyes were entirely eaten out of his head, the gristle of his nose was mostly gone, his tongue was half eaten off, and the skin and flesh of his legs were torn almost literally into strings. In this tattered and poor condition, the poor old veteran stood bracing up in the midst of his devourers."

Barry Lopez (1978, 58) described an incident of prey selection that took place in Wood Buffalo National Park, Alberta, Canada, in 1951.

> Two buffalo bulls and two cows are lying in the grass chewing their cud. Three of them are in good health; one cow is lame. Wolves approach and withdraw a number of times, apparently put off by the human observer [park researcher]. At each approach, though, the lame cow becomes agitated and begins looking all around. Her three companions *ignore* the wolves. When one wolf comes within twenty-five feet, the lame cow gets up on shaking legs to face it alone. It seems clear that prey selection is something both animals play a role in.

That healthy bison will generally adopt a nonchalant, unruffled, general unconcerned attitude toward wolves has been noted by a number of researchers. Apparently, the bison's confidence in its own or the herd's collective strength and power is perhaps part of the reason for the bison to exhibit this type of behavior. The same conduct is demonstrated by a variety of herd animals with respect to other, and even more powerful, predators than the wolf. How often have we seen nature films that feature grazing animals on the plains of Africa being stalked by a pride of lions, and yet the animals continue to just graze or stare at the big cats? After the attack, and an animal is caught and perhaps still in the jaws of a lion, they will continue to go about their grazing as if to say, "Since it obviously was not me they were after, this then is of no consequence." The Indians were well aware of the bison's seeming indifference to wolves, and cloaking themselves in wolf skins, they would creep up on a herd of feeding bison; the animals usually paid little if any attention to them since wolves were a rather common sight. When the bison were in range of their arrows, they would rise up and launch their arrows in the direction of the nearest young animal, or cow, hoping that the stricken animal would not run too far before it would die, and that the remaining bison would not stampede.

Wolves would take the old and sickly, but perhaps preferred bison calves more. According to Jesuit missionary Father Jean Pierre De Smet,

Indians cloaked with wolf skins approaching a bison herd. A painting by George Catlin, drawn sometime during the 1830s. Catlin, who studied the North American Indians from 1832 to 1840, had an uncommon respect for the western tribes and interpreted their culture as no white man had previously done. Courtesy Denver Public Library, Western History Department.

who had spent considerable time with a variety of Indian tribes in the early 1830s, Indians had asserted to him that wolves accounted for the death of one third of the buffalo calves annually. In support of this observation, Frank Roe, quoted from a statement made by Josiah Gregg (*The Commerce of the Prairies, 1831–1839,* 1905, 264) concerning the poor quality of bison calves, suggested that it was primarily due to the "scanty supply of milk which their dams afford, and to their running so much from hunters and wolves." Today, in Wood Buffalo National Park, Canada, wolves regularly and successfully prey on bison. L. N. Carbyn (1992, 170) stated that a pack of ten wolves will kill an adult bison every five to ten days, and that summer predation on calves is extremely heavy, perhaps accounting for 50 percent of the calves before they reach one year of age. Wolves are now considered too numerous in Wood Bison National Park and, as such, present a real threat to the health of the bison herds. Because humans, rather than nature, manage the herd in Wood Bison National Park, we can conclude that the number of wolves will undoubtedly be reduced by park management before predation on bison becomes more serious, or perhaps even a species threatening issue.

Prior to human intervention, bison herds of the Great Plains, and their accompanying packs of wolves, evidently grew in proportionate size, not disturbing what Boulding referred to as "the total system" and their predation relationship. When the great bison herds were reduced (all but eliminated) by the buffalo hunters and hidemen, the remaining wolves (those not already poisoned or shot for their fur) turned to other prey: domestic stock. The sheep and cattle industry was instrumental in placing a bounty on wolves, and *Canis lupus* was all but completely exterminated in the United States by "wolfers."

The North American grizzly bear (*Ursus arctos horribilis*) was, and is now (in its current habitat), the most potentially dangerous and formidable creature found in North America. Unlike the wolf, who eschews all but meat, the grizzly can and will eat almost anything edible. Like its cousin the black bear *(Ursus americanus)*, it is omnivorous, and perhaps over its lifetime will consume more vegetation than meat, but it can, and does, eat a lot of meat.

James Audubon, the American naturalist and artist who prowled the western United States in the early 1800s, ranked the grizzly bear as more dangerous to the bison than the wolf, and in this he was somewhat supported by the equally well-known naturalist Ernest Thompson Seton. I found Seton's claim regarding the grizzly most interesting since this claim was made in volume II of *Lives of Game Animals*, which dealt with grizzly bears (1926, 18, 24). In volume III, under the American Bison (1927, 677), he identifies and lists the chief natural enemies of the "Buffalo herds." His inverse order of enemies began with insects and ended with rivers. Wolves were mentioned but not bear. Neither of these two opinions seemed to be based on fact, however, as very few eyewitness accounts of grizzlies actually preying on bison have been documented. A number of anecdotal observations have been offered to describe encounters between live bison and the grizzly bear, but few were actually substantiated with actual names of the eyewitnesses and dates.

Wayne Gard (1960, 20) said that "a veteran hunter in Dakota once watched a huge male grizzly attack a small herd of buffalo cows protected by five or six bulls. As the bear approached, the bulls closed ranks and lowered their horns. When the bulls charged, the bear struck one of the bulls so hard with his paws that he broke the back of the bull, killing him instantly. But the other bulls used their horns so effectively that soon the bear crawled off with mortal wounds. . . ." Coincidentally, in a somewhat similar vein, Osmond Breland (1963, 7) stated that "a grizzly was once seen to attack and kill four bison bulls one after the other. The first three were speedily dispatched with a single stroke for each, but the fourth was made of sterner stuff. There was a flurry of paws and horns and, although the bison was eventually killed, the bear itself was severely wounded in the encounter." Tom McHugh (1972, 213–214) related a story about how a grizzly lay in wait on a rise above a trail, pouncing on a cow as the herd passed underneath, and a bull eventually dispatched the assailant after a prolonged battle. One of the Indian witnesses to this purported epic battle described it in the following manner:

> The bull would charge the bear, and when he struck him fairly would knock him off his feet, often inflicting severe wounds with his sharp horns. The bear struck at the bull, and tried to catch him by the head or shoulders, and to hold him, but this he could not do. After fifteen or twenty minutes of fierce and active fighting the bear had received all the punishment he cared for, and tried to escape, but the bull would not let him go, and kept up the attack until he had killed his adversary. Even after the bear was dead the bull would gore the carcass and sometimes lift it clear of the ground on his horns. He seemed insane with rage, and notwithstanding the fact that most of the skin was torn from his head and shoulders, appeared to be looking around for something else to fight.

Nat Dodge (1963, 433) indicated that the above story was told by Two-Gun White Calf, the Indian whose profile appeared on the buffalo nickel, but that when White Calf added the part about the bull bison hunting down the bear, the entire account was open to question, as White Calf liked to tell stories that tourists wanted to hear.

Another tale about bear and bison was told by the renowned hunter and former president of the United States, Theodore Roosevelt. This tale was included along with a selection of other writings of Roosevelt by Paul Schullery (1983, 46). Roosevelt is reported to have said:

In the old days when the innumerable bison grazed free on the prairie, the grizzly sometimes harassed their bands as it now does the herds of the ranchman. The bison was the most easily approached of all game, and the great bear could often get near some outlying straggler, in its quest after stray cows, yearlings, or calves. In default of a favorable chance to make a prey of one of these weaker members of the herds, it did not hesitate to attack the mighty bulls themselves; and perhaps the grandest sight which it was ever the good fortune of the early hunters to witness, was one of these rare battles between a hungry grizzly and a powerful buffalo bull.

Both Tom McHugh (1972, 214) and Erwin Bauer (1985, 69) reported upon a bison/bear encounter that occurred in Yellowstone National Park. Park Ranger Joe Wray found the carcass of a mature female grizzly in June of 1951, while patrolling the Lamar Valley. The bear had obviously been battered about, and both sides of the carcass were badly bruised and bloodied; all the ribs were seemingly broken on one side, and the belly was punctured by two holes that suggested they were made by the horns of a young buffalo. Near the carcass were several patches of bison hair and numerous bison hoofprints. Although no dead or injured bison was ever discovered, it was concluded that a bison had probably killed the grizzly.

Numerous legends also exist of battles staged in California between grizzlies and cattle bulls and bison bulls, before California was admitted to the Union. Supposedly the bull would charge, the bear would flick out its paw, and thus would usually break the bull's neck at the first stroke. But no actual record of such confrontations has ever been produced. W. J. Schoonmaker (1968, 84), in following up on the authenticity of some of these purported staged fights, stated that "according to early accounts, when bear and bulls were put into an arena, the grizzly was reluctant to fight."

Whenever an animal known to be carnivorous is found feeding on another animal, the presumption is one of natural predation. In some instances this may be entirely true, but in others it may only be that it was feeding on an animal that was already dead. Lewis and Clark reported in their journals that carcasses of bison found dead from either drowning or fire were eventually eaten by grizzly bears or other carnivores. Similar circumstances have been reported with great frequency. The Yellowstone fires of 1988 serve as an excellent example of this, when a number of burned bison carcasses were quickly set upon by grizzlies and other park scavengers.

Tom McHugh suggests that there were, to his knowledge, only two or three eyewitness accounts of grizzly predation against bison, and he provided a report from a Canadian journal that he claimed was the most detailed: "One bear [grizzly] killed at Hand Hills [Alberta] in 1877 required eight shots before he was disabled. His feet were eight inches across, and were armed with claws five inches long. He was caught in the act of killing a buffalo cow, and had just cracked her spine when he received the first shot. When stretched, his hide was as large as a buffalo bull."

In 1967, Bill Burton bought a cattle ranch on Kodiak Island in Alaska. Kodiak Island is also the home of the famed Kodiak brown bear (*Ursus arctos middendorffi*), the largest meat-eating land mammal on our planet, often reaching three quarters of a ton in weight and eight to ten feet in length. The brown bear attacks its prey much like the common grizzly; it uses its enormous strength to strike with its front paws and can easily break an animal's back with one blow. By 1975, Burton's cattle herd had grown to seven hundred, but cattle prices were low, feed costs were high, and the brown bears were taking twenty-five animals a year. Burton experimented with several breeds — Galloway, Charolais, Angus, Hereford crosses, and even Scottish Highlanders — hoping to find an animal that could hold its own against the brown bear. A friend suggested that he try bison, so he started out with thirty-eight and he now has more than 150 in his herd. In an interview, given in April 1993 to the American Bison Association, Burton offered the following comments: "The buffalo [bison] do a lot better up there," he said, in referring to the high summer range. "We don't get near the loss we get with cattle. When something scares them, they come right together and they are pretty formidable like that. It would take a pretty big bear to try to attack a herd of buffalo." In the eight years he has had bison, Burton said that he had only lost three or four to bears.

E. Douglas Branch (1929, 11) includes the coyote *(Canis latrans)* as a potential enemy of the bison. In discussing the eventual demise of herd bulls Branch offered the following observation:

> And after twenty-five years of vigorous life — the wolves, or the coyotes. The old bulls, gaunt and stiff from age and spotted and torn with scars, were prey to the packs that skulked at the herds edge. Coyotes did not dare attack an old, isolated patriarch; as long as the

bull kept his feet, he lived. But a system of worrying him, of giving him no rest, would win; and when he tottered from exhaustion, his enemies leaped, bit, and held.

Although none of the other earlier or past writers elected to identify the coyote as a serious predator, it is quite possible that young bison calves, if unprotected, might possibly be attacked by coyotes, but this would scarcely be a frequent event. Coyotes would more often feed on the carcass of a bison killed by some other agent. Wolves were also known to accompany herds of cows and calves rather than those that were comprised mainly of bulls. John Bradbury (1966, 133) was of the opinion that this was primarily occasioned by the fact that calves are the much easier prey.

The cougar, mountain lion, puma, or, as occasionally called, panther (*Felis concolor*) also receives little mention as a possible predator of, or presenting a serious threat to, the bison. This I found to be quite interesting since there were, at one time, a considerable number of cougar inhabiting both North and South America. It would seem that a young bison calf should have certainly been a rather tempting morsel for a hungry cougar. John Dunn Hunter, who claims to have observed a number of attacks by cougar on bison, relates the following incident (1973, 66–67):

> In one of my excursions, while seated in the shade of a large tree, situated on a gentle declivity, with a view to procure some mitigation from the oppressive heat of the midday sun, I was surprised by a tremendous rushing noise. I sprang up, and discovered a herd, I believe, of a thousand buffaloes running at full speed towards me; with a view, as I supposed, to beat off the flies, which at this season are inconceivably troublesome to those animals.
>
> I placed myself behind the tree, so as not to be seen, not apprehending any danger; because they ran with too great rapidity, and too closely together, to afford any one an opportunity of injuring me, while protected in this manner.
>
> The buffaloes passed so near me on both sides, that I could have touched several of them merely by extending my arm. In the rear of the herd was one on which a hugh panther had fixed, and was voraciously engaged in cutting off the muscles of its neck. I did not discover this circumstance till it had nearly passed beyond rifle shot distance, when I discharged my piece, and wounded the panther.

Hunter claims to have later killed the cougar; removed, smoked, and dressed the skin; and later arrayed himself in it to "surprise the herds of buffaloes, elk, and deer, which on my approach fled with great precipitation and dread."

A somewhat similar experience was related by noted frontierman Daniel Boone (Young and Goldman 1946, 97–98). Leaving their North Carolina home in 1769 to wander through the wilderness of Kentucky, Boone and his brother began their return journey to North Carolina on May 1, 1770. The following day, May 2, 1770, the Boones encountered a large herd of bison that seemed to be extremely agitated. Timothy Flint, who authored a book on the exploits of Daniel Boone in 1856, indicates that the herd's fury was caused by "a panther [that had] seated himself upon the back of one of the largest buffaloes, and fastened his claws into the flesh of the animal wherever he could reach it until the blood ran down on all sides." Daniel Boone then purportedly shot the "panther," bringing it to the ground.

Although the accounting of the above two incidents cannot, of course, be actually proven, it does fall within the realm of possibility, and for that reason I have elected to at least consider the cougar as being a potential predator of bison.

Natural disasters and afflictions were the cause of greater mortality among bison herds than all four-footed predators combined. Since the bison has been designed by nature to be companionable, the movement of bison in vast herds would thus invite disaster at much greater levels than what would befall the isolated animal. Assuredly, there is greater security offered through the herd, but the herd characteristic may also dim individual awareness of potential dangers. Bison are no more susceptible to natural calamities, such as those presented by fire, water crossings, lightning, blizzards and other storms, or perhaps even drought, than are other animals, but because they travel in such hordes the herd mass tends to magnify losses.

Fire plays no favorites, and even a fast-moving prairie fire will tarry long enough to burn or suffocate any animal or bird unable to escape the scorching flames and/or dense smoke. Frank Gilbert Roe (1951, 159) quotes a November 25, 1804, entry from the Henry-Thompson journals that provides testimony regarding the outcome of one such prairie fire: "plains burned in every direction and blind buffalo seen every moment wandering

Bull bison wandering through a field touched by an early winter snow. Bison readily adapt to most climates and are the supreme survivors. Courtesy American Bison Association.

about. The poor beasts have all the hair singed off, even the skin in many places is shriveled up and terribly burned, and their eyes are swollen and closed fast. It was real pitiful to see them staggering about, sometimes running afoul of a large stone, at other times tumbling down a hill and falling into creeks not yet frozen over. In one spot we found a whole herd lying dead. . . . [we have] seen an incredible number of dead and dying, blind, lame, singed and roasted buffalo."

Tom McHugh (1972, 245) quotes from an individual whom he only identifies as "a settler traversing the Oregon Trail [1804] just west of Council Bluffs [who] viewed the aftermath of one such catastrophe": "There had been a slope of the prairie burned and it had killed hundreds of buffaloes. We saw as many as three hundred lying together with the hair all burned off them while many were roaming around deprived of their eyesight by the fire. Many were shot to put them out of their misery."

The terrifying aspect of dealing with a prairie fire was thoroughly illustrated through a number of eyewitness accounts assembled by Merrill Mattes in his book *The Great Platte River Road.* Mattes indicated that one eyewitness reported (1969, 246) "seeing the carcasses of thousands of buffalo, wolves, antelope, and other wildlife which perished in the 'fiery tornadoes.' J.M. Stewart noted buffalo still alive, singed and blinded, which ran berserk, colliding with emigrant wagons."

It is not only grass fires that can, and have, inflicted deadly impact. Animals who browse in the shadow of the woods or in lush woodland meadows also frequently become fire victims. As an example of this, Yellowstone National Park is often the site of some rather calamitous forest fires. Captain Hiram Martin Chittenden, who was acting superintendent of Yellowstone National Park in 1895, noted in his book, *The Yellowstone National Park,* that "the proportion of the Park territory which has been burned over in the past three hundred years is almost as great as the park itself. Evidences of former fires abound everywhere, from the dead timber of last year's conflagration to full grown forests which still show on close inspection charred remains that have resisted the decay of time."

The summer of 1988 developed into one of the driest years that anyone could remember in Yellowstone. The fire danger was extraordinarily high and all precautions that could be taken were placed into effect. Unfortunately, the forested areas were also clogged with the vegetative debris from insect- and wind-downed trees. On June 23, 1988, a fire near Shoshone Lake was spotted by a fire lookout; by July 21, 1988, a series of lightning- and man-caused fires were still burning and had already involved over 16,000 acres of parkland. National Park and Forest Service firefighters were unable to suppress these fires nor a man-caused fire that was started the following day outside the park — and then promptly moved into parkland. Fueled by gale-force winds these fires began to spread throughout Yellowstone. Although every known resource known to man was brought to bear upon the fires, they basically ranged uncontrolled through the park until winter set in and the fires were finally extinguished by nature. Over 1.4 million acres, more than 63 percent of the park, had been affected by these fires.

In addition to its extensive vegetative and geological resources, Yellowstone National Park is home to a variety of wildlife. The animals and birds are not usually troubled by fire, as they move ahead of it or otherwise stay out of its way. In addition, nighttime generally brings a respite as winds diminish and the dew point rises; animals will then cross into areas that the fire has passed. This did not occur, however, with the Yellowstone fires; the winds continued and there wasn't any dew point. The largest public herd of bison is found within the boundaries of Yellowstone, more than thirty-five hundred animals. After the fires were over with and rangers were assessing damage to wildlife, only five bison were found burned to death, far fewer than the number that would have perished as the result of a hard winter.

Recently the National Park Service was criticized for not electing to rescue a bison that was unable to pull itself over the bank after crossing Yellowstone's Firehole River in winter. The Park Service, by appropriately following its policy regarding interference in natural events, permitted the bison to perish — as had countless numbers of bison in the past when herds were attempting water crossings.

Chronicles and journals that record the history of the early West literally brim with tales of huge bison herds attempting to cross swift rivers and being caught up in the current or rapids. Even if the herds were successful in crossing, some animals would perish in quicksand or drown because they were unable to negotiate a crumbling riverbank. It was quite common that after an early thaw, thousands of bison carcasses would be seen floating down the rivers or becoming washed up on the banks. In 1795, a trader, John McDonnell, actually counted 7,360 dead bison along the Qu'Appelle River.

Col. Richard Irving Dodge mentions one particular ill-fated bison river crossing (1959, 122):

> Late in the summer of 1867 a herd of probably 4,000 buffalo attempted to cross the South Platte, near Plum Creek. The water was rapidly subsiding, being nowhere over a foot or two in depth, and the channels in the bed were filled or filling with loose quicksands. The buffalo in front were soon hopelessly stuck. Those immediately behind, urged on by the horns and pressure of those yet further in rear, trampled over their struggling companions, to be themselves engulfed in the devouring sand. This was continued until the bed of the river, nearly half-a-mile broad, was covered with dead or dying buffalo. Only a comparatively few actually crossed the river, and these were soon driven back by hunters. It was estimated that considerably over half the herd, or more than 2,000 buffalo, paid for this attempt with their lives.

Alexander Henry, of the Northwest Fur Company, maintained meticulous accounts of his activities that were later edited and published in 1897 by Elliott Coues. In late March 1801, Henry recorded in his journals the thawing of snow and its resultant impact upon the ice on the Red River. He soon reported seeing ice drifting by in large masses, many covered with drowned bison. After the river was clear of ice, drowned bison floated by in herds; he claimed that the carcasses formed one continuous line in the current for two days and nights. Captain Hiram Martin Chittenden, in *History of Early Steamboat Navigation on the Missouri River*, who had earlier written about Yellowstone National Park when he was acting superintendent, claimed that in spring the carcasses of bison in the upper Missouri lodged on sandbars, islands, and the shore, to such an extent that many of the river travelers found the air almost intolerable. In Wyoming, one of the small rivers that empty into the Republican River is called the Stinking Water, a name that was given to it by local Indians, who had frequently been forced to abandon their campsite on the stream because of the number of bison carcasses mired in the mud and fouling the air.

Archer B. Hulbert reported in *Historic Highways of America* that the almost obligatory wanderings of bison required them to cross rivers and streams on a regular basis, and he then offered the following observation, also quoted in part by Frank Roe (1951, 179):

In winter, when the ice has become strong enough to bear the weight of many tons, buffaloes are often drowned in great numbers, for they are in the habit of crossing rivers on the ice, and should any alarm occur, rush in the dense crowd to one place; the ice gives way beneath the pressure of hundreds of these huge animals, they are precipitated into the water, and if it is deep enough to reach over their backs, soon perish. Should the water, however, be shallow, they scuffle through the . . . ice, in the greatest disorder to the shore. . . . Small herds, crossing rivers on the ice in the spring, are set adrift, in consequence of a sudden breaking of the ice. . . . They have been seen floating on such occasions in groups of three, four, and sometimes eight or ten together, although on separate cakes of ice. A few stragglers have been known to reach the shore in an almost exhausted state; but the majority perish from cold and want of food rather than trust themselves boldly to the turbulent waters. . . .

John Bradbury, who had been commissioned by the Botanical Society of Liverpool, England, to investigate plant life in the United States, accompanied the expedition of Astorians in 1811 up the Missouri River. Although primarily interested in plant life, Bradbury frequently noted the number of bison carcasses floating down the Missouri. On April 16, after passing Fort Osage (Missouri), he entered in his journal the following comment (1966, 44):

We began to notice more particularly the great number of the bodies of drowned buffaloes, floating on the river; vast numbers of them were also thrown ashore, and upon the rafts, on the points of the Islands. These carcasses had attracted an immense number of turkey buzzards *(Vultur aura)* and as the preceding night had been rainy, multitudes of them were sitting on the trees, with their backs toward the sun, and their wings spread out to dry, a common practice with these birds, after rain.

Although herd numbers are much lower today than they were centuries earlier, bison still cross rivers or are caught up in floods. Tom McHugh (1972, 240) cites two instances that took place in Wood Buffalo National Park, Canada. The first occurred in the spring of 1958 when high water in the Athabasca–Peace River delta took the lives of nearly five hundred animals. The second instance, McHugh cited, occurred during the autumn and winter of 1960, when severe flooding along the shores of Lake Claire was believed to have killed three thousand.

Summer storms are often accompanied by spectacular lightning displays. And, when lightning was present, the flat prairies were probably as hazardous to bison years ago as golf courses are today for human golfers. Merrill Mattes (1969, 481) quoted from the 1833 journals of Charles Larpenteur, which provided his personal observation regarding bison struck by lightning:

> On approaching La Ranie's River we discovered three large buffaloes lying dead close together. . . . the animals had been killed by lightning during a storm we had the previous day. . . . we were ordered to dismount and go to work making a boat out of the hides of the buffalo . . . and the party with all the goods were crossed over by sunset. . . . On the arrival of the trappers and hunters a big drunken spree took place.

In addition to causing calamitous prairie fires, lightning could possibly take out an occasional animal, but it would, in certainty, create more havoc by triggering a stampede whereby weak, tired, or sickly animals became trampled. The swiftness with which the storms developed in the plains left little opportunity for human preparation, let alone any anticipation by lesser species. The wind, heavy rain, lightning, and often immense hailstones would send bison herds into frenzy and panic; they would then promptly thunder across the plains much like a runaway locomotive, crushing underfoot all those who could not keep up. Wayne Gard (1960, 10) observed that a stampede on the open plain might wear itself out with little harm, but elsewhere, "it might leave scores or even hundreds of buffaloes dead. In their blind rush, many would be mired in the quicksands of a treacherous stream or would plunge to their death off a steep cliff." In 1541, some of Coronado's men reportedly saw stampeding bison completely fill a ravine to the extent that those animals rushing from behind crossed on the trampled bodies of those that had been in front.

Although tornadoes have been only infrequently mentioned, in the context of them generally representing a hazard to bison, there have been reports of tornadoes or cyclones striking herds with such force that they would drive the eyeballs of bison out of their sockets and also severely lacerate their backs and flanks. Ely Moore claimed to have observed damage to bison as the result of a tornado in southwestern Kansas. Moore, who was on a bison hunt in 1854, saw where the wind had stripped the prairie of acres of sod and topsoil, and then he came upon two bison, completely divested of hair and with their bones pulverized. It was Moore's opinion that the tornado had picked the two bison up, lifted them high into the sky, and then hurled their bodies to the earth. Tom McHugh also related another purported tornado incident (1972, 244):

> A small war party of Sioux once watched a tornado carefully as the funnel descended toward a herd of buffalo; before the dark cone dipped into the herd, however, torrential rains forced the Indians to take shelter. Emerging after the storm, the men discovered "hundreds" of carcasses strewn over a quarter of a mile, the majority broken and twisted, some stripped of fur and mutilated, many stacked in heaps four and five deep.

One natural calamity that you would not normally expect bison to be exposed to is a tropical storm or hurricane. However, now that bison are found in all fifty states, they are also acquiring hurricane experience. Bill Mowry brought a herd of bison to Kauai, a subtropical island in the Hawaiian chain that receives wide variations in rainfall and has the distinction of possessing the wettest spot in the United States, Waialeale, with an annual rainfall of more than 444 inches. On his 202-acre ranch, Hanalei Garden Farms, Mowry had 160 bison, and because of the lushness of vegetation, planned to expand his herd by another 50 animals. In the fall of 1992, "Iniki," a category five (5) hurricane, struck Kauai, with winds in excess of 100 miles an hour. Mowry lost most of his home, his ranch fences, but not one of his bison was hurt or even visibly bothered.

Of all storms, the winter blizzard was probably the most devastating for the bison. The bison is not a puny or weak animal by any definition. There is absolutely no doubt that bison have the capacity to survive under conditions that cattle and most others of the *Bovidae* family would find intolerable. Even today, bison ranchers do not build barns for their animals, nor do they concern themselves about the well-being of their herd during a blizzard or a period of extreme cold (except, perhaps, if it is in the spring during calving time). One of the reasons given for the bison's capacity to adapt to cold weather or blizzards is said to be that bison face the wind, rather than turn their backs to it as cattle do. And this may possibly be correct; however, there are those who say bison will face any way they want to without regard to the way the wind may possibly be blowing. If natural shelter is available, such as a forested area or canyon, the bison may also seek that out. There also is no evidence to suggest that bison, in their meandering and roaming through the countryside, are seemingly devoid of a sense of comfort and may purposely head north in winter or south in summer. But nonetheless, in spite of their apparent winter adaptability, blizzards and cold still take their toll — even from the bison.

Col. Richard Irving Dodge (1959, 129–130) provided a fascinating description of the effect of a gigantic snowstorm:

> According to hunters' traditions the Laramie Plains were visited in the winter of 1844–1845 by a most extraordinary snowstorm. Contrary to all precedent, there was no wind, and the snow covered the surface evenly to a depth of nearly four feet. Immediately after the storm a bright sun softened the surface, that at night froze into a crust so firm that it was weeks before any heavy animal could make any headway over it. The Laramie Plains, being entirely surrounded by mountains, had always been a favourite wintering-place for the buffaloes. Thousands were caught in this storm and perished miserably from starvation. Since that time not a single buffalo has ever visited the Laramie Plains. When I first crossed these plains in 1868, the whole country was dotted with the skulls of buffaloes, all in the last stages of decomposition and all apparently of the same age giving some foundation for the tradition. Indeed, it was in answer to my request for an explanation of the numbers, appearance, and identity of age of these skulls, that the tradition was related to me by an old hunter, who, however, could not himself vouch for the facts.

Tom McHugh relates an almost similar circumstance (1972, 242) involving a blizzard that was said to have occurred in the Hay River country of northwestern Alberta, Canada, sometime around 1821. Snow accumulated to a depth of fourteen feet, and as a result bison perished by the thousands. This same episode was mentioned by E. W. Nelson in a letter to Joel Allen dated July 11, 1877, which relayed information that Nelson had obtained from two travellers who had passed through the Hay River country in 1871. From the number of accounts of enormous bison deaths attributed to snow, circumstances would seem to suggest that it was perhaps not the blizzards or extreme cold that actually killed the bison in the events described by Dodge and McHugh, but the accumulation of snow to depths sufficient to prevent bison movement or feeding.

Natural catastrophes may have taken more than their full share from the bison herds, but were the same circumstances and events assigned to free-ranging and unprotected cattle herds, the resulting losses would have been astronomical if not cataclysmic. In his most interesting book, *The Trampling Herd*, Paul Wellman reports on the 1871 Kansas blizzard and its effect upon cattle:

> In the winter of 1871 the sheath over the grass was even worse than usual, because the first coating on the ground was solid ice. Only one thing there was for the cattle to do. They turned their meek, protesting tails to the blizzard and began slowly to drift with the wind.
>
> Mile after mile that inexorable drift continued. After a time animals began to drop out, to lie down, and whenever they did so they died. . . . A quarter of a million cattle, hundreds of cow ponies, and nobody knows how many cowboys died in that great blizzard of 1871.

The blizzards of 1885–1886 were even more devastating. The cattle were from the south and not bred or acclimated to withstand winter storms or blizzards. All the stock on the ranges in the Dakotas, Nebraska, Kansas, the Texas Panhandle, and that expanse of land only designated at that time as Indian Territory were on the move with the wind. Even parts of Wyoming and Colorado were somewhat affected. Livestock drifted into rivers and perished, and into fences where they froze standing up. Doc Barton of the OS Bar Ranch had nearly 12,000 head of cattle and lost all but a few. R. K. Farmsworth's Circle M had 6,000 cattle before the storm; afterward 182 were found. Wellman indicates that Charles J. (Buffalo) Jones, upon witnessing the aftermath of the blizzards, wrote:

> As I drove over the prairies from Kansas into Texas I saw thousands upon thousands of carcasses of domestic cattle which had drifted before the chilling, freezing norther. Every one of them had died with its tail to the blizzard, never having stopped except at its last breath, then fell dead in its tracks.

It was said that 80 percent of the cattle in large sections of Wyoming were killed, and ranchers in other states lost cattle in similar proportions.

The storied Buffalo Jones, as quoted in Col. Henry Inman's *Buffalo Jones' Adventures on the Plains* ([1899] 1970, 11), probably summed up better than anyone else the primary advantage bison had over cattle in dealing with the inherent problems of an open range:

> Nature is never more persistent in any of its creations than in that of the buffalo's anatomy, or in its habits so suited to its wild environment. A more perfect animal for the strange surroundings of its habitat could not have been constructed. It is ever prepared for the severest "blizzard" from the far north, or the hottest "sirocco" of the torrid zone. It is so constructed that it faces every danger, whether it is the pitiless storm from the Arctic regions or its natural enemy, the gray wolf of the desert.

6

The Human Accelerator
— Bison Slaughter

Over 10,000 years ago, on a wintery day along the Arikaree River in what is now northeastern Colorado, a herd of bison were driven into a natural trap by Paleoindians. A steep and slippery entrance to the trap prevented the bison from escaping, and most were killed and subsequently butchered. The same scene was repeated at least two more times that winter, and when spring arrived and it was finally over, more than three hundred young, and primarily female, bison had been slaughtered. Anthropologists sorting through the bones and archaeological debris found in what is now referred to as the Jones-Miller site near Wray, Colorado, reconstructed what was probably a common hunting method for the Paleoindians and a normal outcome for the bison those many years ago. Uncovered with the bison bones were a myriad of stone and bone artifacts, including numerous flint spearpoints. One of the more lethal weapons in the prehistoric hunter's arsenal was a six-foot, flint-tipped spear that was propelled by a handheld launcher that scientists have called an atlatl (unlike other peoples who eventually evolved to a point where metals were used in their weaponry, the aboriginal and later North Americans basically stayed in a stone culture). Similar to what Indian tribes in future years would do, this ancient hunt was conducted in a systematic and efficient fashion. The hunters were well organized, perhaps even including a few representatives from several neighboring bands, and when the hunt was over, a butchering assembly line methodically stripped the animal carcasses.

Several noted paleontologists have suggested that people were responsible for the demise of many of the larger Pleistocene land mammals, such as the mastodon, mammoth, camel, giant sloth, and horse. Paul Martin developed a model to support an overkill hypothesis that he feels ·demonstrates that (1) these large animals formerly lived in areas not previously habituated by humans, (2) as the humans moved in, the larger mammals were suddenly faced with heavy and very efficient predation by a growing population of hunters, and (3) without time to adapt to this pressure, these animals were subsequently permanently removed from the ecosystem. Two-thirds of the large Pleistocene fauna eventually disappeared in this manner, leaving antelope, bison, deer, elk (wapiti), moose, mountain goat, and musk-ox to represent the remaining native fauna of the North American continent. Simon Davis (1987, 110*)* and Jerry McDonald *(North American Bison: Their Classification and Evolution)* suggest that those few large mammals that did not become extinct, such as was the case with the bison, survived because their species reached sexual maturity at an earlier age and their reproductive rate exceeded that of predation.

When many of the large mammal species became extinct, early Americans still depended on obtaining food and other necessities of life, through regular hunting and gathering processes. Without horses to give them the same level of mobility enjoyed by their favorite prey, the bison, early humans had to rely on stealth and the use of entrapment hunting methods, such as luring herds into some form of natural enclosure where they could be slaughtered, or driving them over cliffs where they would then fall to their death. Remains uncovered within bison-kill sites revealed that it was a rather common practice for huge numbers of animals to be methodically killed in this manner. At one site in western Saskatchewan, scientists indicated that this same site had probably been used for more than thirteen hundred years, and by analyzing one layer of bones it was estimated that in one single instance over nine hundred bison were immediately dispatched.

It was at least over 5,500 years ago that the bow and arrow emerged, and hunting methods then became more flexible. Using the bow and arrow, it was now possible to bring down animals at considerable distance and it was not necessary to depend upon communal efforts to overwhelm prey.

In spite of increasing predation by man, and the combined efforts of other less technically proficient carnivores, the bison herds of North America continued to grow and prosper. Generations of Native Americans had come to depend upon the bison nearly as much as they did on the unpolluted air that they breathed and the pure water that they drank. William T. Hornaday, chief taxidermist of the U.S. National Museum, and one of the more respected of the early so-called bison experts, probably expressed it best when he stated: "If any animal was ever designed by the hand of nature for the express purpose of supplying, at one stroke, nearly all the wants of an entire race, surely the buffalo [bison] was intended for the Indian" ("The Extermination of the American Bison," *Report of the National Museum*, 1887, 437).

Except for occasional forays into the southwestern United States by the Spanish, no permanent settlements were developed in Canada and the United States until the early 1600s. It was at that time that the English and French formed a number of colonies along the eastern coast. The Spanish, beginning with Santa Fe in 1610, opened the Southwest to settlement and later established additional permanent communities in New Mexico, Arizona, and California. Joel Allen and Alice C. Fletcher, considered by bison researchers to be the top authorities with respect to the maximum range of the animal, did not include the extreme East and West Coasts of America as part of the bison's regular and normal habitat. Thus, the initial development of European settlements in Canada and the United States may not have resulted in immediate impact on the bison in those specific areas since the settlements were not within known bison habitat. However, by the 1750s, settlements began appearing on the western slope of the Alleghenies, and this activity alone would have inhibited bison from spreading further eastward and would have served to drive wildlife further into the interior.

In his research on the maximum range of the bison, Joel Allen also indicated that "immense herds" formerly inhabited the valleys of West Virginia and the adjacent parts of Kentucky and Tennessee (1876, 72–73), and that by 1810 they were all gone. With respect to the above-mentioned Kentucky herds, Frank Roe (1972, 232–233) indicates that prior to 1800 several species wholly disappeared from that state, particularly elk and bison, after the settlement of the Europeans. Roe quotes from F. A. Michaux, who wrote in 1802 about bison in Kentucky:

Their [prior] number was at that time so considerable that they were
met in flocks of 150 to 200. They were so far from being ferocious,
that they did not fear the approach of huntsmen, who sometimes shot
them solely for the sake of having their tongue, which they looked
upon as a delicious morsel. . . . At present, there are scarcely any
from Ohio to the river Illinois. They have nearly deserted these parts,
and strayed to the right [that is west] bank of the Mississippi. . . .

Another eastern state that reportedly contained several large herds
of bison was Pennsylvania. The eastern bison boundary in Pennsylvania
was thought to be situated somewhere between the Allegheny River and
the west branch of the Susquehanna River. Regarding bison in this state,
naturalist Ernest Thompson Seton observed (1927, vol. III, 657):

It is hard to realize now that the woods of Pennsylvania contained
thousands of buffalo as late as 1750. Their pathways through the
woods were the most convenient ways for travel for mankind.
    As late as 1773, when Philip Quigley settled on the West Branch
[of the Susquehanna], Clinton County, Pa., the Great Northern herd
of Buffalo still numbered about 12,000 animals.

Similar assertions and commentary can be found in historical annals
for most, if not all, eastern and southeastern states concerning former bison
population levels. By the early 1830s, however, it was doubtful that any
wild bison were found, or ever ventured, east of the Mississippi River.

European immigrants to America seemingly demonstrated extreme
eagerness, perhaps even an urgency, to kill any wild game that occupied
the same land space that they did. Without game laws, no animal or bird
was spared from potential decimation. Settlers organized game drives with
the sole objective of permanently removing as much wildlife as possible
from the local ecosystem. One such drive was orchestrated in central
Pennsylvania in 1760 by a certain Black Jack Schwartz (Shoemaker 1915),
which led to the eventual massacre of 1,124 animals, including 111 bison.
Only the better hides and some tongues from bison were taken. When it
was over, all of the carcasses were placed in one pile and ignited. It was
claimed that the subsequent stench required settlers to temporarily vacate
their cabins for up to three miles from the site of the holocaust.

All available evidence suggests that the range of bison expanded in
the West and Southwest at approximately the same time as it did toward

the eastern coastal areas. Erik Reed offers the following observation with regard to their historical range in the west (1955, 133):

> Bison disappeared from central and western Mexico, no doubt long before historic times. Evidently they disappeared in much of Arizona before the Christian era. To about 1200 or 1250 A.D. there were still buffalo west of the Rio Grande in western New Mexico, abundant in the high enclosed basin of the plains of San Augustin and perhaps occasional in valleys further west; undoubtedly also in Coahuila and Chihuahua; very likely they were still present in the San Luis valley of southern Colorado, and possibly to be found on the western slope of Colorado and in central and southern Utah and perhaps also in northwestern Arizona.

Although somewhat discredited by Roe, Alice Fletcher was a rather knowledgeable archaeologist who had indicated in an article prepared for the *Handbook of American Indians* entitled "Buffalo" that in 1530, bison "ranged from below the Rio Grande in Mexico, N.W. throughout what is now E. New Mexico, Utah, Oregon, Washington, and British Columbia. . . . " Sir John Richardson, who extensively studied the bison from 1829 to 1837, had indicated that their numbers in the west of Canada were increasing, and he went on to say, "Farther to the southward, in New Mexico and California, the bison appears to be numerous on both sides of the Rocky Mountain chain. . . ." The explorer John C. Fremont *(Narrative of the Exploring Expedition to the Rocky Mountains in the Year 1842; and to Oregon and North California in the Years 1843–1844)* offered the following comment in his narrative, which was later quoted by Roe (1972, 263):

> In travelling through the country west of the Rocky Mountains, observation readily led me to the impression that the buffalo had, for the first time, crossed that range to the waters of the Pacific only a few years prior to the period we are now considering [that is, *circa* 1824], and in this opinion I am sustained by Mr. Fitzpatrick [Major Thomas Fitzpatrick, who was said to be extremely knowledgeable about the Rocky Mountains] and the older trappers in that country. In the region west of the Rocky Mountains, we never meet with any of the ancient vestiges which, throughout all the country lying upon

their eastern waters, are found in the great highways, continuous for
hundreds of miles, always several inches and sometimes several feet
in depth, which the buffalo have made in crossing from one river to
another, or in traversing the mountain ranges.

In considering all of the information provided by the frontiersmen,
explorers, hunters and trappers, scholars, and in some cases early travelers
who either personally viewed or performed limited research on bison, it
can be concluded that at their population peak, commonly estimated to be
sixty million animals, bison meandered over much of the contiguous United
States, Alaska, Canada, and northern Mexico. Their presence in California
and the arid deserts of Nevada and Arizona is, however, somewhat
questionable. To attempt to single out or identify those areas where bison
may never have been, or had been seen, is perhaps an interesting, but not
necessarily critical, issue with respect to development of a profile of
potential herd vitality.

By the early 1830s bison herds still covered the prairies and
grasslands of the middle United States in enormous numbers. Bison could
be found west of the Mississippi River in most states with the possible
exception of California, Nevada, New Mexico, Arizona, and Washington.
Although the fur trappers may each have taken a few bison at one time or
another for food, no significant market demand had yet developed for bison
hides. When William H. Ashley, the cofounder of the Missouri Fur
Company along with Andrew Henry, left Fort Atkinson in early November
of 1824 for Wyoming, he was planning to trap along the Green River and
then meet with other trappers on or before July 10, 1825. History will
always mark this as the time of the first "Rendezvous," but another
interesting element to this trip received less attention but would have
significant later impact upon the free-roaming bison herds — his diaries
mentioned that he left Fort Atkinson with a wagon and a team. This is the
first time that a wagon was used on the northern plains. Ashley later sold
his fur business to William L. Sublette, Jedediah Smith, and David E.
Jackson. In 1830, Sublette came to the Wind River rendezvous with goods
in ten wagons, each hauled by five mules. This innovation was so
impressive that the three partners reported this event to the United States
Secretary of War, saying that wagons could cross the Continental Divide
by way of the South Pass, thus demonstrating "the facility of
communicating over land with the Pacific Ocean. By the early 1840s the

depopulation of the beaver, as well as a changing public interest in and demand for beaver hats, wrote an end to the fur trade, as it was then known, and invited the adventurous to consider other entrepreneurial activities.

If we use Ernest Thompson Seton's estimate, of forty million free-ranging bison still remaining in the United States by 1830 as a starting point, we would perhaps then be in a better position to consider the significance and consequences of events that took place within the following fifty years.

Josiah Gregg was travelling through northern Texas in March of 1840, and was disturbed by the extent of wasteful bison slaughter being conducted. Admitting his own guilt in what had become a common practice (1966, 149–150), he lamented that "the slaughter of these animals is frequently carried to an excess, which shows the depravity of the human heart in very bold relief. . . . Whether the mere pleasure of taking life is the incentive of these brutal excesses, I will not pretend to decide; but one thing is very certain, that the buffalo killed yearly on these prairies far exceeds the wants of the traveler, or what might be looked upon as the exigencies of rational sport."

Today there are literally thousands of organizations established for the sole purpose of protecting and preserving land, air, forests, parks, rivers, seas, wildlife of all kinds, domestic animals — virtually anything and everything. Thus, we currently abide by a cultural ethic of assigned preservation that is based upon certain specific and acceptable wilderness and human interrelationships. Possibly the pendulum has now swayed a little too far in its reach toward a stricter conservationist policy, and the high priority that should logically be given by humans to deserving human needs, rights, and requirements is now often being regularly subrogated in favor of any potentially endangered animals, birds, fish, or plants. Whatever the case may be, early America was certainly bereft of such guardian organizations; and further, if it were possible to convince the general population that the natural resources and richness that they saw about them in such abundance were ultimately exhaustible, they still would have been unwilling to accept and follow restrictive conservation measures.

In 1835, hostilities between the Seminole Indians and the United States government led to a "war" that was to last for nearly eight years. At stake was a government plan to move the Seminoles out of Florida. In this same year, gold was discovered in Georgia on Cherokee land, and the Cherokee Indians were later forced to give up their land and be moved to

Oklahoma. These were the days of "Manifest Destiny," a powerful political movement born out of an expansionist creed that sought that the whole North American continent should belong to the citizens of the United States from one shining sea to the other. In 1841, the first immigrant wagon train left for California; in 1843, more than 1,000 settlers left Joplin, Missouri, for Oregon; in 1844, the first message was sent over a telegraph line; in 1848, the Mexican government ceded their claims to lands in Arizona, California, Colorado, Nevada, New Mexico, Utah, and Texas; and in 1849, gold was discovered in California with 80,000 prospectors immigrating there to seek their fortunes — and in the midst of all of this were the bison herds.

The westward thrust toward eventual occupation of the interior of the North American continent had crossed the Mississippi by 1830, but upon reaching the edge of the plains this western movement of civilization came to a full stop. Independence, Missouri, which was founded in 1827, was still in 1840 the westernmost settlement on the frontier line. The main bison herds had gradually moved toward the center of the continent, and were seldom sighted east of the forks of the Platte River. Into the interior and westernmost areas of the continent plunged the missionaries, geographers, and writers. Washington Irving, the first American professional writer (*Legend of Sleepy Hollow* and *Rip Van Winkle),* told all Americans about this land of adventure and danger in three publications: *A Tour of the Prairies* in 1835, *Astoria* in 1836, and *The Adventures of Captain Bonneville* in 1837. When Irving reached bison country he passed on his excitement to his readers, but also took the liberty of becoming just another person at that time who killed a bison (1983, 218–219):

> The buffalo stood with his shaggy front always presented to his foe, his mouth open, his tongue parched, his eyes like coals of fire, and his tail erect with rage; every now and then he would make a faint rush upon his foe, who easily evaded his attack, capering and cutting all kinds of antics before him. We now made repeated shots at the buffalo, but they glanced into his mountain of flesh without proving mortal. He made a slow and grand retreat into the shallow river, turning upon his assailants whenever they pressed upon him; and, when in the water, took his stand there, as if prepared to sustain a siege. A rifle ball, however, more fatally lodged, sent a tremor through his frame. He turned and attempted to wade across the

stream; but, after tottering a few paces, slowly fell upon his side and expired. It was the fall of a hero, and we felt somewhat ashamed of the butchery that had effected it; but, after the first shot or two, we had reconciled it to our feelings by the old plea of putting the poor animal out of his misery.

When the flow of wagon trains began, each train encountered its own problems and parade of adventures as did all preceding and following wagon trains: the first storm, the first Indian party, the first bison. And, if bison were reasonably available, train members fed upon them as often as possible. Gerald Kreyche (1989, 192), in commenting on what travelers could expect in their daily life along the Oregon Trail, says: "Daily life on the level parts of the trail was fairly routine; the high country brought more variety and problems. But when buffalo were spotted, everything stopped. No one could resist the excitement of a buffalo chase and the promise of badly needed fresh meat." Merrill Mattes, former historian for the National Park Service, describes a similar pattern of trail behavior along the Great Platte River Road (1969, 48):

> In the pristine days of the trail, perhaps 1830 to 1849, when game was more abundant and a case-hardened old fur trapper might be guiding the train, there was considerable living off the land, with feasts of buffalo and antelope steak. Small buffalo herds along the Trail were common enough through the fifties and sixties, and emigrants on horseback frequently gave chase and once in a while shot a buffalo. Usually, however, the kill was too far distant from the train to permit bringing in more than token slabs of the prized meat, preferably ribs, tongue, or hump. Charles Larpenteur, a trapper who lived almost exclusively on buffalo in the thirties, found most of it "tougher than whalebone," although fat cows were somewhat better than bulls.

Another version of the preference for the meat of the bison cow over the bull was offered by John C. Duval when he was recounting *The Adventures of Big-Foot Wallace* (Wallace's full name was William Alexander Anderson Wallace). On October 21, 1837, Wallace and Duval were travelling along the Leon River in Texas when one of their hunters killed a "fat buffalo-cow." Duval noted that (1983, 27):

That was the first buffalo-meat I ever tasted, and I thought it better even than bear-meat. The flesh of an old bull, however, I have found out since, is coarse, tough, and stringy, but the "hump" is always good, and so are the "marrow-bones" and tongue.

The rather rapid depletion of the bison herds was undoubtedly due to a number of mitigating reasons and factors. Orin Belknap (G. O. Shields, ed., *Big Game of North America,* 1890, 279–301) identified what he considered to be the three principal causes, in order of impact: (1) the introduction of the liquor traffic among the Indians of the plains, (2) the invention and development of the modern breech-loading rifle, and (3) the building of the Pacific railroads. Although there obviously are, and were, a number of "experts" who would like to place the blame for the slaughter of the American bison at the feet of the Native American, there are perhaps a more than equal number that place culpability with "Civil War veterans and plainsmen who turned to hide hunting as a livelihood" (Keith, 1948, 329), as well as the efforts of the military.

Frank Roe meticulously recorded observations of human activities that impacted bison. To demonstrate possible Indian culpability, Roe quoted (1972, 351–352) from Josiah Gregg *(The Commerce of the Prairies, 1831–1839)* (1968, 92):

To say the truth, however, I have never seen them anywhere upon the Prairies so abundant as some travellers have represented — in dense masses, darkening the whole country. I have only found them in scattered herds, of a few scores, hundreds, or sometimes thousands in each, and where in the greatest numbers, dispersed far and wide; but with large intervals between. Yet they are very sensibly and rapidly decreasing. There is a current notion that the whites frighten them away; but I would ask, where do they go to? To be sure, to use a hunter's phrase, they "frighten a few out of their skins;" yet for every one killed by the whites, more than a hundred, perhaps a thousand, fall by the hands of the savages. From these, however, there is truly "nowhere to flee;" for they follow them wheresoever they go; while the poor brutes instinctively learn to avoid the fixed establishments, and to some degree, the regular travelling routes of the whites.

In a following paragraph, Roe also offers this additional quote (1972, 352) from Gregg:

> Were they only killed for food, however, their natural increase would perhaps replenish the loss; yet the continual and wanton slaughter of them by travelers and hunters, and the still greater havoc made upon them by the Indians, not only for meat, but often for the skins alone . . . are fast reducing their numbers, and must ultimately effect their total annihilation from [sic] the continent. It is believed that the annual "export" of *buffalo rugs* from the Prairies and bordering "buffalo range" is about 100,000; and the number killed wantonly, or exclusively for meat, is no doubt still greater, as the skins are fit to dress scarcely half the year.

The decade between 1830 and 1840 was a period of time when bison reproduction fell far short from replacing those taken. Indians with their horses and guns began to kill bison in large numbers. In 1832, the artist George Catlin reported that 150,000 to 200,000 bison robes were being offered to traders by various Indian tribes. John E. Foster (1992, 61), in commenting upon the reductions in bison in the Canadian West, offered the following:

> A frequently encountered and enduring historical truism, addressing an aspect of Western Canadian experience, is the statement that the "whiteman" was responsible for the destruction of the buffalo on the Canadian prairies. Like most historical truisms this one needs clarification. If by "whiteman" the truism identifies the commercial system rooted in the industrial cities of eastern North America, which for a time seemed to offer an insatiable market for buffalo robes and a cornucopia of material goods in return, the statement has much validity. If on the other hand it purports to identify the "trigger-men" in the hunting of the buffalo in the Canadian West it is wrong. The overwhelming proportion of buffalo hunters in the decade before extinction, the 1870s, were native peoples.

If they had a choice, Indians preferred young bison and cows. And, if indeed it was their belief that the bison offered them an inexhaustible supply of meat, hides, and other environmental necessities, why should they select the older and less tender animals? The same would be true with the mountainmen, frontiersmen, scouts for wagon trains, and other occasional meat hunters; they would not select an old tough bison specimen unless nothing else was available — or if they were only planning to take the tongues. Without an actual count of animals to work with, we can only speculate that by 1840 the ratio between male and female bison may have been skewed toward the male, and conceivably many of those remaining male bisons were the older animals — but still quite powerful and able to discourage younger males. But, the older bulls would be potentially less sexually vigorous and perhaps some even sterile. If indeed there were more bulls than cows, and further recognizing that the bison heifer does not normally reach sexual maturity until it reaches two years of age, the herd replenishment process would thus have been significantly handicapped.

Dr. William T. Hornaday (1887, 484–486) elected to separate the bison herd reduction process into two segments. The first he described as "desultory extirpation," from 1730 to 1830, the more or less expected result of the western expansionary movement and the resultant demand upon the bison species for food and clothing. The second he called "systematic destruction," conducted on a much larger scale, which he dates from 1830 onward, to secure only the tongues, robes, and hides, or just "sport." He also included in his "systematic destruction" segment the purposeful eradication of bison for military or political aims. It is believed that Dr. Hornaday's selection of 1830 as the beginning of a systemized slaughter may have been just about ten years too early, as 1840 would seem to have been the better choice.

After 1840, the eventual demise of the great bison herds would not have been more certain than if the whole process could have been orchestrated by a supreme being. The occasional plinking of a bison here and there for sport or for food (if only to secure just the choice portions on the animal) accelerated dramatically as more people spread westward and civilization gradually began to encroach upon the remaining wilderness. In response to the variety of economic opportunities offered by the bison, Indians also increased their level of slaughter to obtain trade goods, whisky, money, and perhaps even guns, in exchange for hides and tongues. The often-told story of the hunters from the Canadian Red River settlement is another example of the extent of exploitative measures that were taken against the bison throughout the next forty years.

In 1812, Thomas Douglas, the fifth Earl of Selkirk, established a colony of Scotch Highlanders on the Canadian Red River, two miles below the mouth of the Pembina. Hunting bison was not the initial objective, but it proved to be so lucrative that the Red River settlers formed the Buffalo Wool Company in 1821, with the intended purpose of building a tannery and manufacturing cloth from bison fleeces. Although this company eventually failed, the Selkirk colonists, the French-Canadian fur hunters, and a mixed lot of half-breeds and full-blood Indians went on an annual bison hunt into the Pembina country. This annual hunt began in 1820, and gradually grew in size until in 1840 it had grown to encompass more than 1,630 persons and 1,210 carts pulled by oxen or draft horses. The hunt of 1840 ranged southwest into the Dakota Territory as far as, and perhaps even beyond, the Missouri River. Wayne Gard (1960, 52) suggests that much of the killing was done on the plains around Fort Union (North Dakota). The expedition brought back more than 1,089,000 pounds of meat. According to Alexander Ross, who published a detailed report in 1856 *(The Red River Settlement)*, during the twenty-year span between 1820 and 1840, 652,275 bison were killed by Red River settlement hunters, and of this total it was estimated that less than 25 percent of the meat from the bison killed was actually saved or effectively used.

An enormous number of eyewitness and participant accounts of bison hunting between 1840 and 1870 have been meticulously documented and related by a number of writers. A few examples of these are provided below to ensure the complete understanding of the nature of activities that took place.

James R. Mead (1986, 51), one of the founders of Wichita, Kansas, had earlier established himself as a successful hunter and trader on the Kansas prairie. In a moment of remorse, he admitted to killing over 2,000 bison during a span of nearly nine years on the plains. In 1859, he left Iowa to seek whatever adventure may await him on the Santa Fe Trail. Arriving at a campsite in central Kansas, he and his companions were told that there were plenty of buffalo back from the trail — either north or south. They turned north and struck off across the prairie in that direction. In his written reminiscences of what happened that day, he recorded:

> During the morning I noticed a number of big gray wolves which had been killed by strychnine put out by hunters, and some carcasses of buffalo. Towards noon as we approached the divide between the

Arkansas and the Smoky Hill Rivers, we observed in the distance what appeared to be a belt of timber extending along the horizon in each direction as far as we could see. As we approached nearer we saw that it was a vast herd of buffalo grazing — to our imagination the most entrancing sight the universe afforded — and such a sight as the eye of man can never again behold.

When gold was discovered in the early 1860s along the Rockies, prospectors and miners permeated what was then Indian territory. They eventually moved into western Montana and searched for gold along what they referred to as the "Grasshopper River" near the current town of Bannack. A party of fifteen, led by James Stuart, set out on an early spring day in 1863 to look over new country farther east, along the Yellowstone River and its tributaries. Stuart kept excellent journals, and on May 3, 1863, he reports that his whole party chased a bunch of buffalo just for the hell of it. In *The Bloody Bozeman*, Dorothy Johnson provides the following from Stuart's personal journals regarding this incident (1971, 36):

> They came in [to a waterhole] on a run, and did not halt until they were all in the hole. Four or five of us went out to give them a scare. We went on the bank above, and within ten feet of them, and gave a yell. Such Fun! They run over one another, fell down in heaps, nearly drowned a lot of calves, etc. Just such another stampede a man would probably never witness again in a lifetime. We laughed till we could hardly stand.

A few days later Stuart's party experienced a confrontation with a band of Crow Indians and after suffering their losses, left the area and took their wounded with them.

In his autobiography, William Cody recounts a time in 1867 when he was near Fort Hays, Kansas. Meat was scarce, but word was received that bison were in the vicinity. As he was riding toward the bison, he observed five men coming from the fort. As they came closer he could see that they were all officers who he had presumed also heard about the bison. As he joined them, the officers, all new to the fort, indicated that they planned to kill bison just for the sport of it more than anything else, and after they took the tongues and some of the tenderloin, Cody could have what was left. Cody's account of this hunt was as follows (1920, 113):

Eleven animals were in the herd, which was about a mile distant. I
noticed that they were making toward the creek for water. I knew
buffalo nature, and was aware that it would be difficult to turn them
from their course. I therefore started toward the creek to head them
off, while the officers dashed madly up behind them.

The herd came rushing past me, not a hundred yards distant,
while their pursuers followed, three hundred yards in the rear.

"Now," thought I, "is the time to get in my work." I pulled the
blind bridle from Brigham [his horse], who knew as well as I did
what was expected of him. The moment he was free of the bridle he
set out at top speed, running in ahead of the officers. In a few jumps
he brought me alongside the rear buffalo. Raising old "Lucretia
Borgia" [his rifle], I killed the animal with one shot. On went
Brigham to the next buffalo, ten feet farther along, and another was
disposed of. As fast as one animal would fall, Brigham would pass
to the next, getting so close that I could almost touch it with my gun.
In this fashion I killed seven buffalo with twelve shots.

Shortly after this occurred, Cody, now answering to the name
"Buffalo Bill," reflected on his employment as a hunter for the Kansas
Pacific Railroad, a job that lasted approximately eighteen months (some
suggest that his employment only lasted eight months). During this period
he claimed to have killed 4,280 bison. He was particularly proud of a
shooting contest he had with Billy Comstock, a well-known guide, scout,
and interpreter (1920, 122–125):

Comstock, who was chief of scouts at Fort Wallace, had a reputation
of being a successful buffalo hunter, and his friends at the fort —
the officers in particular — were anxious to back him against me.

It was arranged that I should shoot a match with him, and the
preliminaries were easily and satisfactorily arranged. We were to
hunt one day of eight hours, beginning at eight o'clock in the
morning. The wager was five hundred dollars a side, and the man
who should kill the greater number of buffaloes from horseback was
to be declared the winner. Incidentally my title of "Buffalo Bill" was
at stake.

The hunt took place twenty miles east of Sheridan [Kansas]. It
had been well advertised, and there was a big "gallery." An
excursion party, whose members came chiefly from St. Louis and

numbered nearly a hundred ladies and gentlemen, came on a special train to view the sport. Among them was my wife and my little daughter Arta, who had come to visit me for a time.

Buffaloes were plentiful. It had been agreed that we should go into the herd at the same time and make our "runs," each man killing as many animals as possible. A referee followed each of us, horseback, and counted the buffaloes killed by each man. The excursionists and other spectators rode out to the hunting-grounds in wagons and on horseback, keeping well out of sight of the buffaloes, so as not to frighten them until the time came for us to dash into the herd. They were permitted to approach closely enough to see what was going on.

For the first "run" we were fortunate in getting good ground. Comstock was mounted on his favorite horse. I rode old Brigham. I felt confident that I had the advantage in two things: first, I had the best buffalo horse in the country; second, I was using what was known at the time as a needle-gun, a breech-loading Springfield rifle, caliber .50. This was "Lucretia" the weapon of which I have already told you. Comstock's Henry rifle, though it could fire more rapidly than mine, did not, I felt certain, carry powder and lead enough to equal my weapon in execution.

When the time came to go into the herd, Comstock and I dashed forward, followed by the referees. The animals separated. Comstock took the left bunch, I the right. My great forte in killing buffaloes was to get them circling by riding my horse at the head of the herd and shooting their leaders. Thus the brutes behind were crowded to the left, so that they were soon going round and round.

This particular morning the animals were very accommodating. I soon had them running in a beautiful circle. I dropped them thick and fast till I had killed thirty-eight, which finished my "run."

Comstock began shooting at the rear of the buffaloes he was chasing, and they kept on in a straight line. He succeeded in killing twenty-three, but they were scattered over a distance of three miles. The animals I had shot lay close together.

Our St. Louis friends sent out champagne when the result of the first run was announced. It proved a good drink on a Kansas prairie, and a buffalo hunter proved an excellent man to dispose of it.

While we were resting we espied another herd approaching. It was a small drove, but we prepared to make it serve our purpose. The buffaloes were cows and calves, quicker in their movements than the bulls. We charged in among them, and I got eighteen to Comstock's fourteen.

Again the spectators approached, and once more the champagne went round. After a luncheon we resumed the hunt. Three miles distant we saw another herd. I was so far ahead of my competitor now that I thought I could afford to give an exhibition of my skill. Leaving my saddle and bridle behind, I rode, with my competitor, to windward of the buffaloes.

I soon had thirteen down, the last of which I had driven close to the wagons, where the ladies were watching the contest. It frightened some of the tender creatures to see a buffalo coming at full speed directly toward them, but I dropped him in his tracks before he had got within fifty yards of the wagon. This finished my "run" with a score of sixty-nine buffaloes for the day. Comstock had killed forty-six.

It was now late in the afternoon. Comstock and his backers gave up the idea of beating me. The referee declared me the winner of the match, and the champion buffalo hunter of the plains.

On our return to camp we brought with us the best bits of meat, as well as the biggest and best buffalo heads.

Frank Collinson was born in Yorkshire, England, on November 13, 1855. In September of 1872, when he was only seventeen, he went to work on a cattle ranch near Castroville, Texas. Within a short period of time he became a "hide hunter" and claims that he saw more than 1.1 million hides at Lee Reynold's and Rath's Trading Post in Fort Worth (Collinson 1963, 55). After moving around the country chasing reports of herds, Collinson returned to Texas, and he and his two partners settled in the Texas Panhandle area where in 1879 he reported (1963, 56–57):

We killed a herd of about two hundred animals, mostly cows and calves and young buffalo, with only a few bulls, in a weeks time. Each of us had a wagon and two skinners. When we killed the cows I suggested killing the calves, too, because their little red pelts would be worth something, and there was no need to leave the calves there to die. I have killed, and seen killed, thousands of buffalo cows. They were skinned and their calves left to starve to death or be killed by the wolves and coyotes. That was what killed off the herds so quickly: no calves to replace the slaughtered cows. These little

Forty thousand bison hides in the corral of Wright and Rath, Dodge City, Kansas, awaiting shipment. Photo taken about 1874. Wright and Rath were by no means the only shipper of bison hides, but they did ship 400,000 hides in a season. Courtesy Denver Public Library, Western History Department.

calves were lying by the dead cows. We had to keep driving them away while skinning the cows. I saw some of them try to suck the cows. After the mothers were skinned and the hides were in the wagon, the calves followed. They could smell the hides and would follow them to the hide yard. They were gone the next morning — one back to where they had sucked the last time, either to starve to death or be killed by the wolves.

The slaughter did not just involve Indians, hide hunters, and "sportsmen" from the United States; there were also international participants. Col. Dodge recounted an incident that involved a rather unusual hunting party (1959, 132–133):

In 1872 I was stationed at Fort Dodge, on the Arkansas, and was out on many hunting excursions. Except that one or two would be shot, as occasion required, for beef, no attention whatever was paid to buffalo, though our march led through countless throngs, unless there were strangers with us. In the fall of that year three English

"Stalking the Buffalo," a fanciful illustration of a stealthy approach toward an isolated bison by hunter and guide. Although hunting expeditions by "dude parties" and foreign sportsmen were somewhat common, the bison was so easy a victim the "hunt" brought little glory to the hunter. Courtesy Denver Public Library, Western History Department.

gentlemen went out with me for a short hunt, and in their excitement bagged more buffalo than would have supplied a brigade.

Sir George Gore arrived in St. Louis from Ireland in 1854, and led a hunting expedition on the plains that lasted for over three years, covered more than six thousand miles, and is said to have cost nearly five hundred thousand dollars. It was claimed that the Gore party accounted for more than two thousand bison. McHugh (1972, 248) mentions a hunt by Sir William Drummand in 1843 where this group "left the prairie about the Platte River 'strewn for miles' with the carcasses of slain buffalo." Probably the most notorious of the hunting trips by foreigners was that of the Grand Duke Alexis, third son of Czar Alexander II of Russia in 1872. The Grand Duke arrived in Nebraska by train with two sleeping cars, a diner, and a refrigerator car stocked with grouse, quail, and caviar. With Gen. Philip Sheridan, Col. George Custer, and Buffalo Bill Cody as his mentors, and accompanied by one thousand Sioux, the Grand Duke's party killed less than three hundred bison, of which the Duke had reportedly personally claimed twelve. Flushed with his success, the Grand Duke vacationed at Custer's home in Louisville, visited the New Orleans Mardi Gras, and boarded a Russian warship for his return home.

Collinson related a tale about an English earl, named Alesford, who came to Texas to hunt bison in the fall of 1878 (1963, 80–81). After hunting across the western prairies he purchased a ranch near Big Spring, and died there on his ranch in 1881. By the 1880s, a number of foreign investors had also acquired large tracts of western rangeland and developed some of the greatest cattle ranches the Great Plains were ever to see.

Although the Canadian Red River settlement, mentioned earlier in this chapter, faithfully made annual hunts into the United States and reportedly killed more than 650,000 bison between 1820 and 1840, hunters from south of the border also conducted regular excursions into the United States to kill bison and then pack out the meat. These hunters were referred to as *ciboleros*, or Mexican buffalo hunters, a term that grew out of the former Spanish word *cibola*, for buffalo. Frank Collinson claims that these hunters "cut their trails over the Llano Estacado (Staked Plain) long before the American hunters were upon the scene" (1963, 60). It is generally believed that the *ciboleros* were hunting bison in what is now Texas, and areas even further into the Great Plains, prior to the eighteenth century. Collinson said that these hunters were not often seen, but their well-marked trails were most conspicuous. He first encountered these unusual hunters in Blanco Canyon, Texas, in the fall of 1875. A few of his observations from his chapter entitled *The Ciboleros* is quoted below (1963, 61–64):

> They were Mexican buffalo hunters, part of a big train that had crossed over from Fort Sumner, then called "Bosque Redondo," to kill and jerk meat for the Mexican markets. There were fully two hundred men in the party, and many women and children. There were about fifty wagons, pulled by oxen. This train had come from Chihuahua, Mexico, a distance of eight or nine hundred miles, and had been on the trail three months. The Mexicans had crossed the Rio Grande at Guadalupe and had gone by Big Salt Lake south of Guadalupe Peak, where they had secured salt for camp use and for curing buffalo tongues. From Big Salt Lake they had crossed the prairie where Carlsbad, New Mexico, is now located, and had gone up the Pecos to Fort Sumner. From there they went to Los Portales Spring and thence to the head draws of the Brazos River.

When the *ciboleros* saw a herd of buffalo, they would ride as near as possible and start them on the run. The faster the buffalo ran, the more they crowded together. This was when the hunters attacked them. Running alongside an animal, the *cibolero* struck for the ribs, trying to stab the buffalo in the lungs. Another favorite stabbing place was high on the flank. At times the hunters would cut the hamstring. Sometimes a *cibolero* would kill ten or fifteen animals on one run. He preferred to kill cows and younger stock because they were more easily killed and their meat was better. Some big outfits killed fifty animals a day.

Collinson later claimed to have seen some young bison bulls "roped and broken for work" pulling the *cibolero* wagons. The different methods used by the *ciboleros* and the American bison hunters (i.e., the *ciboleros* wanted the herds to run and the American "still" hunter wanted them undisturbed so that he could drop the whole herd, if possible, with his rifle) resulted in some conflicts.

John R. Cook also had some experiences with *ciboleros* in October of 1874 ([1907] 1967, 80–85). Cook stated that "in those days it was the custom of the Mexicans to go each fall to the border of New Mexico and Texas on meat hunts." On October 10, he left with a group of *ciboleros* to hunt in an area near old Fort Bascom in northeastern New Mexico. As earlier described by Collinson, lances were used to spear the bison while they were on the run. Cook describes the action as follows:

> . . . Buffaloes were reeling and staggering out of line of the run. A lancer would dash up to one that had not been struck yet, make a quick thrust and retrieve, rush on to the next one, and repeat until his horse was winded. Some, whose horses were not as speedy as others, had singled out one certain buffalo and were a mile away before getting to use the lance.
>
> When the chase was over we had sixteen bison for that effort. We dressed the meat and loaded it into empty wagons, and proceeded on to Blue Water, better known in those days as Ona Sula. Here we stayed for several days, jerking and drying meat. The lancers were out every day looking for buffaloes, but found very few.
>
> From this place we moved about four miles. The lancers that went north that day came in and reported that we would soon all

have plenty of work, as the buffaloes were coming south, in a solid mass as far as they could see, east or west.

Bison are predisposed to wander; it is perhaps this innate characteristic that provided some level of legitimacy to historical claims that there were regular patterns of bison migration. This continual movement also served, for a limited time, to mask the extent of herd depletions (i.e., if they are not here, they must therefore be somewhere else). It was commonly accepted that prior to 1860 there were basically two megaherds: a Northern Herd that ranged on the north from the Great Slave Lake in Canada to the Platte River on the south, and perhaps as easterly as Minnesota, to an approximate 8,000-foot elevation in the Rocky Mountains on the west; and a Southern Herd ranging from the Platte on the north to Texas and New Mexico on the south, and from mid-Kansas on the east to the Rocky Mountains on the west. In 1860 it was estimated that there were still more than twenty-eight million wild bison on the Great Plains, but by 1870 the number of bison remaining in both megaherds probably did not exceed fifteen million.

Indians recognized the value of bison hides long before the European arrived in America. Tribes that had access to hides, robes that featured the winter pelage of the bison, and dried bison meat were able to barter for items that were not otherwise locally or readily available. However, the taking of bison just for the hide alone probably did not really occur as a regular practice and as a commerce until about 1830. Gradually this industry increased in scope, and eventually, when the railroads transected the plains, hunting bison for its hide only became big business. Because of the railroads and movement of wagon trains along customary trails, the two megaherds became split into four segments: a Northern Herd, which extended from Montana into Canada and included southwestern North Dakota, northwestern South Dakota, and northeast Wyoming; the Republican Herd (Republican River), which spread from eastern Wyoming through southwestern South Dakota, central and western Nebraska, and dipped into northwest Kansas and northeast Colorado; the Arkansas Herd, which roamed through southwestern Nebraska, eastern Colorado, western Kansas, and the panhandle of Oklahoma; and the Texas Herd, which extended from southeast Colorado, through southwestern Kansas and western Oklahoma, and into Texas. The convenience of the railroads

"Shooting buffalo from the trains of the Kansas Pacific Railroad." Drawing by Theodore R. Davis sketched in the mid-1860s. The Kansas Pacific was referred to as "The Buffalo Route" because the trains frequently had to stop to allow unusually large herds to pass. When the herds ran side by side with the cars, as depicted in the drawing, the windows of the cars would be opened and those passengers so inclined would shoot at the animals. Courtesy Denver Public Library, Western History Department.

exponentially increased the taking and shipping of hides, bison meat, and later, the new market product of the 1870s — bison bones.

After the hides were removed and/or the desired cuts of meat withdrawn from the bison carcass, the remainder was generally left for scavengers and the deteriorating effects of weather and time. Bison skeletons virtually littered the plains, occasionally gnawed on by wolves, small carnivores, and rodents; they initially served no economical purpose and, when located on tempting farmland, every now and then became a source of annoyance to those who sought to till the soil. The "bone picking" entrepreneurs started working the plains in a limited way in the 1850s and 1860s. The bones were shipped by wagon to St. Louis and often to even more eastern industrial locations where, depending on condition, they were used in the manufacture of fashionable sale items and ground into bone black or char used to refine sugar, glue, and fertilizer.

By the late 1860s, the railroads began to crisscross the plains. The slaughter of bison along the Kansas Pacific, Atchison, Topeka and Santa

Fe, and Union Pacific rail lines was greater than perhaps anywhere else on the plains, and thus the railroads began to be a most convenient vehicle for moving the bones to eastern processing plants. In *The Passing of the Buffalo* (1917, 36), J. L. Hill reports that "during 1873, The Atchison, Topeka and Santa Fe carried out 25,443 robes, 1,617,600 pounds of meat, and 2,743,100 pounds of bone." Col. Henry Inman offered another opinion regarding the volume of trade in bison bones (1977, 4), and stated that between 1868 and 1881, "In Kansas alone there was paid out . . . two million five hundred thousand dollars for their bones gathered on the prairies, to be utilized by the various carbon works of the country, principally in St. Louis." According to Inman, it would take one hundred carcasses to make one ton of bones, and at the then average price of approximately eight dollars a ton, he suggests that the above sum of money "represented the skeletons of over thirty-one millions of buffalo."

In commenting on the active trade in bison bones in the 1870s and 1880s, Garretson commented (1938, 160–161):

> Many an early western homesteader obtained money to pay for seed, tools and Government charges on his homestead by gathering and selling buffalo bones. The storekeepers of that period, in many of the small towns, traded groceries, cloth and other articles for old bones and then sold them by the carload to bone buyers who came out from the East.
>
> The period of bone gathering and shipping soon cleaned all the bones from the old buffalo plains, from Missouri to the Rockies. Very few places were missed, and the bones that formerly were everywhere on the plains, disappeared almost as quickly as the buffalo herds had.

Maj. I. McCreight, in his short history of the buffalo bone trade, reported that by 1885, the year that he first began to negotiate the purchase and shipment of bones, Indians, half-breeds, and immigrants were the principal bone gatherers. After describing the negotiating process, McCreight indicated (1917, 28):

> The bones are then loaded into box cars and shipped to the St. Louis market. Freight rate from the region being $8 and later $10 per ton. Delivered at St. Louis, the bones were paid for at prices ranging all

"The End, 1883." Drawing by M. S. Garretson, last president of the American Bison Society. A depiction of how settlers would raise a little cash by gathering bison bones while waiting for their first crops to come in. Courtesy Denver Public Library, Western History Department.

the way from $18 to $27 per ton. Railroads granted favorable shipping conditions and rates, as encouragement for first settlers to survive the test of endurance over the three to five years required to prove up title to their homesteads and pre-emption claims. In most cases that was a severe test.

It was common for the bone gatherers to place collected bison bones in enormous piles close to the railroad tracks. Garretson notes (1938, 161) that "twenty miles from Grenada, Colorado, on the Santa Fe Railroad right-of-way, was a rick of buffalo bones twelve feet high, twelve feet wide and half a mile long — and this was but one of many." The owners would usually mark the piles with their name, initial, or some such sign, and later ship the bones by wagon or rail. As the value of the bones increased, a few lawless people would help themselves from these piles, but only infrequently were they caught and prosecuted. One pile located along the Great Northern Railroad near Minot, North Dakota, was estimated at more than five thousand tons. Although there were still bison bones that were being gathered in Canada in the 1890s, by the late 1880s, the bison bone trade within the United States was basically over.

The massive slaughter of bison began at first like most unorganized projects involving human beings; everyone wanted to do what they considered the "fun" things (i.e., shooting the animals). No one wanted to do the dirty jobs, such as the actual skinning and curing. Many thousands of bison were killed and never even skinned — in some instances perhaps only their tongues were taken. There were also an inordinate number of amateurs on the plains, who had never hunted bison before but were willing to undertake anything for the money. These neophytes frequently only wounded the animals, which then wandered off to die. The Southern Herd, which included the Texas and Arkansas segments, was basically wiped out between 1870–1874. The Northern Herd, including the Republican segment, was systematically destroyed between 1876 and 1883.

Public apathy was not universal; there were a number of public protests over the indiscriminate slaughter of the plains bison, and legislative bills to protect the bison were introduced by members of Congress, a number of times, between 1871 and 1876. Unfortunately, when both houses did pass a suitable bill on June 23, 1874 (during the last days of the session), it was pigeonholed by President Ulysses S. Grant and died for lack of action. Grant's Secretary of the Interior, Columbus Delano, had earlier expressed his opinion in the previous year's Annual Report of the Department of the Interior when he stated: "I would not seriously regret the total disappearance of the buffalo from our western prairies, in its effect upon the Indians, regarding it as a means of hastening their sense of dependence upon the products of the soil and their own labors." It was also well known that members of the military had expressed somewhat similar opinions. Col. Richard Dodge, a well-known name in the American West, expressed his conviction that his troops should "kill every buffalo you can, every buffalo gone is an Indian gone." Gen. Philip Sheridan was equally blunt in his praise of the buffalo hunters: "These men have done more in the last two years, and will do more in the next year, more to settle the vexed Indian question than the entire regular army has done in the last thirty years. They are destroying the Indians' commissary; and it is a well known fact that an army losing its base of supplies is placed at a great disadvantage. Send them powder and lead, if you will; but for the sake of a lasting peace, let them kill, skin and sell until the buffaloes are exterminated. Then your prairies will be covered with speckled cattle and the festive cowboy, who follows the hunter as a second forerunner to an advanced civilization." Although no formal public policy was expressed by the federal government, it was the belief of the Canadian North West Mounted Police, as well as otherwise-informed Canadian traders, that the extermination of the bison was planned by United States military authorities as the only means of bringing the Sioux into submission.

If I can exclude, for a moment, the theory of the United States government having had an ulterior or Machiavellian plan to eliminate the bison, it would be interesting to perhaps consider a somewhat parallel incident with respect to another specie.

The passenger pigeon *(Ectopistes migratroius)* was the most common bird in North America. It ranged from Nova Scotia to Washington, and south to the Gulf of Mexico, but it was principally a bird of the hardwood forests of the eastern and central United States. Nearly half again as large as the still common mourning dove, this slender elegant bird with long wings and powerful breast muscles was a favorite food of the Indians prior to the arrival of the Europeans, and when colonization of America began, the new settlers quickly added the birds to their menu. No one would even hazard a guess as to how many there may have been. Alexander Wilson, who was a noted ornithologist of that day, was astonished by the numbers of pigeons in a flock that passed over him as he was on his way to Frankfort, Kentucky. He estimated from the width and length of this flock that it contained 2,230,272,000 individuals — over two billion birds! John James Audubon, the world-famous American ornithologist, painter, and naturalist, witnessed a flock in Kentucky in 1813 that passed through the area continuously for three days at the rate of one billion birds in three hours! The birds were shot, netted, poisoned, and even dynamited from their nightly roosts; young birds (squabs) were preferred for human consumption; and most of the other birds killed in this manner were shipped east for eventual use as livestock food (primarily pigs). By the 1850s the species was no longer seen in marginal areas within its former habitat, and the last wild pigeon was shot in Ohio in 1900.

Thus, from the fate of the passenger pigeon and the bison, we learned that, at least in these two instances, there is not necessarily safety in numbers. Hunters did not even leave one mated pair of pigeons; the bison were eventually more fortunate. Dr. William T. Hornaday probably summed up this whole dismal chapter of American history more succinctly than anyone else before or after him has been able to put into appropriate words (1887, 464):

> The primary cause of the buffalo's extermination, and the one which embraced all others, was the descent of civilization, with all its elements of destructiveness, upon the whole of the country inhabited by that animal. From the Great Slave Lake to the Rio Grande, the home of the buffalo was everywhere overrun by the man with a gun; and, as has ever been the case, the wild creatures were gradually swept away, the largest and the most conspicuous forms being the first to go.
>
> The secondary causes . . . may be catalogued as follows:
>
> Man's reckless greed, his wanton destructiveness, and improvidence in not husbanding such resources as come to him from the hands of nature, ready made.
>
> The total and utterly inexcusable absence of protective measures and agencies on the part of the National Government and of the Western States and Territories. . . .

When the fury of the hunt was finally over, the last hides were claimed, and dust began to settle on the carcass or the bones of the last wild bison to be killed on the plains, efforts were made to obtain an assessment on the number of bison remaining. David A. Dary (1989, 286) stated that to his knowledge the first bison survey was conducted by *London Field*, a British magazine, that reported on November 10, 1888, its finding that there were only thirteen hundred live buffalo (bison) in the world. William Hornaday, perhaps a more knowledgeable source, proclaimed the existence in 1887 of 1,091 bison: approximately 200 in Yellowstone National Park and 550 in the vicinity of the Great Slave Lake (Canada), 256 in private herds and zoos, and 85 still roaming wild in the United States (1887, 525). If reasonably correct, Hornaday's estimate would mean that there were then less than 600 bison remaining in the United States.

7

The Recovery

When he died at 104 years of age in February of 1954, Frank Mayer represented the last of his breed, a professional buffalo hunter — or runner, as he insisted that he and his peers preferred to be called. In his book *Buffalo Harvest*, Mayer expressed but little regret regarding his participation in eliminating the bison from the Great Plains (1958, 27–29):

> I'm often asked now what my feeling is toward myself that I helped wipe out a noble American animal by being a sort of juvenile delinquent with a high-power rifle. I always am frank in answering. I always say I am neither proud nor ashamed. At the time it seemed a proper thing to do. Looked at from a distance, however, I'm not so sure. The slaughter was perhaps a shameless, needless thing. But it was also an inevitable thing, an historical necessity.
>
> What I mean is this: the buffalo served his mission, fulfilled his destiny in the history of the Indian, by furnishing him everything he needed — food, clothing, a home, traditions, even a theology. But the buffalo didn't fit in so well with the white man's encroaching civilization — he didn't fit at all, in fact. He could not be controlled or domesticated. He couldn't be corralled behind wire fences. He was a misfit. So he had to go.

Mayer also claimed (1958, 29) "that the buffalo [bison] was hunted and killed with the connivance, yes, the cooperation, of the Government itself." He bases his belief on the fact that he was provided with free ammunition from most, if not all, frontier army posts. He then concludes his reflection with the following statement (1958, 30):

Hunting bison by horseback, or "buffalo running," was both exciting and dangerous. Unless the runner was experienced, the outcome was usually a loss in the ammunition supply. Revolvers and bows and arrows were not as effective as the deadly Sharps rifles used in "stands." The scene depicted would have been a rather uncommon event, white men and Indians jointly participating in bison hunts. Courtesy Denver Public Library, Western History Department.

It wasn't long after I got into the game that I began to realize that the end for the buffalo was in sight. I resolved to get my share. I went into the business right. I invested every cent I owned in an outfit. I have no apologies for my participation in the slaughter. I hope that answers the question.

Frank Mayer's personal convictions with respect to the eventual loss of America's large bison herds is somewhat typical of the opportunistic and often selfish attitude prevalent at that time. Although he professes to have no misgivings regarding his participation as a "buffalo runner," it is interesting to note that he dedicated his book *Buffalo Harvest* to Charles (Buffalo) Jones "because he was the only one among us who had sense enough to know that the buffalo could not stand up against the slaughter forever; because he with his own hands and single-handedly captured a few

Bison calf. Calves are usually born between April and June after a gestation period of about 275 days. The reddish brown calves will normally weigh at birth between 35 and 40 pounds, but heavier calves occasionally do occur. Unfortunately the birth of a large calf can lead to the death of the calf and sometimes also the death of the cow. Courtesy American Bison Association.

buffalo and saved the breed from extinction." Charles Jesse "Buffalo" Jones is but one among a number of individuals who have received acclaim over the years as "saviors of the buffalo." Although each of these "saviors" may have been altruistically motivated to some degree, their primary interest was that of an entrepreneur who perceived the bison to be a potential moneymaker.

Probably the first person to take an interest in private ownership of bison was the icon Texas trail herder Charles J. Goodnight. Prior to establishing the Goodnight-Loving Trail from Fort Sumner, New Mexico, to Denver, Goodnight had been putting together a herd of Texas longhorns in the hopes of cashing in on what was a rapidly expanding eastern beef market. Raising cattle in Texas was not an expensive proposition. Grass was free and plentiful and the climate was so mild that stock required little attention. By 1860, nearly 3.8 million Texas cattle appeared on tax rolls, and that did not include a goodly number of wild cattle that roamed the plains. In the fall of 1866, Goodnight, Oliver Loving, and their hired hands were trailing about twelve hundred head of longhorns across western Texas; stampeding bison split the herd in two, but the trail hands were able to put the herd back together again after the bison had passed through. Goodnight had no reason to feel sympathetic to the plight of the bison, but upon his later return to his Texas ranch, he captured six calves (the taking of one calf required him to kill the calf's mother) and placed them with domestic cows who were willing to nurse them. After they were weaned Goodnight took the six calves to a friend at a neighboring ranch with the understanding that the two friends would split any eventual profits. Since bison were not much of a novelty at that time, Goodnight's friend quickly tired of the animals and sold them.

In 1873, Goodnight was financially wiped out when the Stock Grower's Bank of Pueblo failed. He lost his Colorado ranch, all of his money, and the only property left to him was eighteen hundred longhorns that he trailed to the Texas Panhandle. He was able to make an arrangement with a wealthy Irishman, John G. Adair, whereby Goodnight was to purchase, develop, and manage a ranch, stocking it with horses and cattle with money furnished by Adair, and at the end of a five-year period Goodnight would gain a one-third interest in all land, cattle, and horses. It was during this five-year period that Goodnight once again began to gather a few wild bison from the remaining herds, and by 1887 he had acquired a modest herd of thirteen. It was estimated that by 1910 his bison herd numbered slightly more than 125, and besides selling bison to zoos and to other breeders, he had also experimented with bison wool and bison tallow, and experienced some limited success in crossbreeding bison with cattle to produce what was referred to by C. J. "Buffalo" Jones as "cattalo."

Charles Jesse Jones was born in Illinois in 1844. An overwhelming yearning for the West brought him to Kansas in 1866. From 1869 until 1886, he claims to have spent his life as a plainsman, hunting bison and achieving some measure of success as an "Indian fighter." While hunting bison, Jones had occasionally captured calves and later sold them; subsequently in order to differentiate him from "Dirty-Face Jones" and "Wrong-Wheel" Jones, who were also hunting bison on the prairies, he was given the name of "Buffalo" Jones. Having attained some measure of success in the past in the acquisition and sale of native wild animals, Jones was determined to capture some bison calves and "domesticate a race of cattle equal to, if not superior to all ruminants heretofore known." According to William Hornaday, Jones started out in April 1886, and by 1887 he had acquired fifty-seven bison and possessed the largest private herd in the United States. In 1888, he added more bison to his herd, through the addition of eighty-six bison and cattalo from Sam Bedson of Stony Mountain, Canada; but to maintain this growing herd he was obliged to sell bison on a regular basis. Eventually, in 1895, because of a general lack of adequate financing and some poor investments, he was obliged to dispose of all his bison. Some of these animals ended up in Austin Corbin's private game preserve in southwestern New Hampshire, which we will hear more about later in this chapter.

Upon learning that Yellowstone National Park (which at that time was being operated for the Department of Interior by the U.S. Cavalry) was actively recruiting for a game warden, Jones sent his application to President Theodore Roosevelt for the position, and, based upon his supposed knowledge and experience with bison, he was subsequently appointed as a game warden by the Secretary of the Interior, arriving in the park on July 16, 1902. His initial task was to build fences to contain a herd of bison that he later would acquire for the park. According to Robert Easton and MacKenzie Brown (1964, 120), Jones purchased three bulls from Charles Goodnight, fourteen cows from Charles Allard, and "he apparently sold the government several animals from a herd he himself was re-establishing in Kansas and Nebraska." David Dary (1989, 227) suggests that a total of eighteen animals were acquired: "Fifteen cows came from the Allard herd in western Montana, and three bulls were selected by Jones from Charles Goodnight's herd in Texas. . . . " There was no mention of Jones himself providing any animals. Because of a number of personality and supervisory problems that he could not overcome, Jones resigned his position at Yellowstone on September 15, 1905.

Convinced that crossbreeding bison and cattle was practical, Jones acquired thirty bison from E. J. Molera, who had a ranch in Monterey, California, and fifty-seven bison from the Allard herd in Montana. Like most of his other ventures this too failed. The bison he acquired, and Galloway cattle he selected, bred reluctantly and the progenies of any of these successes were burdened with certain genetic problems; male calves from the first crossbreeding either naturally aborted or caused the death of the cow, and heifer calves produced sterile males when bred to bison bulls. Only by breeding back again to domestic cattle could fertile males be obtained. After all animals were sold, the purebred bison became the first state-owned bison herd in Arizona.

A person identified by David Dary as being one of the principal saviors of the bison was a Pend d'Oreille Indian named Samuel Walking Coyote. Walking Coyote has received but little attention from other writers. According to Dary, Walking Coyote lived with the Flathead Indians in western Montana. In the summer of 1872, he left his Flathead wife and the Flathead reservation and travelled east to the Blackfoot reservation where he spent the winter of 1872–1873 hunting bison. He later married a Blackfoot woman but yearned to return to the Flathead reservation. He knew that his return would be fraught with problems because the Jesuit Fathers at the St. Ignatius Mission would find two wives unacceptable. When eight orphaned bison calves "wandered" into Walking Coyote's hunting camp he saw this as his opportunity to return to the Flatheads; he would offer the bison calves to the Jesuit Fathers as a peace offering. With his Blackfoot wife and the eight bison calves he left for the Flathead reservation in the spring of 1873. When he arrived he was welcomed in a rough manner by receiving a beating from the Indian police and being ejected from the tribe. Walking Coyote decided to keep the calves and proceeded to raise them in the Flathead Valley, and when the heifers reached four years of age in 1877, each gave birth to a calf. By 1884, Walking Coyote was said to have had thirteen bison, which he later sold that year to Charles Allard and Michel Pablo for $2,000 in gold. Leaving for Missoula with the gold, Walking Coyote supposedly went on a long binge and was eventually found dead of natural causes underneath a bridge.

E. Douglas Branch (1929, 228), one of the few writers who also mentions Walking Coyote, refers to him as a half-breed Indian who "had driven a band of thirty buffalo from Alberta [Canada] to the Flathead reservation in Montana. Another half-breed, Pablo, bought the herd for two thousand dollars, and protected his property well. . . ."

One of the truly large private herds assembled in the late 1890s and early 1900s was the Allard-Pablo herd. Charles A. Allard was a prosperous and industrious individual who had a ranch on the Flathead River. Hearing of the availability of Walking Coyote's bison (whatever the number may have been), he contacted his longtime friend and fellow rancher Michel Pablo, and convinced him that they should acquire Walking Coyote's bison. In 1893, Dary writes, "the two ranchers bought twenty-six more buffalo and eighteen cattalo from C.J. 'Buffalo' Jones in Kansas." (Jones' *Adventures on the Plains* refers to his disposal of some animals in Salt Lake

City, but doesn't identify Allard or Pablo by name, but Easton and Brown [1961, 140], in reporting on a 1906 purchase of bison by Jones, indicate that they had come from Jones's original Garden City herd and that they had originally been sold to Charles Allard.) Through natural means, or perhaps through unidentified purchases, the Allard-Pablo herd had grown to more than 300 animals by 1895. This same year, Allard suffered an injury that would not heal properly, and he left for Chicago to obtain better medical attention. An operation performed in Chicago eventually proved to be unsuccessful and, a few weeks later, Allard died at his ranch. The Allard-Pablo herd was equally divided between Pablo and Allard's estate. The Allard share was eventually sold by the heirs to Charles Conrad of Kalispell, Howard Eaton (who later sold fifteen bison to Jones for Yellowstone National Park), and a Judge Woodrow of Missoula (who later resold the bison to the Miller Brothers' 101 Ranch in Oklahoma).

Michel Pablo continued to retain his share of the bison herd, which grazed on Flathead reservation land, and by 1906 they were said to number 600 animals. Facing potential loss of future use of reservation grazing lands, Pablo attempted to secure an alternate grazing site for his bison herd from the U.S. government, and failing in this he petitioned the Canadian government for land to graze the herd. The Canadian government instead offered to buy his whole herd at the rate of $200 per animal, an offer that he eventually accepted. It took six years to deliver all of the bison, which by 1912 came to a total of more than 700 animals.

Fred Dupree was a French-Canadian trapper who married into the Sioux Indian tribe and ended up raising cattle along the Cheyenne River (west of Pierre, South Dakota) within the Dakota Sioux reservation. While on a bison hunt along the Grand River in 1881, Fred's son Pete roped five bison calves and brought them to Fred's ranch when they sort of mingled in with his cattle. Over the years Fred and Pete offered an occasional buffalo barbecue to their friends, but otherwise they did little with this small herd. By 1888, Pete Dupree had nine bison and seven cattalo, and in 1898, when he died, it was estimated that there were seventy-five or eighty bison in his herd along with some of the mixed breeds or cattalo. The executor of the Dupree estate was Pete's brother-in-law, D. L. "Dug" Carlin, who was determined to sell all of the bison prior to distributing the estate to the heirs. Carlin subsequently sold all of the bison to a nearby rancher, James (Scotty) Philip, provided that Philip took all of the mixed breeds as well.

James (Scotty) Philip is referred to by his biographer Wayne C. Lee as "the man who saved the buffalo." Lee goes on further to claim that "most of the buffalo east of the Rockies today are descendants of Scotty's herd." James Philip was born in Scotland in 1858, and came to America in 1874 when he was sixteen. In 1875, he was part of that motley group of prospectors who illegally sought gold in the Black Hills, and later he tried his luck as a teamster, cowboy, rancher, and freighter. In 1891, Scotty Philip entered into a partnership with two other people which they called the Minnesota and Dakota Cattle Company. On behalf of the partnership, Scotty bought, grazed, and sold thousands of head of cattle from his Pierre headquarters. Since cattle represented his primary business, throughout the rest of his life it remained his principal interest.

The mixed breeds were promptly disposed of, and in 1904, after all the bison were transferred from the Dupree herd to his newly fenced ranch near Fort Pierre, Scotty had about 80 bison. When Scotty Philip died in 1911, his herd had grown to nearly 400 animals and his two sons, Roderick and Stanley, took over what had now developed into a booming bison business. According to Dary, when financial problems occurred in 1914, the sons sold 36 bison to the State of South Dakota for the new Custer State Park. Further sales took place in the early 1920s, and three shipments of 100 animals each were made to William Randolph Hearst, the Miller Brothers' 101 Ranch in Oklahoma, and Oklahoma oilman Waite Phillips. Hearst placed his animals in an animal preserve he established near San Luis Obispo, California, and Waite Phillips moved his bison to a ranch he owned near Cimarron in northeastern New Mexico. Management of the remainder of the Scotty Philip herd in 1925 was the responsibility of Scotty's son-in-law, Andy Leonard. Leonard staged a big buffalo hunt and brought in a number of important men from nearly every state of the union. Of the near 250 bison remaining, approximately 200 were killed and the remaining were either sold that year or given to a variety of parks and reserves.

There are any number of other individuals and entrepreneurs of the moment who acquired bison, owned them for a while, and then passed them on to someone else. Usually the intention was to make money from these animals by displaying them as a novelty, as did William "Buffalo Bill" Cody in his Wild West show, and later profiting through resale because of their scarcity, or just impulse buying because they were available.

With limited success, bison have been broken to a harness and to pull a cart or wagon. "Buffalo" Jones, Pawnee Bill, and even Bill Cody had previously made such efforts. Cody's bison man, "Old Scotty," is pictured above with his team. Courtesy Denver Public Library, Western History Department.

Although adequately apprised of the critical situation regarding the bison population in the United States, Congress failed to act on any number of bills brought before it. In 1871 a bill was introduced that would have provided for a fine of $100 for each bison killed on public lands for purposes other than food or preserving the skin. The bill was printed but was never reported back from committee so that legislation could continue. In 1872 a similar bill was introduced and it met the same fate as its predecessor. In 1874, two bills were introduced: the first to protect the bison, the second to tax bison hides. The tax bill was killed in committee, but the bison protection bill, which (1) prohibited the killing of a female bison by anyone other than an Indian, and (2) made it illegal to kill more animals at one time than could reasonably be used for food, passed both the House and Senate and went to President Grant for signature. However, Grant failed to act upon the bill in a timely manner and it died as a result of his successful pocket veto.

A number of state and territorial legislatures introduced, and several actually passed, laws to protect bison. But these laws were either unenforceable or contained limitations that basically left nothing but window dressing and empty vapor that were aimed to satisfy eastern preservationists.

On March 1, 1872, President Grant signed into law an Act of Dedication, setting apart "a certain tract of land lying near the headwaters of the Yellowstone River as a public park." The new Yellowstone National Park was to be under the exclusive control of the Secretary of the Interior whose duty was to "provide for the preservation from injury or spoiliation [spoilation] of all timber, mineral deposits, natural curiosities or wonders within said park, and their retention in their natural condition." Nothing was specific in the Act with respect to the animal life within Yellowstone. Regulations to protect the animals were established by the Secretary, but enforcement and punishment of poachers left much to be desired. By 1894, it was estimated that less than twenty-five of the more than two hundred pre-1872 wild bison remained in the park. After the extent of poaching in Yellowstone National Park became well known and developed into a national issue, the Lacey Yellowstone Protection bill was signed by President Grover Cleveland on May 7, 1894, and became law. The new law provided for a jail sentence of up to two years and fines as high as $1,000 for anyone removing mineral deposits, cutting timber, or killing game in Yellowstone National Park. Congress then was sufficiently encouraged to provide the funds to reestablish a healthy bison herd within Yellowstone.

In spite of abundant evidence that the American bison was being methodically eliminated as an extant species in the United States, little public interest had been generated with respect to the bison's predicament. However, one person who was concerned was William T. Hornaday, then chief taxidermist at the U.S. National Museum. Worried over the eminent demise of the bison and the museum's obvious lack of suitable bison skins in its collection, he sought permission from his supervisors to undertake an expedition to the field to obtain appropriate specimens. He arrived in Miles City, Montana, on May 9, 1886, and set out by wagon train to explore the land to the north of Miles in hopes of locating bison. Establishing a base camp on the divide between the Yellowstone and Missouri Rivers in southeastern Montana, Hornaday and his party spent nearly four weeks searching for bison but only collected three. Learning that there was a herd of approximately thirty-five ranging in the badlands to the north, he returned to Washington after making plans to return in the fall when the bison robes would be in the best condition. Returning to Miles City on September 24, Hornaday immediately took to the field. After eight weeks in the field the expedition had collected twenty-five bison. Hornaday commented that he had obtained "as complete and fine a series as could be wished for." When the new bison habitat exhibit opened in the Washington, D.C. National Museum, it was considered to be the most outstanding presentation of its type in the United States.

The following year, authorities at the American Museum of Natural History, recognizing their own lack of bison skins, commissioned an expedition to secure for them suitable specimens from the same area Hornaday had visited a year earlier. When this expedition returned empty-handed — no bison could be found — the scientific and academic community was astounded. What had happened to all the bison? In January 1889, Hornaday attempted to conduct a census of the free-ranging bison in the United States. After compiling the results, he could account for only 85 wild bison, plus some 256 scattered in private herds and zoos, and the 200 that were still presumed to be ranging within the confines of Yellowstone National Park.

In 1904, a private herd of about 160 bison was located in Austin Corbin's Blue Mountain Forest and Game Preserve in New Hampshire. Ernest Harold Baynes, who was either a naturalist who behaved like a journalist or a journalist who behaved like a naturalist, saw the bison and was so impressed that he immediately embarked on a career path to save the bison as a species for the enjoyment of future generations. During the following months Baynes wrote a number of articles about the Corbin herd, and otherwise proceeded to conduct a spirited crusade on behalf of the beleaguered American bison. Urging the establishment of permanent herds by the federal government, Baynes contacted a number of prominent people and prestigious organizations, including President Theodore Roosevelt. Roosevelt encouraged Baynes and urged him to continue his efforts. On December 8, 1905, fourteen concerned individuals met in the Lion House of the New York Zoological Park and established an American Bison Society. William T. Hornaday was elected Society president and Baynes secretary. Shortly thereafter, President Roosevelt accepted the Society's invitation as its honorary president.

One of the fourteen charter members present at that first meeting at the New York Zoological Park was Martin S. Garretson, a somewhat cynical, but extremely knowledgeable and outspoken proponent for bison protection. Eventually Garretson assumed a key role for the Society, publishing bison population statistics from 1918 through 1933, and shouldering the somewhat thankless caretaker role for the American Bison Society from 1949 until 1953, when the Society faded from the scene. Garretson noted in his book *The American Bison* (1938, 207) that there were only two herds of bison under government control at the time the Society was first organized: those few live bison maintained at the National Zoological Park in Washington, D.C., and those remaining free-ranging bison in Yellowstone National Park. Article II of the Society's constitution provided that "the objects [objectives] of this society shall be the permanent preservation and increase of the American bison." Since most of the remaining live bison in the United States were in private hands, and thus subject to the acknowledged vagaries of private ownership, the Society felt that it had to take the initiative to increase the quantity and quality of public herds and ensure the continued government protection of and emphasis on bison. Based upon an earlier recommendation of Hornaday, but with the support and urging of the Society, Congress provided funds in 1907 to enclose 8,000 acres of the National Wichita Forest Reserve in Oklahoma for a bison herd. To stock this new National Bison Range, Hornaday shipped fifteen quality bison from the New York Zoological Park to the Reserve.

With the support of Montana Senator Joseph M. Dixon, the American Bison Society sent Congress a bill proposing the establishment of a bison reserve in Montana. Embarrassed by the loss of the Pablo herd to Canada, Congress quickly approved the proposed action and President Theodore Roosevelt signed the bill into law on May 23, 1908. A new National Bison Range, near the town of Moiese in western Montana, had been established, but it did not as yet have any bison. The Society was asked to come up with the bison, which they did by soliciting more than $10,000 from the public to purchase thirty-seven seed animals. What proved to be an interesting outcome of this show of public support was that most of the money came from the eastern states, and not one red cent was collected from Kansas, North or South Dakota, or Texas, the very locations where most of the bison slaughter took place. Thirty-six bison were acquired from

Mrs. Alicia (Charlie) Conrad, and one bison was donated by Charles Goodnight. The National Bison Range was appropriately fenced by October 1909, and according to David A. Dary (1989, 238–239), the federal government now exercised authority over 158 bison: 7 at the National Zoological Park in Washington, D.C., about 95 within Yellowstone National Park, 19 on the Wichita Game Reserve in Oklahoma, and 37 on the National Bison Range in Montana.

In 1913, the Society donated six bison to start a herd on the Fort Niobrara reservation in north-central Nebraska, and fourteen bison to start the Wind Cave National Game Preserve (now Wind Cave National Park) bison herd. The last effort of the Society to establish a public herd was in 1919 at the Pisgah National Forest and Game Preserve in western North Carolina. The latter effort did not turn out too well, as eventually all the bison died.

The American Bison Society performed the critical role of a catalyst for the public to exert their determination to reestablish a place for the bison in the United States. By 1930 the American Bison Society issued its last report, and although some members remained quite active, the Society as an organization actually accomplished very little after 1933.

When the immense bison herds were eliminated from the Great Plains, this did not necessarily result in any rebirth of vegetation in those lands that basically presented a rather dry and fragile ecosystem. Bison herds were totally dependent upon grass for their food, constantly on the move, wandering seemingly without purpose. If you observe bison feeding today, you will witness the same behavior: going from pasture to pasture without pausing to eat all the good grass first. Although the herds would occasionally stampede across the plains from apparent or unapparent threats, they also spent considerable time lying down or standing, as has been the custom of ruminants. As the bison were moved out, or permanently removed as the case may have been, their place was taken by equal, if not greater, herds of cattle. In 1848, Paul Wellman (*The Trampling Herd*) reported that, exclusive of wild cattle, there were 382,873 head of domestic cattle in Texas in 1848, 1,363,688 in 1855, and 3,786,443 in 1860. In north Texas, by 1869, cattle herds had taken over most of the former bison range. Cattle herds were trailed from Texas to railheads in Kansas, Colorado, and Missouri. They were later trailed to Montana, Wyoming, and other plains states that offered grass and water to "fatten them up." The *Saline County Journal*, published at Salina, Kansas, said on July 20, 1871:

The entire country, east, west, and south of Salina down to the Arkansas River and Wichita is now filled with Texas cattle. There are not only cattle "on a thousand hills" but a thousand cattle on one hill and every hill. The bottoms are overflowing with them and the water courses with this great article of traffic. Perhaps not less than 200,000 of them are in the state, 60,000 of which are within a day's ride of Salina, and the cry is "still they come."

By 1883, an estimated six hundred thousand head of cattle were competing for grazing land in Montana and Wyoming, and each of the other so-called eleven range states (i.e., Arizona, Colorado, Kansas, Nebraska, New Mexico, North and South Dakota, Oklahoma, and Texas) was similarly festooned with vast herds of cattle. Lewis F. Allen (*Improvement of Native Cattle*), a prominent cattle breeder at that time and a productive writer for a number of agricultural journals, wrote that "hostile Indians and the buffalo may retard the settlement of those vast plains, but those obstacles will rapidly disappear before the grand march of civilized industry." Looking forward with an enthused anticipation, he went on further to say that from a hypothetical north-south line west of the Mississippi "the great plain thence to the Rocky Mountains will mostly be devoted to stock growing, as will the great basin west to the Sierra Nevada. In time these plains will grow their herds, to be transported to the richer grain regions east and west for feeding and consumption." In short, what he visualized was cattle to take the place of bison, and, instead of waiting for the usual seasonal fattening on grasses, the cattle could be moved at will to market centers where they would be fattened on grain and sold.

Quickly following the cattle to the free grass were sheep. In Montana the 1870 census recorded a total of 4,212 sheep in that state; by 1900 there were 4.2 million. The overstocked Great Plain range eventually became a battleground as cattle and sheep owners, many of which were actually large corporations, competed for grass and water. The practice of overstocking and overgrazing ultimately ended in the transfer of large tracts of public lands into private hands and the construction of legal fences. But in the process, the short- and tall-grass prairies formerly occupied by an estimated 60 million bison also became history. According to the cattle industry, cattle numbers in 1993 were at their highest level in over six years, more than 102.7 million cattle in domestic herds (U.S. Department of Agriculture statistics suggest that the greatest number of cattle in the United States occurred in 1983, when there were a recorded 115 million cattle). The grass pastures, however, have given way to feedlots with corn, grain, and silage becoming grazing surrogates.

Years ago some of the early bison entrepreneurs were of the belief that if bison could be successfully interbred with domestic cattle, the resultant crossbreed, if it inherited all the perceived good qualities of each, would be superbly equipped to meet the rancher's optimum maintenance, handling, and production needs. Charles J. "Buffalo" Jones, writing of what he referred to as his "cattalo" experiments in the *Farmers Review* on August 22, 1888, stated that:

1. We want an animal that is hardy.
2. We want an animal with nerve and endurance.
3. We want an animal that faces the blizzards and endures the storms.
4. We want an animal that will rustle the prairie and not yield to the discouragement.
5. We want an animal that will fill the above bill, and make good beef and plenty of it.

For many reasons, interbreeding between bison and domestic cattle has never really worked well. First of all, the domestic bull wants little to do with the bison cow — and artificial insemination has not proven to work successfully with bison cows. Secondly, although bison bulls are normally willing to breed with the common domestic cow, only slightly more than 50 percent result in successful live births — and this usually occurs only if the calf is a heifer. Bull calves are frequently aborted or lead to the death of the cow. If the bull calf survives, it is normally sterile. Fertilized embryo transfer has also been tried, but has not as yet proven to be an effective method of producing bison or bison-cattle crossbreeds. With the exception of the so-called beefalo, which is three-eighths bison and five-eighths of some type of cattle breed, crossbreeding (except by accident or as an "experiment") does not now take place — nor is it recommended by any of the bison associations.

We are indeed fortunate that the few bison that remained were nurtured and protected and that an unadulterated or manufactured species was not created, such as with the auroch and tarpan experiments at the

Munich Zoo and the quagga in South Africa. Although only a few white men may have historically held hopes for a healthy return of the American bison, most Native Americans desperately held on to this dream. The Ghost Dances of the 1880s were fed by visions of Indian holy men and rumors of recent bison sightings. The Ghost Dance swept through Plains Indian tribes and was considered something that was profoundly mystical as well as deeply religious. These visions and rumors spoke of a time that the buffalo would return, the white man would disappear, and all would be as it once was. The bison has now returned, perhaps not in the numbers the former herds once commanded, but they are flourishing to the degree that they now form the basis of a full-fledged bison industry.

The common North American plains bison (*Bison bison bison*) can now be found in all fifty states, Canada, and a number of other foreign countries. The few remaining wood bison (*Bison bison athabascae*) are predominately under governmental control in Canada, but there are a smattering of wood bison that can be viewed in about a half-dozen zoos in Germany and the United States. Plains bison ranching is becoming quite popular in Canada, and because governmental regulations on exporting live bison are seemingly not as restrictive as they are in the United States, Canada has, to this moment, proven to be the origination point of choice for shipment of live bison to a variety of European countries. Canada does not now have anywhere near the number of plains bison that are found in the United States. However, this was not always the case. Canada placed into effect a Buffalo Protection Act in 1877, and the Canadian Northwest Mounted Police provided effective protection beginning in 1897. When the Pablo herd was acquired in 1906, the numbers rapidly increased to the degree that plains bison were rapidly depleting their range and overcrowding their designated preserves. In 1972, David Dary attempted to conduct a survey of the numbers of bison in North America; he arrived at an estimated total of 30,114 animals; approximately 15,000 in the United States and 15,114 in Canada. Since that time, the United States herds have increased exponentially, whereas those in Canada, although somewhat larger than they were projected to be in 1972, have not quite doubled.

It is extremely difficult for humans to visualize, grasp the complexity, measure the extent, or appreciate the inherent qualities of any issue or problem that addresses or invokes numbers of objects, or subjects, without knowing precisely just how many there were and/or are. If someone is describing to you his or her new home, what you really want to know about this home is (1) how many rooms are there? (2) how many square feet of living space does the house contain? By doing this, we are simply expressing our need to place parameters on things that we haven't as yet seen but are attempting to envision. There really is no way to re-create the total number of bison that once roamed the plains of North America, but the statements that there were "lots" of them, or that they were "as numerous as the locusts of Egypt," or "The plains were black and appeared as if in motion," do little to satisfy the truly inquisitive. For this reason, the figure of sixty million bison formerly occupying North America, although merely an estimate, gives us the parameters that place the bison in context with their former environment.

After nearly all the bison were slaughtered, they were then much easier to count. Hornaday's 1889 survey of 1,091 bison in the world, and Ernest Thompson Seton's 1895 survey of 800 bison (1927, 670), are presumed to be their best count of all the bison that they knew about or each felt comfortable including in their survey. The American Bison Society conducted a survey, or census, of bison for seventeen of the years between 1908 and 1933, and their 1933 census reported the existence of 21,701 bison — a very precise figure to be sure, but in reality it could only have been, at its very best, perhaps only a close estimate. Henry H. Collins, Jr., of Bronxville, New York, was reported by David A. Dary (1989, 287–288) to have compiled a census of bison in North America in 1951 and concluded that there were 23,154. Since that census or survey was conducted thirteen years prior to the time Dary began his research in 1964, Dary obviously had good reason to seek some updated figures. Using Collins's 1951 census data as a starting point, he obtained names and addresses of bison owners from a variety of sources, and mailed out questionnaires to 490 known or suspected owners of bison in North America. Dary received 210 responses (slightly less than 43 percent) by January 1, 1970. When the results were tabulated, 10,131 living bison were reported in the United States and 15,114 in Canada, or a grand total of 25,245 bison. Dary suspected that the reported figures were low, since only 43 percent of the questionnaires were returned, and by conducting additional research he came up with a count of "nearly 15,000 living buffalo in the United States or about 50 percent more than had been confirmed in my 1969 survey. In Canada, the figure of 15,114 is felt to be reasonably accurate for 1972 since nearly all buffalo in Canada are owned by the government and the herd sizes are controlled; private buffalo owners in Canada have less than 400 buffalo." Dary printed a revision of his 1974 *Buffalo Book* in 1989, and in the revision he provided estimates of 83,000 bison in 1982 and 98,000 bison in 1989, but did not indicate how he arrived at these figures.

After having spent more than thirty-four years with the National Park Service, I had a number of opportunities to observe bison and became somewhat familiar with that fiercely independent and stubborn animal's errant and almost schizophrenic behavior: seemingly stoical one moment, but bordering on ballistic the next. Later on, after accepting the position of executive director of the American Bison Association, I was able to meet and perhaps try my best to better understand the people who owned or wanted to own bison. As one bison owner observed: "We are a lot like the animals we own, we don't like to be regulated." Bison owners also seem to be somewhat reluctant to fill out long questionnaires or divulge information that they may possibly view as privileged ownership data. It was, and still is, important for the bison industry to know just how many bison there are. Without these figures, there really isn't any way to acceptably measure availability and project growth, or respond to market supply and demand inquiries. The United States government does not elect to separately assemble or report information with respect to numbers of bison. The Census of Agriculture, conducted by the U.S. Department of Commerce, Bureau of the Census, includes bison under a summary category of "Other Livestock and Livestock Products," along with goats, mink, rabbits, etc. Unlike cattle, bison are not subject to the Federal Meat Inspection Act, but under the Agricultural Marketing Act of 1946, bison owners can request voluntary meat inspection, at the owner's expense, at United States Department of Agriculture (USDA) plants. The USDA, however, includes bison in the "other" category when it reports the number of animals slaughtered at these plants.

Because of the foregoing, and for other substantive reasons, the American Bison Association (ABA), through its Dr. Ken Throlson American Bison Foundation, decided to undertake a census, or inventory, of bison in the United States as of December 31, 1992. As executive director of the ABA at that time, I assumed the responsibility for conducting this inventory. To ensure that bison owners would not find the inventory form too onerous or have reason to be suspicious of the purposes of the census, a stamped, addressed census card was provided to every known owner of bison in the United States along with a letter that identified the purpose and need for the bison count. The census card asked the bison owner/manager to provide only three figures with respect to his/her bison herd. They were asked (1) to provide the total number of animals in their herd, (2) the number of cows and heifers included in this total, and (3) the number of bison slaughtered for meat in 1992. Although the initial response to the mailing could be considered as excellent by most of the abstract statistical standards, two follow-up mailings were conducted and estimate inventories were developed for those known owners/managers who failed to respond.

Unlike previous bison censuses or surveys, bison owners in the private sector today are often members of some established bison organization or association. In fact, many private sector owners may enjoy more than one such affiliation. In 1992, the largest and most active bison association was the American Bison Association headquartered in Denver, Colorado, and the second largest was the National Buffalo Association, located in Fort Pierre, South Dakota. The membership lists from both of these national organizations, as well as those from the then six active state associations, were obtained and 1,260 mailings were made. From these 1,260 mailings of stamped and addressed census cards, 721 were returned (approximately 57 percent). A number of individuals (41) responded by indicating that although they were listed as active members of a bison association, they did not own bison. However, nearly half of them (20) also mentioned that they would soon be acquiring animals. Those who did not respond to the initial mailing were either contacted by telephone or received a second mailing. However, in spite of these remailings and telephone contacts, 465 individuals still refused to respond; several expressly indicated that they did not want anyone knowing how many bison they owned — even after receiving assurances that census information would only be made available in summary form.

In order that bison owned by these 465 individuals would be considered in the survey/census, estimates were obtained from knowledgeable people reasonably familiar with the size of these unreported herds (neighbors, peers, etc.). Where accurate estimates could not be reasonably obtained, mean herd values applicable to reported herds were used. To avoid the possibility that extremely large privately owned herds (over 500 animals) would unduly influence or distort the mean herd averages used, these large herds were excluded in arriving at the mean computation.

Throughout the survey/census process it was quite apparent that there were a number of bison owners who did not belong to either of the then two national associations or to a state organization. When the presence of these unreported animals was subsequently uncovered, these animals were then included in the survey/census. However, a later comprehensive state-by-state review of herds that were reported revealed that there still were significant numbers of bison that had not been counted. For example, only one herd was reported in Maine, but three other small herds were later identified and recorded. In Illinois, twenty herds were reported but one unreported herd of over 250 bison was eventually uncovered as the result of a newspaper article on bison. The same circumstances were present in reviews of Texas, Oklahoma, and California. Because of the time and cost associated with conducting further state reviews, a statistical estimate, determined from those states individually reviewed, was used to compensate for any potential error in this survey/census of bison. Information on public and tribal herds was rather easily obtained, and, for the most part, readily available.

INFORMATION FROM THE 1992 SURVEY/CENSUS:

Public Herds:

Federal	6,463
State	4,685
City and County (includes all municipalities, zoological gardens, etc.)	1,988
Total Public Herds	**13,136**

Tribal Herds:	3,599
Private Herds:	108,854
Total bison:	**125,589**

| Heifers and Cows: | 81,620 |
| Slaughtered for meat in 1992: | 10,823 |

In February 1995, the newly incorporated National Bison Association mailed a questionnaire to all active and associate members requesting (1) information to update its membership directory, and (2) data relative to the number of bison owned, breeding cows, and proposed sales. It was interesting to me to learn that the responses the Association eventually received that included herd count data numbered 767, only slightly more than the number of responses the American Bison Association received in 1992, in spite of the now joint (American Bison and National Buffalo) Association membership reported to exceed 2,000 members.

No attempt was made in 1992 to secure information with respect to the number of bison in Canada or Mexico. Canada does, however, maintain some rather good records on the numbers of bison within Canada, and it was understood that in 1993 it was determined that there were slightly more than 25,000 plains bison in Canada. Because of the number of bison imported from the United States, and the remarkable reproductive capacity of bison, a consultant who was involved in the bison industry in Canada has projected that, by the year 2000, Canada could conceivably have over 120,000 bison.

The January 1, 1993, census of bison in the United States did not attempt to include or project the 1993 calf crop, which conservatively could have represented some 35,000 additional animals. However, it was noted that a number of late returns received in May 1993 may have included some 1993 calves. Like any census or survey conducted by mail, reliance is placed on the respondents' answers, and some of the respondents may not necessarily maintain current herd totals or they may not have been recoverable at the point of time requested. In addition, there are always those human frailties that lead to the reporting of information that some bison owners may feel "more comfortable with" (i.e., after some animals have been sold, slaughtered, or purchased, or perhaps adjusted to allow for other projected events, such as an upcoming calf crop).

It is doubtful that many of the early bison entrepreneurs could have envisioned a time when bison would again be assembled in herds that contained thousands of animals. Nor is it probable that those early bison conservationists could have foreseen a time when the herd health of bison on public lands would become threatened because of overcrowding and overgrazing. But what would really be startling to William T. Hornaday and those early pioneers who formed the American Bison Society is that it was the private sector that has proved to be the eventual major player, and as such, is primarily responsible for the return of the American bison.

8

The Industry

They were the harbingers of a new agricultural industry, those indefatigable and sometimes crusty individuals who forged their livelihood from the remnants of a western wilderness soon to pass from the scene; people such as Scotty Philip, Charles Jesse "Buffalo" Jones, Charles Goodnight, Michel Pablo, Gordon W. "Pawnee Bill" Lillie, Samuel Walking Coyote. The fledgling Bison Industry also owes much to individuals and organizations, such as William T. Hornaday and the American Bison Society, who did not seek personal profit and strived equally hard — but altruistically — on behalf of the bison. When "Buffalo" Jones jotted down what he considered to be the fifteen primary assets of a bison, the first item he thought of was that they were "made for the Great Plains climate;" the second asset that came to his mind was that bison had "flesh superior to any domestic animal under similar conditions." However, each of these early entrepreneurs either displayed his newly acquired bison for its curiosity value, or considered schemes where the bison would become a beast of burden or crossbred with cattle in an effort to develop a superior breed of western range cattle. Not yet fully promoted were the principal advantages of the bison: its hardiness and high quality of meat.

The Plains Indian hunted the bison for its meat, its hide, and for the many other nonfood by-products that they obtained from the animal. Although there is no way that this assumption can now be proven, many people attribute the superior health and great endurance of the early Plains Indians to their near exclusive diet of bison meat. Over the years a number of claims have been made as to the believed nutritional qualities of bison meat. In addition to it being touted as higher in protein and lower in calories, fat, cholesterol, and calories than other red meats, it reportedly contains a number of other salubrious properties and is non-allergenic. The limited research that has been conducted thus far would appear to support most, if not all, of these nutritional contentions. A recent study by Dr. Marchello, North Dakota State University meat scientist, suggests that bison steaks contain about one-third the fat of choice-grade beef rib-eyes.

Since production-line bison meat is not marblized with fat, portion cuts of bison meat could not possibly produce anywhere near the levels of cholesterol that would be obtained from the same cuts of domestic red meats such as beef. Endorsements from American Heart Association advisors have also provided validity to industry claims that bison meat represents a healthy red meat alternative. In today's marketplace nearly every part of the bison is used, much as it was when the massive herds roamed the prairies and were referred to by the United States Army as "the Indians commissary." However, it is the meat from the bison that essentially forms the economic basis and substance of the Bison Industry.

If the meat is the economic basis of the industry, it could also become the catalyst that could drive bison breeders and producers perhaps even further toward development of genetic change in the physical structure and temperament of the American bison. The structural changes could come about through selective breeding to encourage the production of bison that have longer backs and larger hindquarters; this would serve to improve carcass appearance and enhance the extent of market return from the higher-priced loin and round cuts. The current practice of certain producers to remove the more obstreperous of bison from their herds may make handling easier, and perhaps reduce some fencing problems, but the ensuing result could also be the eventual development of progeny that are more complacent and perhaps exhibit other prosaic but unbisonlike characteristics. Although genetic change is not necessarily an inevitable consequence, or outcome, of selective breeding, it certainly is a possibility. Currently a number of breeders elect to dehorn their bison, including cows. Dehorning tends to make the animals more submissive, and obviously more manageable. Dehorning would seem to be particularly advantageous with respect to confined locations, such as feedlots, where horns could damage hides and meat. Although genetically polled cattle have been around for quite some time, it is unlikely that polled bison could ever become a viable option.

Mature bull bison that has been dehorned. This animal exhibits the long body that is sought by breeders, and although bison are easier to handle without their horns, some breeders are of the opinion that removal of horns ruins the animals' appearance. Courtesy American Bison Association.

Why do people get into the bison business? Perhaps a few because of the so-called romance that American people have with the bison, or just having an opportunity to own a part of the Old West. The remainder are basically in the business to make money, and if they are essentially good businesspeople, they will make money. The same ancestral ingredients that economists call the factors of production — land, labor, capital, and entrepreneurial ability — still come into play, but the options are endless. If a person owns land, and is currently raising cattle or crops, or perhaps nothing, he or she may decide that it is more profitable to raise bison. If they do not have land, and are not interested in investing in land but do want to raise bison, there are absentee owner programs where they can place their bison on someone else's land. Maybe they only want to distribute bison meat, that is, buy animals from a producer, have them slaughtered, and distribute the meat to a variety of wholesale and/or retail outlets. Perhaps they are interested only in by-products such as the hides, horns,

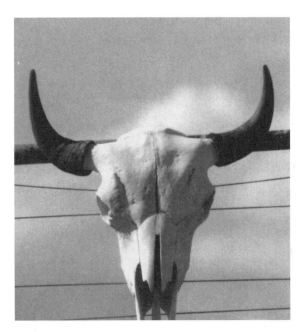

Bison skull "curing" on a fence. The horn caps are usually removed and treated with mineral oil so they do not become too dried out. In the past few years it has become popular to decorate and paint these skulls, usually adopting a southwestern or Native American design. Courtesy American Bison Association.

skulls, or mounted heads. Whatever their choice may be, they are all viable options. Some people have even carved a business for themselves out of processing what is referred to as "bison wool." That is the soft, downy winter insulation that bison acquire in late fall and shed in the spring. Mature animals will produce nearly two pounds of this furlike material, which can be woven into an almost cashmere yarn. If that doesn't sound like it is too economically promising, sweaters made from yarn of bison wool are currently, and rapidly, selling for over $500.

Probably the best way to explain the Bison Industry and its functions is to take a closer look at the individual bison owners, the breeders/producers, the distributors of bison products, and some of the problems of the industry.

There are more than two thousand individual owners of bison in the private sector. Most owners are small ranchers, and perhaps some of these may only be considered as hobbyists. Unfortunately, the Internal Revenue

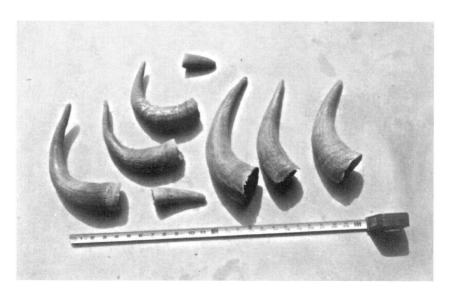

Bison horn caps. Calves have just nubbins for horns and yearlings have straight spikes that begin to curve upwards before the animal reaches two years of age. After three years of age the horns should have achieved a complete curve and the point nearly perpendicular to the base. Annual growth rings on bison horns, however, are not as easy to count as the internal growth rings on trees. Courtesy American Bison Association.

Service, which is not renowned for its ability to distinguish certain businesses that may not make a profit each year from hobbyists, takes a rather dim view of the economic practicality of a small bison rancher. A census of bison, conducted by the American Bison Association in 1992, indicated that an "average" bison owner possesses 23 bison, and, of this total, approximately 15 are cows and heifers; the remainder are bulls of varying ages. Generally those who own fewer than 50 bison are considered to be maintaining a "small" bison operation, those who have from 51 to 200 bison a "medium" sized operation, and anything over 200 bison a "large" operation. The largest single owner of American bison in the world is Ted Turner, the communications and television magnate. On his numerous landholdings, Mr. Turner maintains bison on the Flying D Ranch, Gallatin Gateway, Montana; the Ladder Ranch near Caballo, New Mexico; the Vermejo Park Ranch, a huge holding covering over 578,000 acres north of Cimarron, New Mexico, and running to the Colorado border; the

Typical small cow/calf operation, Omaha, Nebraska. Cows have an anticipated 20-year breeding life span and are expected to calve at three years of age. The desired ratio of breeding bulls to cows is 1 to 10, but this will often vary based upon circumstances and conditions.

Armendaris Ranch near Engle, New Mexico; and the Spike Box Ranch, north-central Nebraska. These five ranches, totaling well over one million acres, are home to more than ten thousand bison. Not only do these ranches serve as home for numerous herds of splendid-looking bison, the unspoiled natural beauty of the land and surrounding scenery of these ranches are just simply magnificent.

Besides the Turner bison ranches, there are also any number of large privately owned ranches and bison operations located across the country that maintain equally well-flourishing herds of healthy and robust representatives of the species. It is now not uncommon to see bison herds numbering in the thousands of animals in many of the western states.

As was the case in years gone by, bison still thrive as a part of the South Dakota grassland environment and many excellent herds are now situated in that state. One of the more notable of the larger herds is that which is located on the Triple U Buffalo Ranch, Fort Pierre, South Dakota. This bison herd was formerly owned and managed by Roy Houck, and was the prime feature in Kevin Costner's movie epic, *Dances with Wolves*. Another rather large herd of bison can be found in the western part of the

Entrance to the Flying D Ranch, Turner Properties, Gallatin Gateway, Montana. Ranch buildings are located behind the butte to the left of the picture.

Distant herd of bison trailing through the vast hills and valleys and magnificent grasslands on the Flying D Ranch, Montana. The scene is reminiscent of what may have been a common spectacle hundreds of years ago.

state on the Triple Seven Ranch near the town of Hermosa. Although not necessarily numbering in the thousands of animals, the bison raised on Larry and Dixie Byrd's Trails End River Bison Ranch near Presho are considered to be among the best, if not the best, in the country. The Byrds have been consistent winners of the Producer of the Year Award at the ABA, now the National Bison Association, Gold Trophy Show and Sale.

Wyoming was the home of what was, in all likelihood, the last free-ranging herd of bison in the United States outside of Yellowstone National Park. In 1889, it was reported that a band of at least twenty-six head were seen grazing in the Red Desert. Today there are two private herds within the state that contain bison numbering in the thousands. The Flocchini family has been actively involved in bison ranching since 1965; their Durham Ranch, which is adjacent to Gillette, accommodates one of the largest bison herds in the world. Their current plans call for a cow herd that would level out at around two thousand animals. Ron and Janice Thiel operate the Iron Mountain Bison Ranch near Cheyenne, and in addition to marketing live animals and selling meat and bison by-products, they offer guided tours of their ranch and the bison herd. Located near Cody, in the southwestern part of the state is the Diamond Eighty Eight Ranch of Richard and Peg Bryan. This ranch is an excellent example of what a medium-sized operation is all about. The Bryans field slaughter, market their bison meat, sell hides and other by-products, irrigate and maintain pastures, repair fences and all ranch buildings — and they do all this without any permanent ranch help. Since the Bryans are adjacent to the Shoshone National Forest and near Yellowstone National Park, they also need to keep a wary eye out for marauding grizzlies.

Although North Dakota may not have any privately owned bison herds that would number in the thousands of animals, it does have several top ranching operations, and one in particular, Dr. Ken and Marlys Throlson's RX Ken Mar Buffalo Ranch near New Rockford, is regarded as one of the nation's best. In addition to producing top bison, Dr. Throlson is considered to be one of the more knowledgeable of people when it comes to matters of bison health.

More than 150 years ago wild bison were commonly found in Colorado as far west as the Pikes Peak and South Park area of the state, but the great herds usually ranged east of the present city of Pueblo. Colorado is now home to many privately owned bison herds, three of which can be

Slaughter bulls in a holding pen on the Diamond Eighty Eight Ranch near Cody, Wyoming. The ranch owner field slaughters his own bison and also processes most of his bison by-products on site.

included among the largest in the country. Gene and Shirley Linnebur are the owners of probably one of Colorado's most conspicuous bison herds. Located on the plains east of Denver, their Linnebur Grain and Buffalo Ranch is convenient to nearby I-70 and the town of Byers. Hisayoshi Ota's Rocky Mountain Bison Ranch, located adjacent to Mosca, contains the largest single bison herd within the state. It gets cold in the San Luis Valley in the wintertime, but bison are equipped to endure the most severe of weather conditions.

One of the more successful bison promoters in the country, and clearly the most enthusiastic, is Will McFarlane. His Denver Buffalo Company not only markets bison meat products in restaurants and grocery stores within Arizona and Colorado, but throughout the United States by catalog mail order. Recently McFarlane appeared on a nationwide television shopping channel, QVC, to promote the Denver Buffalo Company's bison meat package. In addition to buying bison from other

Part of the Diamond Eighty Eight herd. Note the six-strand barbed wire fence. The ranch owner has initiated a program of ranch tours that bring visitors close to the herd and their gigantic herd bull.

producers, the Denver Buffalo Company has a ranch southeast of Denver, near Kiowa, that is home to over a thousand bison.

Perhaps no other state can boast of the number of quality bison herds that are held within its borders as can Colorado. Although it is not possible or practical to attempt to name them all, the Colorado Bison Company ranch of Merle and Susan Maass has clearly one of the better of the medium-sized ones. Like the Byrd's Trails End River Bison Ranch of South Dakota, the Maasses' emphasis is on breeding and excellence rather than just meat production.

There are only two other bison herds within the remaining continental United States that can lay claim to close to a thousand animals: the Duff Land and Cattle Company, Rich and Susan Duff, of Scott City, Kansas; and Oleson's Foods Stores and Farms, Gerald and Frances Oleson, Traverse City, Michigan. There are, however, a considerable number of ranches across the United States that maintain bison herds of more than two hundred but less than one thousand animals.

Bison grazing on the Rocky Mountain Bison Ranch near Mosca, Colorado. The bison herd on this ranch approaches 2,000 animals and is currently the largest herd in the state of Colorado. There are now at least four other ranch operations in the United States that maintain bison herds in excess of 2,000 animals: the Flying D Ranch, Montana; the Ladder Ranch, New Mexico (both ranches are owned and operated by Ted Turner); the Triple U Enterprises/Standing Butte Ranch, South Dakota (as featured in the film Dances with Wolves); and the Durham Buffalo Ranch, Wyoming. Besides the above-cited private sector bison operations, Custer State Park, South Dakota, and Yellowstone National Park, Wyoming/Montana, have herds of more than 2,000 bison. Courtesy American Bison Association.

Regardless of size, each operation has its own unique problems and concerns — but one problem that none of them will have is a lack of demand for their marketable bison. The so-called small operator probably is working with limited space and would like to market his/her excess animals by either selling them to another breeder or butchering some of the bulls. Whether the operation is small, medium, or large, heifers and productive cows are too valuable as breeding stock to slaughter for meat. The medium and large operator may also have to make some critical choices regarding disposal of excess animals, but these choices are simply business decisions whereby excess animals represent occupational products, and disposals are timed and influenced by existing economic conditions.

One of the most frequently asked questions by prospective bison owners is "How many bison can I put on an acre of land?" Although bison are conceivably more efficient in processing their feed than are cattle, experienced breeders and producers suggest that the best rule of thumb is not to exceed the ratio of bison per acre (or acres per bison) that has been recommended for cattle by the local agricultural extension agent. Bison will eat the same types of feed as cattle, but they will also eat a few items that cattle will pass over. Because of this, feed costs and pasture needs for bison are essentially the same as that for cattle. Similar to any other species, if they are not well fed, bison cannot be expected to provide a top calf crop. Therefore, where the primary differences between bison and cattle occur are in care and facilities acquisition and maintenance.

Generally accepted standards of the Bison Industry declare that low-level antibiotics and hormones are not given to the animals to stimulate growth, as is the case with cattle. It is the unadulterated, pure organic nature of bison meat that stimulates market interest and forms the basis of its demand as the healthy red meat alternative. Another significant difference between bison and cattle is that bison cows do not need any help in calving; in fact, they prefer to be totally by themselves if it is at all possible. Bison are not in need of constant veterinarian care and only a few veterinarians are skilled in working with bison. It is not that tending bison represents a particularly difficult medical specialty, it is just that the infrequency of need offers little opportunity for many veterinarians to acquire experience with bison. Bison also have a remarkable immune system and, because of this, they only rarely become ill. They are vulnerable, however, to a number of cattle diseases — especially anthrax, brucellosis and tuberculosis — but their resistance is phenomenal. Bison are not known to develop malignancies; in those that have, the tumors were externally induced. It is perhaps the fact that most private sector bison are, of necessity, confined that they even develop the limited health difficulties that they do. This is particularly true with respect to parasitic conditions.

Bison generally require much stronger and higher fences than cattle. Although both are members of the Bovidae family, the bison is the Superman of the family: it can leap small fences in a single bound. The fence needs to be higher than the bison's line of sight; if it can get its head over the fence it will likely jump the fence — if it happens to feel like it. Making a fence sturdy enough to contain a bison depends a lot upon how

A variety of fencing has been successfully used by bison ranchers, including the simple five- and six-strand barbed wire (pictured above). Exterior fences tend to be stronger and taller, with interior fencing perhaps less formidable. Exterior barbed wire fences are often electrified and/or used in combination with high tensile wiring. If a bison can get its nose over the fence and is serious about wandering, it is quite probable that the bison will jump the fence or push it over. Courtesy American Bison Association.

determined the bison may be to leave. If there is enough feed within the boundaries of the fence, there may not be enough incentive to test the fence. However, if there happen to be bison on the other side of the fence, there may be an all out effort taking place. Some bison ranchers claim that five- or six-strand barbed wire is all that they need; others add to this a high tensile electric wire about three feet off the ground and one foot from their perimeter fence. Other fences that are used include non-electric high tensile, woven wire, pipe and/or cable, and all electric. However, I once saw a bison leap a six-foot wood corral fence from a standing start, and I also saw an adult bull bison knock down two six-foot woven wire fences that were spaced about one foot apart. There are quite a few bison ranchers who claim that their bison do not require much more than reasonable fencing. However, unless ten-foot concrete walls and bastions are planned, it is doubtful that any economically priced or "reasonable" fence would be impregnable to a suitably determined adult male bison.

Six-strand electric fence used on the Flying D Ranch, Gallatin Gateway, Montana. With the superb natural conditions of the ranch, along with abundant space and the absence of exterior attractions, it is doubtful that these fences would be subject to testing by Flying D bison.

Handling facilities also need to be sturdy and dependable to accommodate these brawny, muscular animals. Bison corrals, squeeze chutes, crowding circles, alleyways, and sorting pens could easily be used for cattle, but similar cattle facilities are really not suitable for bison. They just are not big enough or strong enough. Bison do not like being handled or manipulated and will generally resist forced movements; however, it is necessary to occasionally move bison into corrals, sorting areas, and squeeze chutes for a variety of reasons. The larger the herd, the more diverse are the reasons. If cows are not being bred when they come in heat, the bull(s) may need to be semen tested, and if you have ever seen this being done you would certainly understand why the breeders want squeeze chutes. Besides testing, medications, vaccines, and drugs can be more easily injected through use of a squeeze chute. Sick and injured animals need to be isolated from the healthy, and bison selected for sale or slaughter need to be separated. Bison facilities and fencing need to be considered by the prospective rancher before the animals are acquired. It is just like going

Feeder bulls being readied for slaughter. Optimum feedlot circumstances would place a yearling bull, hopefully weighing more than 400 pounds, on feed for not more than nine months and process him at 1,000 to 1,100 pounds. For tenderness and quality of meat, animals slaughtered should be under 30 months of age. Older bison should be slaughtered only for burger and/or sausage. Courtesy American Bison Association.

shopping for a dog and a cat: you buy the cat first — and get a good firm grip on it before you buy the dog. If you acquire the bison first, then start to rebuild or construct fences and facilities; you have theoretically bought the dog first.

There are several distinct market differences between bison and cattle. Cattle are given a variety of growth stimulants, are genetically bred as a meat supply, and normally are moved to a feedlot at fifteen months of age, where they are grain finished for approximately ninety days. Bison receive no growth stimulants and feeder bulls are normally finished between twenty-two and thirty months of age. Unlike cattle, there is no advantage to castrating market bulls. Feeder bulls are normally slaughtered before they reach a mature breeding age, and there is no evidence that castrated bison bulls get larger; in fact there is more evidence to suggest that their rate of growth becomes lower. With bison, animals slaughtered are usually the young bulls with a finished weight of about 1,000 pounds, and the older, the unproductive, or the cull animals usually end up as burger or sausage. There is no bison equivalent to the Beef Industry's method of producing what it refers to as veal. Veal is just simply the meat from extremely young, milk-fed beef, from three weeks to fourteen weeks old. In some instances it is understood that meat from young grass-fed beeves that are from fifteen weeks to one year old have also been sold as veal, but the meat from the older calves is usually easy to identify because of its much redder color. The heralded qualities of veal are its tenderness and absence of fat — which are precisely the known qualities of bison meat.

There is some controversy about the advantages and disadvantages of grain-fed, as opposed to grass-fed, cattle as well as bison. Over 160 years ago, farmers in the Midwest experimented with feeding their surplus corn to cattle. This gradually became a common practice, as grazing land, particularly in the eastern United States, was consumed by industrial interests and increasing population density. Foreign demand for corn-fattened cattle, along with the mutually beneficial alliance between corn growers — who now depended upon this market — and cattle growers — who no longer could afford to graze cattle for extensive periods of time on grass — ensured the continuance of this relationship. To further cement this affiliation, the United States Department of Agriculture (USDA) devised a grading system in 1927 to measure the value of beef. The grades were based upon the amount of finish, or fat, on the animal. These quality grades were prime, choice, select, standard, commercial, utility, cutter, and canner. Meat inspectors from the USDA will examine the carcass, check the amount of marbling, and attempt to assess the age of the animal. After their examination a stamp is placed upon each individual carcass that designates the grade it was given. Since prime and choice are the favored grades, it is understandable that producing fat beef would be preferred to that of lean beef.

The market primarily is skewed toward grain-fed animals. Grain feeding, particularly corn, changes the texture and flavor of bison meat in the same manner as it does beef, with the exception that the meat of bison bulls does not marblize with fat as does beef. You can usually tell an animal that has been finished on grass; not only does the meat have a slightly gamey taste, any visible fat is more yellow than white. However, taste is not the primary reason for grain finishing bison; it is because the producer has the flexibility of selecting the time for marketing, an economic choice that is available because grain feeding permits the animals to pack on prime weight even during non-pasture seasons. Nevertheless, there is also a market for bison that have been fed only on grass, as a considerable number of consumers opt for what they submit is a "more natural" product.

Bison producers do not feel that they are in competition with the Beef Industry. First of all, as bison producers are very quick to point out, they are in no position to satisfy all of the red meat needs of current beef users. There are more than 105,000 head of cattle slaughtered *each day* in the United States as opposed to the approximate 10,700 bison in 1992. In other words, there are nearly as many cattle slaughtered each day as there are live bison in the United States. Secondly, although bison meat may represent a more healthy product, its cost is quite a bit higher than beef because the economies of scale will always favor quantity over quality. As bison become more numerous, and if more cattle ranchers elect to convert to bison ranching because of market and economic advantages, the cost difference between bison meat and beef should become less. The Beef Industry is quite aware of consumer interest in buying red meat that has less fat and less cholesterol than their current product, and they are attempting to correct this; however, it is the fat that generally provides the recognizable and sought-after flavor in quality beef. Crossbreeding bison and cattle to genetically produce a meat that contains less fat and cholesterol than beef is exactly what the so-called Beefalo breed attempts to do. The Beefalo is precisely three-eighths bison and five-eighths bovine. What produces the lower levels of fat and cholesterol is not the combination of breeds, but the addition of the three-eighths bison. Another bison breed mix is the "Cattalo," which has more than three-eighths but less than seven-eighths bison blood. For most purposes, anything over seven-eighths bison is considered to be a bison. While handling of the animals may be somewhat easier if they have a greater representative proportion of cattle blood, the nutritional qualities and hardiness are also proportionately decreased.

A rapidly developing international market demand for bison meat has placed greater stress upon what is already a fragile national supply. There are obviously more bison today in the United States than there have been for over one hundred years. The higher prices sought for bison meat as opposed to other red meats would normally underscore the marginal utility concept espoused by economists; however, this can become a control measure on consumer demand only when the price generally exceeds that which consumers are willing to pay. Because bison meat offers a quality and a uniqueness not found in other meats, the higher, but still reasonable, price for bison meat is not a significant deterrent to the gourmet, the health diet devotee, or the specialty food buyer. The Japanese have been importing bison meat for many years, and have also become actively and economically involved in a number of activities within the Bison Industry. Recently, kosher bison meat has also become available and will be sold in the United States and in Israel. Heretofore it was not possible to provide kosher certification in volume amounts because most available bison slaughter facilities could not meet the strict processing requirements needed to conform to Jewish religious dietary requirements. Although present sources are still somewhat limited, with the completion of its new slaughter facilities at New Rockford, North Dakota, the North American Bison Cooperative is capable of processing kosher meat for all of its bison meat distributors.

In the past few years the Bison Industry has had to ponder competitive claims of other non-cattle breeders and suppliers professing to offer healthy red meat alternatives — "buffalo," yak, and ratite breeders and importers. It was precisely because of the sale of imported "buffalo" meat that the American Buffalo Association changed its name to the American Bison Association in 1987. The American bison has been, and still is, commonly referred to as a "buffalo." A number of writers consistently refuse to use the word "bison," even if it is the proper name for the animal, and self-righteously support the name "buffalo" because that "is what most Americans still call the animal." Some may also assert that it is only the scientific world that insists upon use of the term "bison." Capitalizing upon this identity issue, certain individuals had elected to market the meat and hide of the African cape buffalo (*Syncerus caffer)* and the Asiatic water buffalo (*Bubalus bubalis)* as being from a "buffalo." Although this did not necessarily misrepresent what their product was, it did possibly mislead consumers into thinking that they were acquiring the meat, or perhaps other by-products, of the American bison. The yak *(Bos gruniens)*, an Asian mountain ox, is still few in number in North America, and except for yak meat representing an exotic entry on a restaurant bill of fare, it is not expected that yaks would exert any foreseeable impact on an alternative red meat market.

Ratites are the large flightless birds commonly known as the South African ostrich, the Australian emu, and the smaller South American rhea. The breeders of these exotics claim that the meat of the ratite, which looks somewhat like beef, contains less fat and less cholesterol than beef, chicken, or turkey. In addition, it is claimed that nearly every part of these birds can be used, much as the bison has been for centuries in America. The meat, when available, sells for about $20 a pound, and although the biggest ratite, the ostrich, will only weigh about three hundred pounds, a bred female ostrich can lay an average of thirty-five eggs a year. When you compare this level of reproduction to that of bison cows, who normally have but one calf a year, there should be no surprise to discover that there already are more than two hundred thousand ratites in the United States. Unlike bison, ratites are really not receptive or responsive to wide fluctuations in climatic conditions; consequently, Texas, Arizona, and Oklahoma are three of the prime breeding states. The primary advantage of ratites is their low maintenance cost (less than $350 a year for feed), minimal land needs, and high profitability. Some ranchers claim that they can get up to $150,000 in a year from just one breeding pair.

The importation and active cultivation of exotic animals may be more of a "get rich quick" preoccupation for those involved than it is necessarily a statement or conviction of species preeminence. People are, unfortunately, quite susceptible to the wondrous claims and lauded benefits of strange and foreign products because they truly want to believe that someone has discovered the better mousetrap. This is particularly so if it could be the nostrum to better health. Exclusive of any of the controversial claims of other alternative red meat products, probably the greatest source of contention for the bison is within the bison industry itself.

More than eighty years ago, Dr. John Lee Coulter, who was at that time Professor of Rural Economics for the University of Minnesota, wrote an interesting little book that he entitled *Cooperation Among Farmers*. His thesis was simply this: farmers must become businessmen, they must organize, and they must be better farmers. Coulter felt that it was extremely important that those involved in the production and marketing of animals for meat develop a local marketing cooperative, rather than depend upon traveling buyers or "self-appointed middlemen trying to get the animals at the lowest possible prices." Fortunately for the bison breeder and producer, demand for bison is extremely high, and the subsequent competition between meat distributors for quality animals is now quite intense. Because of this competitiveness, prices for slaughter bulls and feedlot bison fairly reflect this healthy market.

Most owners of smaller bison herds tend to be individualists first, bison breeders second, and businesspeople third. And, for this reason, few small operations are usually profitable. This lack of profitability is what precipitates Internal Revenue Service questions about whether some of these small operations are really businesses or perhaps just hobbies. Another problem for the smaller operation is that the information exchanged within the industry leans toward the generic rather than the specific, with the privacy and privilege of individual ownership seemingly taking precedence over most cooperative ventures or industry interests. Since smaller herds are most often owned by novices, they either learn the hard way — by trial and error — or are obliged to seek help from the more experienced or one of the established state or national bison associations. Two rather recent examples of this hesitancy to freely provide information were the American Bison Association's 1992 bison census and the research effort in the spring of 1992 by Colorado State University to complete a program that would determine the better finishing feeds for bison. Every industry needs to be responsive to the primary issues of supply and demand, and the Bison Industry did not have reliable figures on the United States supply of bison. The American Bison Association attempted to put this information together, but it was quite disappointing to discover the number of bison owners who purposely withheld their herd totals because they were (1) either suspicious of how this information would be used, or (2) were just reluctant to compromise their personal privacy. One owner claimed that "it is like asking how much money you may have in the bank." The same predicament faced Colorado State University researchers when they sought information from producers on finishing feed. Thirty-four producers who had the ability to measure the rate of finishing grain for their animals were contacted. Only one producer responded to researcher inquiries. This information could have been of significant value for the small-scale producers, prospective investors, and certainly beneficial to others new to the industry. It should be noted, however, that the one producer who responded to the finishing feed inquiry of Colorado State University did join in with the university to complete the research project. The eventual research report, "A Study of Bison Finishing Rations at Four Energy of

Concentrate Levels," was made available to the industry through its publication in the National Bison Association's January/February 1995 *Bison World.*

Medium- and large-size bison operations are usually owned by people who have been in the business for a number of years and have the experience, or have recourse to others on their staff who do possess these qualities. However, just like the smaller operations, they are obliged to learn by trial and error unless they, and others within the industry, are willing to share knowledge and otherwise work together — cooperate — for the common industry good. Toward this end, a variety of formalized bison or buffalo associations have been formed.

In 1959, L. Roy Houck purchased a 50,000-acre ranch near Fort Pierre, South Dakota. A native South Dakotan and longtime cattle rancher, he began slowly to acquire small lots of bison for his new ranch. After making a purchase in 1963 of slightly over four hundred bison from Custer State Park, he began to phase out his cattle operations. Today the ranch that Houck acquired, the Triple U Enterprises/Standing Butte Ranch, is home to more than thirty-five hundred bison. Like so many of the earlier bison pioneers, Houck found that bison not only possessed a certain indescribable charisma, they did extremely well under conditions that would have been intolerable for cattle. Familiar with the workings of cattle and stock grower associations, Houck was frustrated by the lack of market focus and industry direction that he was forced to deal with almost on a day-to-day basis by raising bison. He contacted a number of other concerned bison ranchers, and on March 11, 1967, the first bison industry organization, the National Buffalo Association (NBA), was formed, with L. Roy Houck elected as its first president.

The National Buffalo Association had four primary objectives:

1. To promote buffalo and buffalo products, namely meat and hides.
2. To seek fair and equitable regulations in the control of disease and in the movement of buffalo and buffalo products, both intrastate and interstate.
3. To promote and develop recreation where it is connected with buffalo.
4. To advance any and all ventures wherein we can better our position in the promotion of the buffalo.

Succeeding meetings of the NBA were held annually, and later semiannually, to address collective problems and issues impacting the Bison Industry. Two issues that were often discussed were uniform bison meat prices and cooperative marketing. With communications between owners still at the embryo level, and perhaps less than 10 percent of all bison owners belonging to the NBA, very little could be accomplished that would influence industry practices. At NBA formal meetings, educational seminars were offered, but progress on the NBA's four primary objectives was very slow. The NBA continued to work on building its constituency and membership, but was never able to establish the same measure of control, direction, and guidance within the Bison Industry that the powerful, and politically astute, cattle associations enjoyed within the Beef Industry. This was not necessarily the fault of the NBA, but was primarily due to the reluctance of members, and nonmembers as well, to permit their association to exercise the authority it needed to accomplish industry objectives.

Research was another area that was grossly inadequate and woefully underfunded. Association dues were very modest, and the NBA was barely able to meet normal and ongoing administrative expenses. It therefore became obligatory that attendance fees be developed to cover the costs of meetings and any scheduled social events. In some instances directors and officers assumed the responsibility for certain NBA expenditures and obligations. With these meager resources, there wasn't any way that the NBA could commission even the most essential and basic of research projects. Any research that was conducted was either accomplished through individual bison ranchers or by academic organizations upon their receiving approval for an earlier grant application. Unfortunately the NBA was not consulted with respect to research priorities, research was not coordinated within the industry, and research results were not often published or made generally available to others.

Perhaps it could be just attributed to the sometimes confounding vagaries of human nature, but there soon appeared several indicators of dissatisfaction within the industry with the decision-making and basic organizational processes of the NBA. In any organization you would expect to find a normal amount of political intrigue and factional scheming, but this was a much broader problem, and it was apparently centered on membership participation. Under its existing bylaws, membership in the NBA did not grant active members the right of voting on who would be on the NBA Board of Directors or hold association office. In addition, during NBA conferences or when meetings of the board took place, board meetings were closed. Although it may not have been essential for the general membership to have a vote or a veto, the membership at least wanted the opportunity for the board to hear them out and try to accommodate their wishes — or at the very least, explain why they couldn't.

In the summer of 1975, a group of fourteen bison owners, frustrated by what they felt was a policy of continued unresponsiveness by the NBA to their needs, founded a new bison organization, the American Buffalo Association. The founders met with the dream of creating an association that would promote the production, marketing, and preservation of bison, and serve all the people in the Bison Industry equally. Its bylaws provided for membership voting on all important issues and membership nomination and election of all board members and officers. In 1987, the membership approved a change in name to the American Bison Association (ABA) to better represent the animal and the Bison Industry. Membership in the ABA grew rapidly, and eventually its membership far exceeded that of the NBA. Some of the more positive accomplishments and innovations spearheaded by the ABA were the Gold Trophy Bison Show and Sale, a bison meat cut poster, an industry video film, and the establishment of a set of quality control guidelines for bison finished on grain.

With the exception of the Gold Trophy Bison Show and Sale (which is held in conjunction with the National Western Stock Show in Denver, Colorado), the North American Bison Registry, and the quality control guidelines for grain finished bison (all of which were developed and/or administered through the ABA), neither of the two national associations, or any of the state associations for that matter, was individually able to provide the type of leadership and direction that the Bison Industry needed. These failures could not be any more evident than they are even at the present time with respect to marketing practices, research requirements, legislation, and resistance to governmental regulations.

Although the American Bison Association provided average wholesale and retail prices for various bison meat cuts and by-products in its *Bison Breeder's Handbook*, third edition, 1992, this information became quickly outdated. The industry still needs some way to regularly provide the average prices, at least nationally if not geographically, for not only the more common bison meat cuts but also for half and quarter dressed weights. Efforts to develop such data are usually stymied by the reluctance of individual breeders/producers to provide their prices — they are seemingly interested in seeing the results of the averaging, but are somewhat reluctant to divulge their own prices. The NBA had avoided becoming involved in this rather sensitive issue by indicating that by publishing such price lists "we might be contributing to setting a floor or ceiling for bison meat. This we don't do. You have to do your own research here" (*Buffalo Producer's Guide to Management and Marketing*, 1990, 281). However, the two industry publications, *Buffalo!* (NBA), and *Bison World* (ABA), did list auction prices for live animals. If a bison breeder or prospective buyer had access to either one of these publications, it was not too difficult for him/her to get an idea of the probable purchase or sale prices of live animals.

Another marketing need is a grading system for bison meat. Bison have historically been considered to be wild animals by the United States Department of Agriculture (USDA), and as such are not subject to regulations or requirements covering cattle or other common domestic farm animals. Since USDA does not promulgate grading criteria for bison, as it does beef, bison carcass grading does not now exist. Without grading, there is no way that an inexperienced consumer knows whether he/she is purchasing the meat of a young and well-nourished bison, or that of an old and neglected animal. The same is true with regard to meat from grain- or grass-fed bison. Some time ago, when I was with the ABA, I was contacted by a butcher in a midwestern state who had recently purchased the half carcass of a field-dressed bison bull. He bought the half because some of his better customers were asking for bison meat and one of his competitors regularly offered bison meat for sale. He wanted to know a little bit about the customary aging practices for bison meat before he began to start filling some of the steak and roast orders he had received. During our conversation he mentioned that the dressed half weight was nearly eight hundred pounds, and that the limited fat cover on the carcass was yellow. From that and other information he told me, it was quite obvious that someone sold him the half-dressed carcass of a very old and grass-fed bison bull. Upon learning what he had hanging in his cooler he was disappointed — but still planned to sell high-priced primal cuts to his customers from an animal that should have been used only for burger or sausage.

Field slaughter of bison is fraught with a number of problems if the owner plans to sell the meat. At this time, there is no federal requirement for bison meat to be routinely examined prior to sale. Fortunately most commercial establishments will not buy uninspected bison meat, but, as noted in the preceding paragraph, some will. In its Quality Control Guidelines for Bison Finished on Grain, the former ABA, and its successor organization the National Bison Association, provide that:

> The American Bison Association (National Bison Association) supports inspection to the extent necessary to assure that all bison meat entering commercial or consumptive channels is wholesome and processed and distributed under sanitary conditions. It is therefore recommended that all bison meat is either state or federally inspected.

The USDA Food Safety and Inspection Service provides for voluntary inspection of bison under the Agriculture Marketing Act, as amended. However, this inspection is not free for bison owners as it is for the owners of cattle, sheep, and swine. If a USDA-approved plant is not reasonably close, owners can apply for a field inspection option. Field inspection would still entail a field antemortem inspection by an examiner, as well as a postmortem examination of the carcass at the USDA inspection plant. In order for this option to be exercised, a federal examiner would have to first approve a designated area on the owner's ranch, and secondly determine that the skill and facilities for stunning, hoisting, bleeding, and prompt transport of the carcass to the nearest USDA inspection plant are adequate. The cost of the examiner's travel time and any other expenses must be paid by the owner. In addition to all of this, if delays occur that may impact upon the wholesomeness of the meat, or other defects are discovered by the postmortem inspector, he/she may condemn the carcass.

Some states have a mandatory state inspection service. Since it is mandatory, there is usually no charge for these services. State inspections normally provide the same benefits and assurances of federal inspection, but if the meat is shipped out of state, regulations of both states will apply: the state of shipment and the state of destination.

There are a number of instances where governmental regulations and/or nonregulations prove to be far more burdensome for the Bison

Industry than they are for the Beef, Pork, Lamb, or Poultry Industry. As noted above with respect to meat inspection, the absence of required inspection regulations doesn't mean that the obligation to have the meat inspected no longer exists, it simply means that this commonsense inspection operation has to be paid for by the individual bison owners — whereas the federal government (taxpayers) covers the cost of USDA inspections of cattle, sheep, and swine.

Another branch of the federal government, the Food and Drug Administration (FDA), is responsible for approving the use of preservatives that are added to processed meat products. Because meat products made from beef, pork, lamb, and poultry had sodium nitrite, a common meat cure and preservative, added prior to passage of the Food, Drug and Cosmetics Act of 1958, these meats were considered to be "prior sanctioned" under USDA regulations and are therefore permitted the continued use of sodium nitrite. The FDA is of the belief that sodium nitrite may be a carcinogen, and, because of this, restricts the use of sodium nitrite in any food that the FDA regulates. Since bison meat is regulated by FDA rather than USDA, the use of sodium nitrite in bison meat products has been prohibited. Only by including more than 3 percent of beef, pork, lamb, or poultry within each processed bison product is the use of sodium nitrite permitted. No other preservative has yet been discovered that is as efficient or as effective as sodium nitrite. By restricting bison meat in this manner, the industry is not able to market 100 percent bison meat products.

The FDA is also responsible for nutritional food labeling for packaged foods and processed meats regulated by the USDA. Fresh meats regulated by the USDA, specifically beef, pork, lamb, and poultry, are excluded from the labeling regulations of FDA. Fresh bison meat is required to meet the labeling regulations of FDA. There is some flexibility for small businesses. Subject to later changes, FDA regulations would place the nutritional labeling threshold for manufacturers and packers (small business) at 100,000 units, and retail sales that total less than $500,000, or if in excess of that figure, total sales of food of not more than $50,000. In other words, if a manufacturing and packing business sells less than 100,000 pounds of fresh bison meat in a year, it would not be required to place nutritional statements on its fresh meat packages.

Bison meat producers have no problem with disclosure of the nutritional contents of their fresh meat packages; they see this as being an advantage if consumers compare their product with other red meat products. What they object to is the potential cost of research and labeling that they are required to furnish, and other fresh meat suppliers are excused from this compliance. FDA has indicated that they would like to see the Bison Industry develop a data base that supports its nutritional claims. Once such a data base has been approved by the FDA, bison products would not be seized if problems should later develop. The former ABA board urged its members to share their nutritional research information, and had agreed to work with the FDA in establishment of a Bison Industry nutritional data base. However, given the current state of coordination and cooperation within the Bison Industry, it is doubtful that such a data base could be developed without considerable difficulty and it would quite probably lack industry-wide support.

The fledgling Bison Industry does not, however, possess the constituency or have the funds to conduct the extent of legislative lobbying that is commonplace for the Beef, Pork, Lamb, and Poultry Industries. In the United States the Beef Industry reigns supreme; it is big business with a capital "B." Information on meat production and consumption figures provided by the Economic Research Service, USDA, indicates that more than 24 billion pounds of beef were consumed in the United States in 1990. Farm marketing of livestock and products (other than bison) in 1990 was nearly $90 billion, which represented nearly 53 percent of all farm income. And, according to Marvin Harris (1985, 109), in any given week, 91 percent of all United States households purchase beef. This level of market domination could not have occurred without the Beef Industry receiving a certain amount of governmental support and regulative sanction. A good example of this is found in the evolution of the common hamburger.

Although range wars were fought between sheep and cattle interests, the real market competitor for beef had always been pork. When the bison were being methodically slaughtered, pig farmers would fatten their animals on the stripped bison carcasses. Even Scotty Philip, who credited himself as being "the man who saved the buffalo," acquired pigs before he did cattle. In 1877, when grain prices became higher than he could afford to pay, Philip shot wild game (including bison) near his ranch near Fort Robinson, South Dakota to feed to his pigs. It was not until the American public discovered the outdoor grill and a compulsion for fast food that beef was able to totally dominate its chief rival, pork. Fast food and outside cooking became synonymous with pink and juicy meat. Because of the potential health risk from eating pork that was not thoroughly cooked, the USDA and the American Medical Association, of which the United States Surgeon General was a member, embarked upon a determined public education program in the 1930s to inform the American public on the need to cook pork until it turns fully gray instead of pink. When you thoroughly cook ground pork patties on an outside grill, they become gray, dry, and crumbly, and not ideal for family barbecues — or fast food restaurants. The beef hamburger also reigned supreme because of a legislative lobbying coup. Marvin Harris (1987, 124) very effectively described how the Beef Industry successfully lobbied into law a little publicized, but rather far-reaching, USDA regulation in 1946 that defined hamburger as "a ground meat patty which contains no meat or fat other than beef or beef fat." If a hamburger contained even "a smidgeon of pork or pork fat," it could not be categorized as a hamburger. By including the exclusive "beef fat" in this regulation the hamburger patty could be moist, could be pink, and also would not crumble.

For many years, the two former national associations (ABA and NBA), as well as a number of individual bison ranchers, had attempted, without success, to persuade members of the U.S. Congress to introduce legislation that would relieve the Bison Industry from inequitable regulatory actions. Senator Larry Pressler (R-SD) did seriously consider legislation that would give USDA jurisdiction over bison inspection. His proposed bill would have amended the Federal Meat Inspection Act (21 U.S.C. 6701 et seq.) by inserting the parenthetical phrase "(American bison/buffalo)" after "cattle" each place it appears. However, Senator Pressler elected not to take action because (1) the administration and his cohorts would probably not support this particular bill, (2) it would increase the federal budget and deficit, and (3) there would be a reduction in federal revenue because of the loss of inspection fees now collected from bison owners.

Of all the acknowledged needs of the Bison Industry, none is more essential for the animal and the industry than a continuing program of research. Although the Board of Directors from both the American Bison Association and National Buffalo Association had previously expressed sincere interest in bison research, they lacked the funding necessary to commission studies. The American Bison Association had even established a separate organizational entity, the Dr. Ken Throlson American Bison Foundation, in a continuing effort to solicit funds for the protection, preservation, and reestablishment of the American bison. The Throlson Foundation is a chartered 501(c)(3) nonprofit, tax-exempt public charity, the goals and purposes of which are to:

1. Provide scholarships and financial assistance to persons engaged in the study of agriculture, animal husbandry, veterinary medicine, nature conservation, human and bison nutrition, and other fields affecting the Bison Industry.
2. Conduct and support research on bison, including bison health, prevention and treatment of diseases, reproduction and genetics, human and bison nutrition, and environmental impact.
3. Foster public education, awareness, and appreciation of bison and their history and role in American life.
4. Generally promote the reestablishment, protection, and preservation of the bison population.

To get the Foundation started, the ABA had donated $29,000. Now managed through the successor organization, the National Bison Association, it is understood that public donations are still somewhat disappointing. This may be due, in part, to the Foundation's low-key subscription efforts. There are now so many not-for-profit agencies and charitable appeals that people are becoming a little hardened and perhaps a little callous. Some time ago the former ABA received a letter from an individual from the West Coast who expressed profound interest in bison and the Bison Industry. He asked that the ABA send him "all the information that you have on buffalo." The ABA did send him a packet and retained his name and address on its mailing list. Shortly thereafter, he was sent a fact sheet about the Throlson Foundation along with a letter that extended an opportunity to contribute to the fund. Using the Foundation's "no postage necessary" reply envelope, he wrote back and said: "Tell me where they are so I can come and shoot them!" He obviously was not planning on making a contribution.

One of the most essential research needs is the extensive analysis and examination of bison meat. Research conducted thus far has been limited, and perhaps not all of the research efforts were performed with the same exacting level of scientific rigor and impartiality. However, enough research has been performed for the industry to forcefully contend that bison meat contains more healthful properties than any other red meat. What is needed is for the industry to thoroughly prove this contention by establishing an inquiry process that assures that (1) all conditions of parallel relationship and environment have been met between the various animals tested, (2) the nutrient composition of the meat taken from the animals is secured from similar carcass locations, and (3) sampling size is sufficient to avoid challenge to the significance of research findings. To avoid a repeat of the past proprietary tactics with respect to research findings, it would appear that bison nutritional research (as well as all other forms of bison research for that matter) should be performed under the umbrella of an association or foundation that is not in itself an active and competitive player in the bison market.

It is understood that a continuing research project, conducted through the College of Agriculture, North Dakota State University, titled "Nutritional Composition of Bison," and endorsed by the National Bison Association, has produced some positive, but limited, results with respect to nutritional analysis of bison meat. Much more still needs to be done, and hopefully, this project will just be the beginning of a cooperative industry effort to support bison research.

Probably the least known of all of the attributes of bison meat is its nonallergenic qualities. People who are allergic to most meats, as well as a number of other staple foods, have found that they can freely eat bison meat without difficulty. Why? No one really knows why. It could be because the human body is naive as far as bison meat is concerned, or perhaps there are still some unknown attributes of bison meat that research has not yet uncovered. We do know that bison are not exposed to regular injections of low-level antibiotics, they do not receive hormone treatments to accelerate growth, nor are artificial substances or chemicals added to the meat. One prime example of what bison meat can do for a person who may be suffering with severe food allergies is Billy Casper, the professional golfer. Casper was basically allergic to every major protein food, and because of this he quickly learned that he would no longer be competitive or successful on the PGA tour without a normal diet. Alerted to bison meat by his doctors, Casper quickly returned to top form and shortly went on to win the 1966 United States Open, held at San Francisco's Olympic Club, over Arnold Palmer. By overcoming his allergy problem in this manner, Billy Casper acquired the colorful nickname of "Buffalo Billy."

The annual Gold Trophy Bison Show and Sale (GTSS) is the Bison Industry's equivalent of the Motion Picture Academy Awards (Oscars) presentations. Held in conjunction with the more well-known National Western Stock Show and Rodeo in Denver, the GTSS has done more for bison breeders than any other single event or activity. Managed and orchestrated originally by the ABA, the first GTSS took place in 1981, and has eventually become not only the final event scheduled each year for Denver's National Western, but has proven to be their most popular event next to the rodeo. There were 161 animals judged during the 1996 GTSS, and the owners elected to auction off 151 of these. A yearling bull, which had earlier won the Canadian Grand Championship, not only won the yearling bull class but also later became the GTSS Grand Champion. The next day this animal was auctioned off for $61,000, which was the record amount ever paid for a yearling bull bison. In addition to the live auctions of GTSS bison, the National Bison Association conducted a video auction on 149 additional bison. Although the GTSS is deservedly the premier show event for the *Bison bison bison* (plains bison) subspecies, it may also result in becoming a catalyst for genetic change. This could possibly come about if too much acclaim or credit in judging is given to the animal possessing a less pronounced hump or straighter back and fuller hindquarters. Although perhaps desirable as far as eventual meat production may be concerned, some of these features would seem to be more characteristic of the *Bison bison athabascae* (wood bison) than *B. b. bison*. The question of bison that reflect some wood bison heredity being entered in the GTSS was brought up at a meeting of the Board of Directors during the 1992 ABA summer conference in Bartlesville, Oklahoma, but since there was no effective way of evaluating possible breeding except by arguable visual appearance, the subject was dropped at that time and no future action was proposed to attempt to differentiate in judging between the plains and wood bison.

In an effort to be more competitive with the ABA and respond to membership desires, the NBA changed its bylaws in 1992 to permit the election of board members and to open its board meetings to all members. The ABA and the NBA, together with the Canadian Bison Association (CBA), cohosted an International Bison Conference in La Crosse,

When bison auctions are held, animals of the same sex and approximate age are segregated for sale. Based upon the number of bison that are to be sold, they are often sold in pens or lots of three or more animals. Video auctions, where only films of the animals to be sold are shown, are also quite popular. At the January 22, 1994, Bison Video Auction held in conjunction with the American Bison Association's 1994 Gold Trophy Bison Show and Sale, 260 head of bison sold in less than one hour. Bison shown in the above photos were auctioned by the Denver Mountain Parks in a recent sale. Courtesy American Bison Association.

Wisconsin, July 27–31, 1992. For several months prior to this conference, members of both the ABA and NBA expressed the opinion that the Bison Industry would be best served if there were but one national association. During the International Bison Conference the ABA and NBA jointly met to discuss the options and possibilities for merger, and decided to put the merger proposal to a vote of their joint membership. A ballot was mailed to each active and associate member of the ABA and the NBA, and the memberships of both organizations overwhelmingly concurred with the establishment of a joint task group to consider a merger. As the memberships of both organizations were strongly in favor of the merger, the process simply evolved into the introduction of resolutions to change ABA bylaws to (1) change the name of the American Bison Association to the National Bison Association; (2) provide for the creation of a joint ABA/ NBA Board of Directors which would provide guidance for the merged associations until January 1996 (at that time, formal elections would take place to elect officers and directors for the newly combined organization); (3) proceed with the disestablishment of the National Buffalo Association (NBA) and the transfer of capital, franchise, and power to the successor association; (4) discontinue the business of the American Bison Association (ABA) as such; and (5) accept all NBA and ABA members who are in good standing without payment of membership fees to the successor organization, the National Bison Association,

Hopefully, the newly created National Bison Association will continue to grow and become the strong and vibrant national association that the Bison Industry so urgently needs, and will subsequently provide the necessary guidance and direction to ensure continued research and economic growth. If these events do not eventually occur within a reasonable time span, it is possible that we would again see the founding of another competitive national association by bison breeders who are either dissatisfied with the progress made or the management policies of the new association and wish to offer bison owners the option of an organizational choice. The latter could be a strong possibility since there are a number of unaffiliated state bison/buffalo associations eagerly seeking memberships from bison breeders and producers even from outside their state boundaries. The Northwest Bison Association, for example, has its headquarters in the state of Washington but has members that are located in over seven other states.

The Bison Industry could learn a lesson in cooperation and teamwork from the bison. As James (Scotty) Philip is reported to have once said (Lee 1975, 248): "If a man wants to get a fine lesson in the advantage of 'standing together' he need only watch a buffalo herd in stormy weather."

9

Public Sector Involvement

As the American frontier moved slowly westward, it was not just prairies, grasslands, and forests that were absorbed by the rapidly advancing civilization; total ecosystems fell before an unyielding onslaught of national growth. To make the land adaptable for purposes of civilization, it was determined at that time that it was essential to first remove all resident Indians and the bison. Since cattle were the prescribed successors to the bison, and European occupancy was to replace that of the Indian, potential predators of cattle and all other domestic animals were considered as unsuitable residents within these newly refined lands. This also meant an end for the wolf and the grizzly. Fate, however, is sometimes not inevitable, and in its aimless way of determining the outcome of human-caused events it will occasionally spare a species seemingly destined for extinction, as it did with the bison.

Fate, in this instance, offered the bison another chance at continued existence through the intervention of journalist Ernest Harold Baynes. Baynes, who was one of the first crusaders for the cause of the bison, wrote a sequence of articles in 1904 for the *Boston Evening Transcript*, as well as a number of other newspapers and magazines, on the predicament of the bison. Through his efforts, the American Bison Society was formed and, eventually, legislation was proposed that would establish governmental preserves for the American bison. Therefore, although the carefully crafted, but thinly veiled, political campaign to eliminate the bison from the open range was successful, because of the efforts of a few private entrepreneurs and existing remnants of the former vast plains herd in Yellowstone National Park, the bison was not totally eliminated.

As most bison in the United States in 1905 were in private hands, Baynes and the American Bison Society were concerned that the bison's future would not really be secure until governmental bison preserves could be established and stocked with bison. In addition to bison being protected within the boundaries of Yellowstone National Park, under provisions of the National Park Protective Act of 1894, the Society successfully lobbied Congress to set aside eight thousand acres of prairie within the National Wichita Forest Reserve, Oklahoma, in 1905 for use as a bison reserve. Congress came up with $15,000 to fence the land, and William Hornaday, president of the American Bison Society, donated fifteen bison on behalf of the New York Zoological Society as a nucleus herd for the new Wichita Mountains Wildlife Refuge. The second bison reserve, the National Bison Range, was established three years later in 1908 in western Montana. As with Wichita Mountains, Congress provided land, but provided no funds to purchase bison. Through public subscription the American Bison Society raised more than $10,000 and acquired thirty-four bison that were released on the new reserve on October 17, 1909.

There are now four National Wildlife Refuges that maintain herds of bison: Wichita Mountains, the National Bison Range, Fort Niobrara (which is located in northern Nebraska), and Sully's Hill (situated in northeastern North Dakota near Devil's Lake). Wichita Mountains is now perhaps the showplace of the whole Wildlife Refuge System, with more than 59,000 acres devoted to bison, deer, elk, and Texas longhorn cattle. Although originally meant to be a bison refuge, other wild animals were later added to more or less complement a total wildlife theme. Beginning with the original donation of fifteen bison from the New York Zoological Society in 1907, four bison bulls were added from Fort Niobrara in 1940, and the Wichita Mountains herd now ranges between 480 and 675 animals. Consistent with genetic management policies within most public herds, the refuge managers attempt to maintain an equal ratio of bulls to cows. Bison herd reductions are accomplished through public auction sales of live animals and donation to other governmental or tax-supported organizations. Although elk hunts are permitted on the refuge to control elk populations, refuge managers are not considering any public hunting of surplus bison.

Hunting of bison is offered as a potential recreational opportunity to the public by a variety of public sector land managers and private sector entrepreneurs. It is quite possible that just the word "hunt" may create the vision of a stealthy search eventually culminating in a courageous encounter by the hunter with his/her worthy quarry. With only a few limited exceptions, bison hunting opportunities usually end up being less like a sport and (as one private herd owner elected to express) more like ritual killings. With the possible exception of two Alaskan state parks, under no circumstances would a hunter be permitted to wander around a designated hunting area and pot any bison he or she feels like shooting. The objective of permitting a hunt is to cull the herd of surplus animals, and at the same time to make a profit. Thus, by necessity, every opportunity is quite selective — no bison owner wants to put up his or her prize breeding bulls or top productive cows as potential hunting targets.

Some private ranchers try to make the "hunt" as interesting as possible, suggesting the use of bow and arrow and single-shot black powder rifles, and offering extended tours for the hunter to absorb and savor whatever historical and natural features that the area may offer. Most will assist in dressing out the animal, take the meat to a local butcher (if desired), and arrange for taxidermy services or robe and hide tanning. Based upon services provided, the normal ranch fee runs between $2,500 and $5,000. Expect to pay additional for any taxidermy, tanning, or meat processing that you may request. The "hunt" can end up being as simple as having the owner point out to you which bison in his/her pasture you can shoot, or it can be a more elaborate process where you will stay overnight in some rustic accommodations, and then later be taken on a circuitous route over the ranch property to where the preselected bison or bisons are located.

Except for hunts on public lands, official bison hunting licenses or permits are not required. Public lands bison hunts are limited to specific state herds located in Alaska, Arizona, and Utah, and limited bison hunting permits are issued for certain designated public lands within Grand Teton National Park. Montana has also issued hunting permits for bison that have strayed out of Yellowstone National Park and into Montana. No amenities are offered with respect to public land hunts. You purchase your license and permit and pack out your own animal. With the exception of the Alaskan herds and one of the Utah herds (Bureau of Land Management, Henry Mountains), the hunting success rate on public lands will be 100 percent because the bison are as captive on the public lands as they are on private lands.

The National Bison Range was set aside in 1908 as a bison sanctuary. This single purpose and objective has been broadened over the years to where the United States Fish and Wildlife Service now maintains, at the National Bison Range, a representative wildlife sampling of animals that were endemic to the Flathead Valley of western Montana. This means that in addition to bison, the approximate 18,500 acres of the range also support resident herds of antelope, bighorn sheep, deer, elk, and mountain goats. The desired bison herd size is between 370 and 475 animals, and to keep it at this level, surplus live animals are sold through sealed bid. Management attempts to maintain a 40 percent bull to 60 percent cow ratio, with less than 10 percent of the herd reaching ten years of age on site. Bison calves are year branded for identification purposes.

Fort Niobrara National Wildlife Refuge, established in 1912, has antelope, bison, deer, elk, and Texas longhorn cattle all grazing on its 19,122 acres. Eight bison were donated in 1912 to start the refuge herd, and over the years a number of methods had been used to try to control herd size, including donation and sale of live animals and slaughter and sale of carcass meat. The size of the herd is now maintained only through public auction sale and intragovernmental transfers and donations. An equal ratio of bulls to cows is maintained, and to assist refuge managers in their efforts to appropriately manage the herd, all bison calves are branded on the left hip with a four- or five-digit identification code. Fort Niobrara staff have made some real efforts to mitigate inbreeding by introducing new bulls into the herd on a yearly basis. Currently, bison herd size fluctuates between approximately 400 and 600 animals.

Sully's Hill National Game Preserve is a nice little area (1,674 acres, of which 700 acres are reserved for hay production) that was originally set aside in 1904 by United States President Theodore Roosevelt as a National Park (lacking any other appropriate federal land reserve classification at that time) for preservation of big game. In 1914, it was officially established by Congress as a Game Preserve. Management attempts to maintain the herd at between thirty and thirty-five bison, as elk, deer, and a variety of other small animals and birds also occupy the limited rangeland. Herd size is primarily controlled through a lottery slaughter method. Beginning in 1990, all bison calves have been age branded to assist refuge managers in their herd control measures. All Federal Wildlife Refuges are managed by the Department of Interior's Fish and Wildlife Service. The Department of

Interior also exercises administrative jurisdiction over the National Park Service, which has responsibility for managing bison herds in Badlands, Grand Teton, Theodore Roosevelt, Wind Cave, and Yellowstone National Parks, and Chickasaw National Recreation Area.

National Wildlife Refuges and National Parks are but two segments of a total network of publicly owned and government-managed sanctuaries where nature is the primary focus and, dependent upon available space, wildlife is permitted to exist as wildlife and carry on its struggle without artificial help, or, in some instances, are merely exhibited for public viewing and enjoyment. Although the primary federal shelter for bison is National Wildlife Refuges and Parks, bison may be found in a few other federal locations; however, the greater amount of public exposure to bison actually occurs through an extensive and generally outstanding system of state and city reserves and zoological parks that exist throughout the United States.

There are some rather obvious differences between management of public and private bison herds, but there are also considerable variations in the development and implementation of public sector bison management plans. The private owner possesses much more flexibility in what he or she plans to do with his or her bison. They can easily dispose of part or all of their herd or they can elect to acquire more land and expand the herd. Public herd managers have firm and fixed land boundaries to deal with, and within a bureaucracy they are usually accountable to a number of people, as well as the public, for their actions. One of the more significant problems that the public sector bison owners face is overpopulation.

Without the ability to precisely measure probability outcomes on bison births throughout the years, it would be safe to say that the chance is fifty-fifty, or that there would be bull calves and heifer calves on an equal ratio. Private herds are not by any means a replica of wild herds; they are managed to optimize the reproductive values of the bison and, as such, seldom would you find fewer than seven or eight breeding cows to each bull. If a public bison herd with an equal sex distribution was permitted to reproduce without the introduction of any herd reduction measures or other herd losses, over six years the herd would increase by 560 percent. This would also presume that only 10 percent of the breeding cows would not be with calf and that all heifer calves are bred in their second year.

As an example of this, if we assume that a bison herd consists of thirty mature animals, divided evenly between fifteen bulls and fifteen cows, and if we accept the above assumptions of reproduction potential, we would arrive at the following:

Year	Bulls	Cows	Calves	Yrlg. Heifers	Total	% Increase
1	15	15	13	0	30	0
2	21	15	13	7	56	87
3	28	22	22	6	78	160
4	39	28	28	11	106	253
5	53	39	39	14	145	383
6	73	53	53	19	198	560

This, of course, represents the optimum of all breeding circumstances but it clearly demonstrates the enormity of the problem. If we carried the above example into the seventh year we would find that the resultant herd increase would have amounted to 800 percent.

With the exception of the bison in Yellowstone and Grand Teton National Parks, and the bison roaming Bureau of Land Management land near the Henry Mountains of southwest Utah, all other public bison herds are at least restrained by perimeter or boundary fences. Without fencing to impede their movement, most, if not all, of the small herd (approximately 250 bison) at Grand Teton National Park will drift, in the winter months, into the National Elk Refuge outside Jackson, Wyoming, where they compete with the elk for feed. When homesteaders fenced the normal winter range of elk for cattle in Jackson Hole, it was necessary to provide supplemental feeding for the thousands of elk who still make their annual pilgrimage to the refuge. During the winter of 1993–1994, more than 10,000 elk were in the vicinity of the National Elk Refuge, and approximately 8,500 were receiving supplemental feeding. At first only a few bison found out about this free feed, but now the number has now grown to about 180. The bison swagger through the refuge and intimidate the elk, much to the displeasure of refuge staff. The free movement of Yellowstone

Bison within Grand Teton National Park on the east side of the Snake River. Unless they become a casualty of a fall herd reduction program, these bison will migrate in the winter to the National Elk Refuge near Jackson, Wyoming.

Bison cow and early spring calf, Grand Teton National Park. It was not unusual to also find some extremely small calves in the herd, as some cows in Grand Teton will calve as late as August.

and Grand Teton National Park bison herds also presents another problem for their neighbors outside park boundaries: an unknown number of Yellowstone and Grand Teton bison have brucellosis, a systemic bacterial disease that can cause the cow to abort the calf during the last months of her pregnancy or to give birth to immature and weak calves.

Brucellosis is not endemic to bison; it was originally communicated to bison from cattle, and through testing, vaccination, and removal of sick animals, brucellosis has been all but eradicated in domestic herds of cattle and bison. The presence of the *Brucella abortus* bacteria in Yellowstone National Park bison has been known since 1917, but there is no evidence to suggest that the herd is heavily infected or that the presence of brucellosis has significantly impacted the reproductive capability of the bison in Yellowstone National Park. Irrespective of these two considerations, however, there still is no reason for ranchers outside the Yellowstone boundaries to welcome intrusions of potentially infected bison on their properties while the question of transferability of brucellosis from bison to cattle has not been fully resolved.

Montana State Veterinarian Dr. Clarence Siroky argues that an experiment that was conducted in Texas, involving the injection of brucella into captive bison and the later successful transfer of brucellosis from the bison to cattle, proves that free-ranging park bison harboring the brucella bacteria can be a threat to neighboring cattle herds. This argument is not very convincing to Dr. Meagher or Dr. Meyer, who claim that the manner in which the experiment was conducted caused "distortion and magnification" of results (Wuerthner 1995, 38).

In the late fall months of 1996, there were probably more than 4,000 bison in Yellowstone National Park. According to Yellowstone National Park biologist Dr. Mary Meagher (1993, 388), this was probably 1,400 bison above the level that could be normally accommodated during the snow months without the bison having access to additional winter range. From the early 1920s to 1966, the population of the bison herd within Yellowstone was maintained at a rather constant level by the park staff "cropping" the animals. When I was assigned to Grand Teton National Park during the late 1950s, it was not an uncommon practice for Yellowstone to ask the Grand Teton–based ranger staff for assistance in their reduction program. I can recall rather vividly how this particular assignment was not met with much enthusiasm. After 1967, it was decided that the better policy

Bison roundup in Yellowstone National Park. Unlike today's free-ranging and mainly uncontrolled herds, Yellowstone was granted authority in 1923 to sell surplus bison or transport them to zoos and other public organizations. Other forms of herd reduction also took place until 1967. With the close of the Lamar Valley "Buffalo Ranch" operations in the 1950s, routine bison handling at Yellowstone ceased. Courtesy Denver Public Library, Western History Department.

was to let nature determine what the viable bison population should be. The bison population in 1967 at Yellowstone was 397 animals, and within the ensuing twenty-six years the number of bison increased by more than 800 percent. The bison have adjusted to the problem of adequate winter range by using the Yellowstone road system to facilitate their movements. They have also attempted to expand their range by moving out of the park to the north; when this occurs, the State of Montana has reacted in a forceful way to eliminate these strays and wanderers by issuing hunting permits.

The winter of 1996–1997 was particularly devastating for the Yellowstone herd. The harsh winter drove a record number of bison out of the park and toward presumed better pastures in Gardiner and West Yellowstone, Montana. Those that were not immediately shot were later captured and then transported to a slaughterhouse. However, there were a few bison among the many that did not test positive for brucellosis that were spared. It was estimated that between the winter kill and those leaving the park for Montana, never to return, 2,000 bison perished.

Grand Teton National Park and the State of Wyoming still attempt
to control the size of the Grand Teton herd by issuing a number of bison
hunting permits for hunter use on designated parklands.

Bison are unwelcome guests for basically three reasons:

1. Since they are not actually game animals, they do not have a
   legitimate hunting season, and thus add little to the state
   economy.
2. They are powerful, they can damage property and kill domestic
   livestock, and they are also potentially dangerous to people
   (according to National Park Service Regional Safety Officer
   Richard Powell, from 1989 through 1993, there were two
   incidents involving bear and humans at Yellowstone National
   Park, but during the same period of time, there were fourteen
   incidents where humans were gored by bison).
3. Park bison are perceived by the ranching community to harbor
   the *B. abortus* bacteria.

From December 12, 1988, to March 20, 1989, park biologist Mary
Meagher and Margaret Meyer, researcher from the University of
California, Davis, and a leading authority on *Brucella*, estimated that at
least 700 Yellowstone bison crossed the park border into Montana, and
while some were hazed back into the park, 570 were shot (Meyer and
Meagher 1993, 369). According to George Wuerthner (1995, 36), since
1985 more than 1,500 Yellowstone bison have been killed after wandering
from the park. Adding those killed in the winter of 1996–1997, the total
would probably be currently close to 2,500. Thus far, this method of control
selected by the state has proved to be a very unpopular decision as the
successfully designated state "hunters" needed little skill to shoot the
unwary and basically disinterested bison — as the media and public had
vociferously noted. The State of Montana tried to wriggle out of this public
relations dilemma by suggesting that it was the responsibility of the
National Park Service to destroy these so-called trespass bison, a suggestion
that was not actively pursued by Yellowstone. In an attempt to resolve the
bison issue, the National Park Service, the National Forest Service, the State
of Montana, Departments of Fish and Game and Livestock, cooperatively
prepared a bison management plan in 1994, which I have not yet been able

to get a copy of, that purportedly addresses not only how to deal with the problem of bison brucellosis, but what should be done about the more than 10,000 elk that inhabit the greater Yellowstone ecosystem and also have acquired brucellosis. Since the elk are legitimate game animals and, through the normal hunting process, add significantly to the economies of the states of Wyoming and Montana, it is doubtful that the state agencies would be willing to treat the elk as harshly as they would Yellowstone or Grand Teton National Park bison.

Yellowstone National Park was perhaps *terra incognita* to the Indians who had formerly dwelled nearby, but to poachers the park was more like *terra familia*. The 1872 Act of Dedication of Yellowstone as a public park unequivocally provided for the preservation of its "timber, mineral deposits, natural curiosities or wonders within said park, and their retention in their natural conditions . . . and shall provide against the wanton destruction of the fish and game found within said park and against their capture or destruction for the purposes of merchandise or profit." The Act did not offer a code of laws, nor address how indiscretions should be punished. As was customary with the early congressional appropriation processes for National Parks, little if any funds were allocated for Yellowstone. The park was expected to obtain operating funds from leases that they would grant for business use within the park. Without legal protection or adequate funds, conditions became so bad within the park that it was necessary for the Secretary of Interior to call upon the Secretary of War for assistance in managing Yellowstone. In 1886, Captain Moses Harris became acting superintendent, and soldiers of the First United States Cavalry assumed responsibility for protecting the park. In spite of a military presence, without the authority to do other than escort poachers and vandals from the park, the army seemed powerless to protect the park and preserve park values. It was not until a poacher was caught in the act of killing bison in the Pelican Valley area that Congress was finally spurred into passage of a National Park Protective Act. However, by this time the damage was done; it was estimated that in 1901, there were not more than twenty-five wild bison left in Yellowstone National Park.

The intrepid Charles J. "Buffalo" Jones, who actively sought (and was subsequently appointed to) the position of game warden for Yellowstone, arranged in 1902 for the purchase of eighteen bison and the donation of three more. This would then have given the park a nucleus bison

Bison along the roadside in Yellowstone National Park. The bear jams of yesterday have now seemingly given way to "bison jams" as bears are seen less often and the number of bison in park herds has increased significantly.

herd of somewhere between forty and fifty animals (Meyer and Meagher 1993, 367, claim that there were forty-four). Thus, from what was seemingly a rather skimpy beginning, the current Yellowstone herd has evolved.

The four other areas within the United States National Park System that have bison — Badlands National Park, South Dakota; Theodore Roosevelt National Park, North Dakota; Wind Cave National Park, South Dakota; and Chickasaw National Recreation Area, Oklahoma — are somewhat different in their method of interpretive approach. Whereas bison at Yellowstone and Grand Teton are only a small part of what really are magnificent panoramas of geological and natural wonders, the bison of Badlands, Theodore Roosevelt, Wind Cave, and Chickasaw represent one of the primary visitor attractions for each of these park areas. Because of the size of Yellowstone and Grand Teton, visitors may or may not even see a bison during their stay within the park, but they have a far greater opportunity to see bison at these four other National Park areas because the acreage is smaller and the bison ranges are fenced.

Not the normal Yellowstone fly-fishermen, two bull bison occupy one of the many turnouts along the Madison River.

Badlands National Park tries to maintain its bison herd at between 500 and 550 animals. Like all National Park areas, hunting is not considered to be a legitimate recreational pursuit or an accepted wildlife management practice on parklands. There is not enough land within Badlands to allow the bison to roam freely or reproduce normally and expand their range. Surplus bison are donated to Indian tribes or to individual Native Americans upon approval of appropriate Indian authorities. The seed bison for the Badlands herd came from Theodore Roosevelt National Park and Fort Niobrara National Wildlife Refuge. In 1983, the National Park Service decided that a small bison herd maintained at Colorado National Monument was inappropriate because it was the Service's belief that bison were not previously native to that part of Colorado. Consequently the twenty bison from Colorado National Monument were transferred to Badlands. The herd is brucellosis-free and probably genetically acceptable, even though the only new bison that have been introduced within the past thirty years were the Colorado National Park bison.

The National Park Service does not ignore the potential of inbreeding within park herds, but neither does the Service necessarily attempt to prevent the practice by the insertion of outbred animals from other herds, as the United States Fish and Wildlife Service occasionally attempts to do. When the enormous herds of wild bison were common to the Great Plains, inbreeding was not a problem; primary and secondary herd bulls had limited reproductive responsibilities and they were also usually subject to constant challenge by other determined suitors. In this way, the strongest and most fit were the species progenitors. After the near bison genocide that took place and culminated in the late 1880s, there were so few animals left that it was literally impossible to avoid active inbreeding if the species were to propagate. According to Dr. James H. Shaw (1993, 3), between seventy-four and seventy-nine individual bison were responsible for creating all of the foundation herds from which the current crop of bison came. With this in mind, the absence of genetic diversity needs to be mitigated by the practicality of circumstances and options available. The bison of Yellowstone National Park are probably the closest that any public bison herd can now attempt to replicate reproductive circumstances and conditions that were prevalent with the former wild herds. At Badlands National Park, as at all National Park areas, surplus animals are not genetically selected, but more often removed from the herd through the process of opportunity or availability. Since neither Badlands, nor any other National Park Service area currently blood types, registers, and regularly earmarks its bison, it is not possible to establish paternity. But what these National Park herds do have going for them are relatively large herds and a near equality between the breeding bulls and cows to ensure that more than just a few bulls are doing all the breeding.

One of the more interesting public bison herds is that managed by Theodore Roosevelt National Park. The park itself is split into three sections or units (one unit is the 218-acre Elkhorn Ranch Site) and, within its more than 70,000 acres, two of the three units can comfortably support between 400 and 650 bison. Bison were endemic to the Little Missouri Badlands area of western North Dakota, and were the reason for Theodore Roosevelt's initial visit to and subsequent acquisition of the Elkhorn Ranch north of Medora in the mid-1880s. The National Park was established in 1947, and, since there were obviously no wild bison inhabiting the park, twenty-nine bison were obtained from Fort Niobrara National Wildlife Refuge in 1956 to round out the historical and natural resource interpretive themes. The current bison population of more than 400 animals is the result of the breeding of just the original 29 bison. Bison are ear tagged but not branded or tattooed. Surplus bison are live-shipped to Indian Tribal Agencies, and governmental and other public and/or educational organizations. An example of a governmental transfer was the shipment of twenty bison in September 1969 to the Land Between the Lakes, a Tennessee Valley Authority demonstration project. Unfortunately, the National Park Service has seemingly been granted by law, agreement, and regulation the authority to only give its surplus bison away, with provisions that permit the recovery of handling and shipping costs. The primary recipient of surplus bison from Theodore Roosevelt National Park has been the Three Affiliated Tribes from the Fort Berthold Reservation. Park management is extremely interested in maintaining a healthy and vibrant bison herd, but genetic manipulations thus far have been restricted to movement of animals between the North and South Units and the objective observation of gene frequencies in tested bison.

Wind Cave National Park is located in western South Dakota, near the city of Custer and Custer State Park. In 1913, Wind Cave National Park and, in 1914, Custer State Park (Game Preserve) became the recipients of starter herds of bison. Wind Cave received either thirteen or fourteen through donation from the New York Zoological Society — thirteen if you want to believe park records, and fourteen according to Dary (1989, 239) and McHugh (1972, 303). Custer received thirty-six bison by way of purchase through the State of South Dakota from the heirs to the James "Scotty" Philip herd. Yellowstone and Theodore Roosevelt National Parks later contributed some of their surplus bison, and there could also have been some fugitive bison exchanges between Wind Cave and Custer State Park. The park has a bison management plan that suggests that the Wind Cave bison herd should be kept at around three hundred animals. There are a number of good management reasons for this, and the vegetative carrying capacity of this 28,285-acre park, considering all its wildlife needs, would probably be one of the principal reasons. Surplus bison at Wind Cave are usually given to the adjacent Indian tribes upon their request. In recent years the park has elected to use the yearling-class animals to cull the herd. Beginning in 1993, the park retains ten male and ten female yearlings (to replace losses and mitigate the nonproductivity of older animals), and all remaining yearlings are excessed.

Wind Cave is also notable for its role during an emotional, but perhaps legally questionable, "return" by a group representing the Dakota American Indian Movement (AIM) to the Paha Saba (Black Hills). To demonstrate their conviction that a major portion of the Black Hills should be returned to tribal authorities, a camp named Yellow Thunder (after Raymond Yellow Thunder who was killed in Gordon, Nebraska, in 1972) was established on April 4, 1981, by the AIM group approximately twelve miles south of Rapid City on Forest Service land. To demonstrate its solidarity with AIM, the Oglala Sioux Tribal Council planned a similar "occupation" on June 25, 1981, within the borders of Wind Cave National Park. Granted a two-week permit by the National Park Service, the camp, called "Crazy Horse Camp," was to be part of a demonstration of commitment and solidarity to Indian belief in legal right to the Black Hills lands. Although it may have been originally intended to permanently occupy the campsite, these plans were eventually discarded and the camp was abandoned. The National Park Service later determined that one of the park bison had been slaughtered during the time the camp was occupied.

Chickasaw National Recreation Area maintains a small herd of bison, currently one bull and seven cows, that are the continuance of a bison program that had been in existence since the area was formerly called Platt National Park. The bison occupy a ninety-acre pasture and are one of the more popular visitor attractions within the area.

In southern Utah, near Hanksville, the Bureau of Land Management (BLM) is responsible for more than 650,000 rugged acres of land along the Henry Mountains upon which the State of Utah has placed a herd of free-ranging bison. Originating from the Yellowstone National Park herd many years ago, the herd multiplied, but when it reached a total of about 100 animals it was discovered that some of the animals carried the *Brucella abortus* virus. The whole herd was rounded up, those that tested positive for brucellosis were destroyed, and all others were vaccinated. Whenever a bison is now removed from the herd it is examined for presence of the Brucella virus, and thus far it has not been found to be present in the herd. BLM does not own corrals, squeeze chutes, or maintain fences to contain the bison herd that now numbers in excess of 400 animals. Occasionally the bison will wander into either private or public land (more often on land belonging to nearby Capitol Reef National Park). Until such time as the grazing/carrying capacity of the land is determined, no specific herd size limit has been established. Control measures are now restricted to limited hunting (Utah issues approximately sixty hunting permits annually) and transfers to nearby Indian tribes.

The BLM has also accepted a small herd of bison (currently numbering about twenty-four head) from the State of New Mexico on the 263,000-acre El Malpais National Conservation Area near the city of Grants. Managed by the New Mexico Department of Fish and Game, the animals had to be moved from their former home at Fort Wingate. Now part of BLM's "Watchable Wildlife" program, the acquisition of the bison herd by El Malpais was the result of a rather unusual cooperative effort among the state, BLM, and a private sector holder of the grazing allotment upon whose leased land the bison were liberated.

There are a few other federal agencies that have bison, but having bison is a corollary duty, a sort of "nice" thing for them to display, as interpretation of wildlife is not really one of their primary features, such as is the case with the Department of Interior's National Park Service and Fish and Wildlife Service. An example of one of these "nice" installations is the Tennessee Valley Authority's (TVA) bison herd located in southeastern Kentucky on a sort of peninsula between Kentucky Lake and Lake Barkley. The TVA was established in 1933 as a unique federal corporation that was designed to improve the standard of living in the Tennessee River Valley, primarily through the adoption of a variety of flood control and navigational measures. The 170,000-acre Land Between the Lakes was designated as a recreation and environmental project in 1963, and the TVA established a herd of bison within this area in 1969. The bison are maintained on two 100-acre pastures with abundant trails and roads that provide for maximum viewing by area visitors. Since the Land Between the Lakes does not have corrals or bison handling facilities, culling is accomplished by field slaughter. The meat is served at environmental education centers located within the area and a few carcasses are sold.

The Daniel Boone National Forest, which also is in Kentucky, recently acquired a small number of bison. This is the only United States Forest Service installation to maintain a herd of bison. The Department of Energy's Fermi National Accelerator Laboratory, in Batavia, Illinois, supports a medium-sized bison herd (55–135 animals) "only to remind people that where the laboratory is now was once open prairie and grassland." Surplus bison are sold through public auction. Nearly the same reason for keeping bison, as expressed by Fermi Laboratory, was declared by the keepers of bison at Fort Riley, Kansas, as to why they maintain a small herd (7) of bison at Fort Riley. They said that "it was to remind people that bison were formerly common in Kansas." Fort Riley gives its excess bison to the Kansas State University of Agriculture, which has a school of veterinary medicine. Bison caretakers at the Fort are also the recipient of the progeny from a small herd of bison that are kept within the walls of the federal penitentiary near Leavenworth, Kansas. The bison were originally acquired as a gift from the Buffalo Bill Cody Society in the early 1970s, and the four or five bison that are maintained are cared for by prisoners. Currently there are two bulls and two cows; the calves are paroled and the adult bison currently serve life sentences.

Next to National Park and Wildlife areas, the largest governmental owner of bison is the various state park systems. Like their federal counterparts, most state parks that have and display bison are in the western United States. Two of the larger state park herds are those now supported at Custer State Park, Custer, South Dakota, and Antelope Island State Park, Syracuse, Utah.

Custer State Park was originally established in 1913 as a game preserve and its 47,000 original acres was where the State of South Dakota released its initial acquisition of thirty-six bison in its beginning effort to stock the preserve. Custer was not designated as a state park until 1919. If it were necessary to choose one governmental bison enclave where the bison herds are managed in the most businesslike manner, it would have to be Custer State Park — but Antelope Island would be a very close second. There are approximately 1,500 bison contained within the current 73,000 acres of Custer State Park. In accordance with the objectives of their bison management plan, park management attempts each year to dispose of roughly 550 bison in an effort to control the bison herd size. Most are sold through on-site live sales (auctions), sealed bid sales, and through the American Bison Association's video auction. The park removes about 10 of its overmature bulls each year through authorized hunts. Custer State Park conducts one of the most aggressive herd genetics programs in the United States; because of this and the fact that they do have quality animals, competition, as well as the price, for surplus Custer bison is high.

A live bison auction is not the least bit similar to a cattle auction, or the auction sale of any other form of domestic livestock for that matter. It

Bison cow sold through auction at Custer State Park. When the animals are released from the chutes or gates they usually depart forcefully. Unlike cattle, bison seem to do everything at full speed and power. For this reason, adult bulls are unpopular candidates for auction sales. Courtesy American Bison Association.

would be like comparing a photograph to a motion picture film. Bison will come out of squeeze chutes like cannonballs out of a cannon, ricochet around the sale pen until sold, and then depart into the adjoining corral when the gate is opened, with the speed of light — as if they had been planning to make a break for it all along. Mature bulls are extremely difficult to handle, and two-year-old bulls are right on the cusp. When the American Bison Association holds its annual Gold Trophy Bison Show and Sale, the oldest bulls that are accepted for show and sale are the two-year-olds. Even though these two-year-olds are still accepted, the bison handlers in the yards are somewhat apprehensive about working with these animals. Two-year-old Custer bulls are, however, eagerly sought after for herd bulls, or herd bull replacements, and the handling aspect is just an accepted part of the process. At the Custer State Park live bison auction in mid-November, stock trailers and trucks fill the parking area. Most of the successful bidders will leave with their bison the same day, for destinations as far away as California and Ohio.

At Custer, public viewing opportunities for bison are excellent. And, as is the case with any other park attraction, the public has to be constantly warned that bison are indeed wild animals — people just do not seem to be aware that there could be a risk involved through their close contact with bison. There have been three goring incidents since 1987, but fortunately none were fatal. Custer State Park is not unique with respect to visitors suffering injuries from their contact with bison. Yellowstone as well as other National Parks have had their share of human/bison incidents in spite of a wide distribution of warning literature and use of a number of cautionary devices.

Antelope Island State Park is Utah's largest state park, located on the east side of the Great Salt Lake just west of Syracuse, Utah. Antelope Island's 28,000 acres are also home for a number of mule deer, elk, and pronghorn antelope; however, bison represents the park's primary wildlife program. Herd size will range from about 750 animals to approximately 550. The then park superintendent, Mitch Larsson, reported during the July 27–29, 1993, North American Public Herds Symposium that the park had 589 bison. The size of Antelope Island's bison herd is controlled in two ways: sealed bids and hunts. Park management would like to maintain a breeding ratio of eight cows to each bull, and to accomplish this they sell each year all their nine-year-old cows and one-half of all their two-year-old and yearling bulls. The older, and potentially nonproductive, mature bulls are either culled or hunted (six permits issued) during the first week of December each year. Antelope Island is unique for its use and sale of a microchip ear tag and microchip implant system for bison. The park claims that the microchip has proven to be simply outstanding for the storage of specialized information such as life history, vaccination dates, or any other information about the animal that they wish to maintain from year to year.

The State of Alaska maintains three wild bison herds that are located in the southeastern and central part of the state. Although there is some predation on the part of wolves, bear have little, if any, impact upon these wild herds. The principal concern of the Alaskan bison is available forage. Since two of the three herds have demonstrated healthy growth, bison hunts have been permitted by the Alaska Department of Fish and Game with respect to the Big Delta and Farewell herds. In 1928, twenty-three bison were acquired from the National Bison Range and released near Delta Junction. After a number of years, it was possible for the state to transfer some animals from its Big Delta herd and establish a Farewell herd near McGrath. Another small herd, Copper River, was later established near Glenallen. Bob Hunter, Alaska Department of Fish and Game, reported that at the end of 1993, there were slightly more than 500 bison in the Big Delta herd, approximately 350 in the Farewell herd, and perhaps slightly less than 50 in the Copper River herd. Mr. Hunter does not believe that the Copper River herd can, or will, survive, and unless they are moved they will eventually just disappear because of lack of adequate forage.

Although some bison from the Farewell herd may be occasionally taken by wolves, herd growth for the Big Delta and Farewell herds is primarily maintained through the issuance of hunting permits. There are over 10,000 applications received for the approximate 200 permits the state will issue. In the past, most of these have gone to Alaskan residents. The permit fee is $10, but successful nonresident applicants must also buy an Alaskan hunting license ($85) and pay for a bison tag. The tag currently costs $450. The state plans to issue not more than 120 tags for the Big Delta herd and 80 for the Farewell herd. Because prospective hunters have relatively easy access to the Big Delta herd, the success rate has been nearly 98 percent. The Farewell herd is basically deep in the back country along the Kuskokwim Mountains where motor vehicles are useless and horses are not reasonably available. Permittees have to pack in and pack out. Bob Hunter indicated that there was only one successful Farewell permittee last year. No hunting is permitted on the Copper River herd.

The State of Arizona has experienced a rather interesting bison history. From archeological discovery it is known that bison were native to Arizona in prehistoric times, but, according to Erik Reed (1955, 133), they were not to be found in Arizona after the beginning of the Christian era. They were reintroduced by Charles J. "Buffalo" Jones on the Kaibab Plateau, north of the Grand Canyon, near the Utah border. Shortly after their arrival on the plateau, the bison were moved to the nearby House Rock Valley. Jones intended to experiment with raising a crossbred animal, using bison and Galloway cattle. Moving in nearly 120 bison from Montana and California, and an unknown number of Galloway cattle, Jones met with but limited success. He rounded up all the bison he could in 1909, and shipped them to a ranch near Fort Sumner (Raymond Lee 1993, 182); however, some fifteen to twenty bison were still left in the House Rock area. These stragglers were acquired, in some unknown but permanent manner, by

James Owens, although the Grand Canyon Cattle Company also apparently exercised some limited ownership over the bison, and in 1924 shipped about twelve to a ranch in Mexico. Whatever number of bison were left in the House Rock Valley in 1927 — and it has been suggested that there may have been around 100 at that time — were sold by Owens to the State of Arizona.

The bison herd maintained on the 65,000-acre House Rock Ranch has varied over the years from less than 100 to slightly over 300. A second herd was started at the Raymond Ranch (located southwest of Winslow) in 1945. The bison herd at the Raymond Ranch began with 52 animals and after transfer of 166 bison from House Rock in 1950, the new total of 358 became too much for the available forage and a reduction program was promptly initiated. Ninety-one were removed by hunters, and 175 were transferred to abandoned Fort Huachuca near Sierra Vista (southern Arizona, about fifteen miles from the Mexican border). In 1949, the Arizona State Game and Fish Department (ASGFD) acquired some 35,000 acres of land from the United States Army for wildlife study. The herd was kept within a 13,000-acre enclosure, and after addition of bison from the National Bison Range, Yellowstone National Park, House Rock Ranch, and Raymond Ranch, there were slightly more than 350 bison on the Fort Huachuca range. In 1954, bad news was received by the ASGFD: the United States Army Signal Corps intended to reactivate Fort Huachuca. Chances of continuing this herd appeared to be rather slim, so it was decided to hold a hunt in January of 1955. ASGFD moved 39 bison back to the Raymond Ranch, gave 20 to Mexico, and removed 217 through its hunt. Ensuing hunts removed the rest of the bison herd at Fort Huachuca.

Currently, permits are still issued for bison hunts at House Rock and Raymond. The number of animals culled from each herd is based upon range conditions at the ranch sites. The target herd size for both ranches is about 200 animals; thus, the number reduced each year would be somewhere between 50 and 100 animals. Hunting fees vary, dependent upon whether or not you are a resident of Arizona. Residents will pay $753 for a bull permit, $453 for a cow permit, and $243 for a yearling (either sex). Nonresidents pay a much stiffer fee: $3,753 for a bull, $2,453 for a cow, and $1,243 for a yearling. At House Rock you are on your own; you can shoot whatever animal you want to. At Raymond, rangers will tell you which permit animal you can take. Because of the earlier crossbreeding efforts of "Buffalo" Jones, rangers at House Rock and Raymond suggest that there still may be a small amount of cattle blood in these two herds. The State of Arizona also retains a small herd at the 1,180-acre Lyman Lake State Park, which is located eleven miles south of St. Johns. The six bison were acquired through donation by the Chamber of Commerce and are maintained by the Lyman Lake Buffalo Club.

The state park systems of the United States are unmatched, even by the federal park system, in geographic dispersion and diversity and numbers of plants and wildlife they embrace. Because of space limitations not all state park areas can, or should, include bison as part of their display of animals that are, or more properly were, endemic to the area. Nonetheless, in addition to those state parks already mentioned, a number of other state parks feature bison as part of their natural wildlife presentation. A few of the major park bison collections are identified below:

Prairie State Park is located about thirty miles north of Joplin in southwest Missouri. The National Park Service has continually hoped that one day there would be a Prairie National Park, where the Service could present and interpret for future generations what tall-grass prairies were formerly like. Tall-grass prairies covered nearly one-half million acres of this nation; however, Prairie State Park is now interpreting for its visitors what these massive prairies were like, but with only 2,560 acres. The park has four pastures set aside for bison; they now have about fourteen animals but plan on letting their herd grow to forty or fifty. The bison were originally obtained from Wichita Mountains and Fort Niobrara National Wildlife Refuges. All surplus bison are sold through auction sales.

In the extreme northwest corner of Nebraska, near Chadron, is historic Fort Robinson and 22,000-acre Fort Robinson State Park. Along with its museums and military buildings, the park also offers a prairie panorama and a bison herd that currently boasts a total of nearly 400 animals. Bison meat is served in the park lodges and cafes and even sold to a number of restaurants in the nearby communities. In order to keep the herd at its present level, besides processing some of the younger (over eighteen months but under three years old) bison for meat, some of the animals are sold through auction sales locally and in Kansas. The park experiences an 80 to 90 percent birth rate for its breeding cows, and tries to maintain a ratio of approximately one bull for every ten cows.

In far western Nebraska, ten miles south of Gering, a small herd of bison are also kept at Wildcat Hills State Park. The 935 park acres do represent some fairly rugged terrain, and to avoid buying feed for the bison, except in the winter months, only two bulls and five cows are now permitted to occupy the 628-acre bison pasture. After breeding season surplus bison are sent to Fort Robinson.

Blue Mounds State Park is located in Minnesota about five miles north of Luverne in the extreme southwest corner of the state. The bison management plan proposes that the park will keep sixty-five bison in the summer and forty-five in the winter. They currently have two breeding bulls and twenty cows, along with a variety of calves, yearlings, and assorted younger animals. There are two pastures of 150 acres each in this 2,000-acre park. Surplus animals are sold by auction sale. One three-year-old is butchered each year for the Blue Mounds open house celebration — first Sunday in June. The original herd started in 1916 by transfer of three bison from Fort Niobrara; six additional bison were acquired in 1970 from Sibley city park in Mankato.

Two other states have very active bison management programs: Kansas and Wyoming. The State of Kansas maintains bison herds within four of its very popular public areas: Maxwell Game Preserve, Byron Walker Wildlife Area, Crawford State Lake and Wildlife Area, and the Finney Game Reserve. The largest herd, which often exceeds 200 animals, is kept at the Maxwell Game Preserve near Canton. To keep herd size within a manageable size, bison auctions are held in mid-November of each year by the Kansas Department of Wildlife and Parks. The State of Wyoming does not currently maintain as many bison as Kansas (54), but it is considered to be one of the better programs because, in addition to preserving a bison presence, it actively promotes the bison as a commercial asset to the state. Surplus animals are given to Indian tribes to encourage increased tribal involvement in the Bison Industry, and productive bison are traded out for nonproductive animals that are used to provide bison meat for a variety of Wyoming boosting functions.

There are a number of other state government organizations that support and display bison for public enjoyment. In Iowa, for example, County Conservation Boards, under the direction of the Board of Supervisors for each county, manage small herds in six different counties. Although the herds may be small, each park area provides a generous allotment of space for their bison and the interpretation and educational programs are superb. In addition to zoological parks or gardens, a rather impressive number of cities still include bison among their wildlife displays in the public parks. The Denver Mountain Parks, for instance, have more than fifty bison contained in pastures along one of the major interstate highways going through Colorado. However, there are probably fewer now displayed by the cities than there were ten to fifteen years ago because (1) city government, like its state and federal counterparts, no longer has the tax base that it may have had formerly, and (2) the resident bison became older and died, were not replaced, or were just phased out.

Although not often considered a part of the public sector involvement with bison, the public zoological parks have exercised a vital role in preserving the bison specie. They currently possess an absolutely unparalleled capacity to inform the public regarding the nature and value of all wildlife, which would include the American bison. Through an international computerized animal inventory process (International Species Information System or ISIS), it is now possible to identify those major zoos that have bison and the number that they maintain. From ISIS totals and random calls to a few of the smaller zoological parks that did not belong to the ISIS network, it was a rather simple process to locate more than nineteen hundred bison that are currently on display. Unfortunately, this number is dropping, as are the number of zoological parks that are willing to devote space to bison. The National Zoo in Washington D.C., has but two bison, a male and a female. The Bronx Zoo in New York City, which has a budget that is only surpassed by the San Diego Zoo, has fewer than ten bison, and the most prestigious and cosmopolitan of all United States zoological park systems, the San Diego Zoological and Wild Animal Parks, have *no* plains bison, the one animal that is most representative of the United States.

When I started contacting the zoo curators at most of the larger city zoos, I was, at first, both astounded and disappointed by what appeared to be the preoccupation of these zoos with the acquisition and display of rare and exotic (to North America) animals and birds. It seemed to me that public zoos have a certain responsibility, particularly to the inner-city youths, to at least provide specimens of the one mammal species that is more commonly associated with the history of this nation that any other animal or bird — the American bison. After a great number of calls and visits, it was quite clear that taxon policies, funding, and politics have at least as much, if not more, impact upon zoo practices and exhibit management than the need for public enjoyment and education.

Zoos are now faced with the simple fact that they cannot save everything. According to Larry Killmar, curator at the San Diego Zoo, there are probably fewer than 20,000 acres available to all United States zoos combined — and approximately 10 percent of this landmass is in San Diego. Killmar contends that it is not possible or practical for zoos to provide captive space for noncritical animals. In the case of bison, a species that is not endangered or threatened, zoos therefore have no choice but to rely upon the private sector, and other public entities, to provide the public with whatever exhibit and viewing opportunities these facilities may offer. In the introduction segment of his book, *Last Animals at the Zoo*, Colin Tudge theorizes that conservation is now the principal and primary focus of zoos, and that education and entertainment are of secondary importance. He later suggests that "captive breeding" is perhaps the only way to save endangered species, particularly those animals in countries with turbulent political climates. If carried to the extreme, the United States would then also have to assume the role of world species protector.

To complete the discussion on public sector involvement with bison, I have elected to include in this chapter information on two bison-managing organizational entities that cannot comfortably be considered as public sector organizations, nor can they be considered part of the private sector: The Nature Conservancy and American Indian tribes.

The Nature Conservancy is a nonprofit international organization that owns and manages its own preserves and is renowned for its scientific expertise and ecological diversity. Throughout the world, the Conservancy owns more than 1,300 preserves. However, for purposes of this book, we are interested in just five of the nature preserves in the United States that support bison herds. The first of the five preserves that the Conservancy acquired was the 7,800 acre Samuel H. Ordway Memorial Prairie Preserve near Leola, South Dakota, in 1978. In 1984 and 1985 a total of 40 bison were acquired, and another 20 were purchased in 1987. Within Ordway's near 1,500-acre bison pasturage, herd size currently fluctuates between 85 and 125 animals. The second preserve stocked with bison was the 53,000-acre Niobrara Valley Preserve near Johnstown, Nebraska, which was acquired in 1985. Nearly five times the amount of land that was earlier set aside for bison on the Ordway preserve has been set aside for bison at

Niobrara Valley; approximately 7,500 acres. The size of the Niobrara bison herd at its low point will normally be about 250 animals; after the spring calf crop it will increase to about 400 animals. The third preserve that the Conservancy acquired and stocked with bison was the Cross Ranch Preserve near Hensler, North Dakota. Herd size on this preserve varies between 75 and 105 animals. The fourth is the Konza Prairie Research Natural Area, which currently has approximately 210 bison that are subject to a controlled study program while they roam over 2,500 of the Konza's 8,600 acres.

The fifth, and to this point, the last prairie preserve that the Conservancy has elected to introduce a herd of bison on, is the Tallgrass Prairie Preserve near Pawkuska, Oklahoma. This was a sort of opportunity project, since the 300 animals that were released on preserve lands in 1993 were the result of a donation from the Ken-Ada Ranches, Bartlesville, Oklahoma. The size of this herd will be permitted to increase over the next eight to ten years until approximately 30,000 acres of grassland will provide forage support for a herd of from 1,100 to 1,700 bison. All surplus Conservancy bison are sold by sealed bid; no public hunting or other herd reduction measures have been considered. The presence of bison on these five preserves is only a small part of the overall total mission of the Conservancy, which is basically aimed toward the preservation of plants, animals, and other communities that represent the diversity of life on earth. The Conservancy tries to accomplish this primarily by protecting the lands and waters that these divergent life communities need to survive and exist. This seemingly is a mission that a number of governmental agencies have been charged with; but then the Conservancy is not similarly burdened by the sheer volume of regulations and the number and variety of special-interest groups that governmental agencies must face, and thus can get something done very quickly.

Perhaps there has never been a more logical agricultural and entrepreneurial arrangement than that which should exist among the bison, the Native American, and the associated Indian tribes. While many of the early tribes had been partially dependent upon gathering, and later farming, the pursuit of wild game was more often a continual process. By the time that the Europeans arrived and began to settle on the east coast of North America, cultural differences between tribes became more distinct and agriculture began to increase in importance as the abundance of wild game

Bison grazing in a pasture on the Ken-Ada Ranch adjacent to downtown Bartlesville, Oklahoma. Bison from this ranch formed the nucleus of the herd recently transferred to The Nature Conservancy's Tallgrass Prairie Preserve near Pawhuska, Oklahoma. Courtesy American Bison Association.

in the East And Southeast gradually diminished. After tribal relocations had been brought about under the auspices of the Indian Removal Act of 1830, the lands that the affected Indian tribes were eventually given in exchange for their former homelands were generally not fertile, lacked water, and wild game was not abounding on these more or less barren lands. The Dawes Allotment Act of 1887 took this divestiture process one step further by then permitting the resale of "surplus" reservation land.

The motives of policymakers who supported the Dawes Act were possibly well intentioned, but the objectives of others, particularly those reflective of western interests, may have been questionable. The basic concept was to allot reservation land in the following manner: 160 acres to the head of each Indian family; 80 acres to unmarried Indians over eighteen and orphans regardless of age; and 40 acres to each unmarried Indian under eighteen living prior to the effective date of the Dawes Act. After this had been accomplished, any surplus land remaining could be bought by the government and then made available for homesteading. Title to the acreage allotments that the Indians would receive would be held in "trust" by the federal government for twenty-five years, after which time clear title would be granted and the individual Indian owners would be free to do whatever they desired with this land — including selling it. After most of the allotments had been made, efforts to teach the owner Indians the principles of modern industrial agriculture (farming and stock raising) generally led to failure. The problems were basically those of climate, soil, equipment, and availability of money, but there were also a number of critical cultural barriers that could not be overcome.

With the federal and state governments now partly out of their way, the Native American and tribal authorities are beginning to make some headway toward agricultural self-determination and accomplishment. An Intertribal Bison Cooperative (ITBC) has recently been formed that is "dedicated to the restoration of bison to Indian people in a manner which is compatible with the spiritual and cultural beliefs and practices of Native American Tribes . . ." (Heckert 1993, 305). In addition, a number of tribes have begun to build bison herds that support a variety of management objectives including those directed toward religious and aesthetic as well as income-producing purposes.

Obtaining information from the tribes about their bison herds was not necessarily more difficult than it was to obtain information from other Bison Industry entrepreneurs, but their social mores and tribal customs dictated a somewhat constrained and less vainglorious comportment than their non-Indian peers. I was able to identify twenty-six Indian tribes that maintained bison herds, the combined total of which amounted to approximately 3,600 animals. The largest single bison owner, at the time of my inquiry, was the Crow tribe of southern Montana, with slightly more than 900 animals, and the second largest was the Oglala Sioux tribe of South Dakota. As provided by law, surplus bison from federal herds are available without cost, except for handling and any provided transportation, to Indian tribal authorities. Wind Cave National Park, for example, was the source for the present herd of 140 bison managed by the Lower Brule Sioux tribe of South Dakota. It is also understood that the State of Wyoming has plans to assist the Northern Arapaho and the ITBC in their efforts to develop a bison herd on tribal lands in Wyoming.

Because of the present demand for bison meat, Native Americans and Indian tribal authorities have no difficulty in marketing their bison products, and, in fact, they have a distinct edge when it comes to certain bison by-products that emulate art form and embody Indian culture. Bison meat products are also eagerly sought, not only in the United States but in foreign countries as well. According to Gael Benoteau ("Marketing American Bison Meat in Europe," *Bison World*, January/February 1994), when asked to choose between American- and Native American–produced bison, European marketers preferred the Native American bison. From interviews conducted, Benoteau observed: "it appears that Native-American bison has the connotation of being a product naturally raised in its traditional environment, and symbolizes the ever-popular Western image of strength and power, and exhibits the true western taste. . . ." The latter is in reference to the European marketers' predilection for young grass-fed bison, rather than feedlot-fattened animals that are preferred by most Americans.

> *How bright is the moonlight*
> *How bright is the moonlight*
> *Tonight as I ride with my load of buffalo beef.*
> *Tonight as I ride with my load of buffalo beef.*
>
> Arapahoe Song
> in "The Ghost Dance Religion and the Sioux Outbreak of 1890,"
> by James Mooney, 1896, 967

10

A Bison Tomorrow

For as long as humans have existed on the North American continent, there were also bison. Believed to have originated as a species in Asia over two million years ago, ancestors of our current-day bison expanded their range into Europe and eventually crossed a then existing land bridge between Siberia and Alaska (referred to by scientists as Beringia) perhaps more than 250,000 years ago. They reproduced and flourished. In pursuit of the large mammals, Pleistocene hunters are thought to have crossed the same land bridge between 25,000 and 40,000 years ago and also began to populate the North American continent.

Bison bison bison, the common American plains bison, is the product of a gradual evolvement process that has resulted in nature fashioning a somewhat different animal from that of the earlier intercontinental bison traveler. Although smaller in size, the current-day bison still exhibits the same degree of courage and strength that had been attributed to its larger ancestors. The ancestral bison's former human adversary has also evolved. Physically, today's humans are larger than their ancestors, perhaps smarter, and unlike the bison, their numbers have increased to the degree that it is now the human that blankets the North American continent and commands the former habitat of the American bison. No longer the free-roaming monarch of the plains, the bison is held captive by whatever segment of environment that is allotted to it by its human stewards. Without necessarily adopting an anthropomorphic guise, we can accept as a precept that the bison does not harbor any false expectations and, like any animal, accepts whatever fate the future may have in store for it. Human expectations, however, cannot be as simply stated since each person is subject to his or her own individual beliefs and desires.

If we can, however, attempt to set aside for just a moment some of our traditional beliefs with respect to agricultural land uses, we may find that there still is room for bison as well as humans. Francis Haines, in *The Buffalo* (1970, 215–216), expressed a rather limited view of the value of the bison:

> The buffalo then, is an interesting wild animal, unfit for domestication or crossbreeding. It can thrive on the open range with no more attention than being protected from men. The species is picturesque, an important feature in our western parks, but of little economic value to civilized man even though it was the staff of life for many thousands of hunters on the western plains for 10,000 years or more.

The point that Haines was attempting to make was not that the bison was not without worth, but that it did not have the same economic value to humans as did cattle. Haines was also a believer in the mental superiority of cattle. When commenting on crossing rivers or establishing trails he noted (1970, 15): "Cattle on the open range, when left to their own devices, follow a pattern of behavior similar to that of the buffalo, except that they are smarter than the buffalo and less apt to get into trouble by trying a new, difficult place." Not wishing to single out Haines for faulty observations, even the usually knowledgeable William Hornaday had expressed in his often quoted publication, *The Extermination of the American Bison* (1887, 429–430): "The buffalo of the past was an animal of a rather low order of intelligence, and his dullness of intellect was one of the important factors in his phenomenally swift extermination." Contrary to these and other similar opinions, bison are reasonably intelligent, quick learners, and are extremely curious. I have often felt that the claim of being the earth's stupidest creature would quickly become a simple contest between the domesticated rabbit and the common chicken for this dubious honor; but it is very probable that their wild counterparts have maintained greater mental capacity as well as physical dexterity. I believe that the same comparison can be drawn today between bison and domesticated Bovidae.

The growth of the Bison Industry has obviously been based upon the economic value of the American bison. No longer just merely a viewing curiosity, bison ranching is now an indisputable agricultural investment alternative to cattle ranching, and it potentially offers a far better return because the worldwide demand for bison far exceeds the supply. Frank and Deborah Popper offered an extremely controversial proposal in 1987 (*The Great Plains: From Dust to Dust*), which was quickly dubbed a "Buffalo Commons" plan because it envisioned returning nearly a quarter of the Great Plains into an ecological reserve and wildlife refuge primarily for bison. That this suggestion was not eagerly adopted is quite understandable because in its infancy the idea reeked of bureaucracy, loss of private land — perhaps even through condemnation — and geographical denigration. In spite of their earlier insistence upon the need for governmental intervention, it would appear that the Poppers have now settled upon an alternative measure that should mitigate most of the expressed environmental and economic problems allegedly attributed to the selected ten-state area. In their presentation during the July 27–29, 1993, North American Public Herds Symposium, Frank and Deborah Popper provided a draft paper entitled "The Future of the Great Plains," and in this paper acknowledged that bison are substantially more than just scenic diversions:

> Plains ranchers are increasingly finding that buffalo offer a better living and more opportunities than cattle. Ranchers can easily switch to buffalo and then sell hunting rights, meat, hides, horns and skulls at healthy prices. Buffalo turn out to be less laborious to tend than cattle and better able to withstand Plains winters. They drink less water than cattle, eat less grass, graze more widely and put less pressure on riparian areas — important advantages in the semiarid, quickly overgrazed plains. They need less care than cattle during calving. The supposed fencing and disease problems of buffalo tend to be much exaggerated. Buffalo meat has more protein and less fat and cholesterol than beef.

> Buffalo, unlike cattle, look like a growth sector, one that in many ways is only now forming. Buffalo producers, for example, still have a chance to avoid the present alienating, many-middlemen, feedlot style of large-scale corporate agriculture that often harms cattle producers and consumers. Thus in recent months state-level buffalo producers' associations have appeared in Kansas, North Dakota and Wyoming. The North Dakota group, for instance, has ambitious

plans for a marketing cooperative and a processing plant that was specifically built for buffalo meat and its byproducts. The new buffalo ranches exemplify the local and private-sector creation of the Buffalo Commons.

There is a nascent economic realism pervading the Bison Industry that has convincingly drawn investors initially attracted by the physical charisma of the bison but who also want to make money. Although many bison producers were former cattle ranchers, a number of producers had little or no previous agricultural experience before they decided to raise bison. Ron Thiel, who manages a herd of more than 2,000 bison on his Iron Mountain Bison Ranch near Cheyenne, Wyoming, is an experienced bison rancher. Thiel recently suggested ("Getting into the Bison Business," *Bison Breeder's Handbook*, 3rd edition, 1993, 27) that "one of the best reasons for getting into the bison business is for fun, but there is a limit to how much fun you can have. Therefore, you have to examine the economic side of raising bison and try to ascertain what level and type of production you want to start out with." Other experienced ranchers also counsel new investors in the bison business to proceed with caution, perhaps start slowly and with young animals that you can grow and learn with. One thing is clear, however: the numbers of bison and bison ranchers are increasing at a far greater level than even the most optimistic of predictions.

The return of the American bison is really not as much a miracle as it is a factual phenomenon of a environmental process. Thanks to legislating an end to de facto annihilation and eliminating their only natural predators, the wolf and grizzly, the fecund bison species has accordingly responded and prospered. Probably one of the more significant issues applicable to full species recovery is those factors that are specifically related to inbreeding. Scientists tell us that the numbers of breeding animals needed in any total animal population to avoid inbreeding problems will vary by specie, but 500 has generally been accepted as the normal minimum. It would seem that for the bison this number may have been perilously close to the total number of animals surviving after the herd slaughters of the late 1800s. Presuming minimal genetic variation, the genes, or versions of genes (referred to as allele), that a bison inherits are extremely important. Since genes will also mutate, recordkeeping and blood-testing of breeding animals become even more critical if problems consistent with inbreeding are to be avoided or mitigated. Progeny may inherit the same allele of any one gene from its parents (homozygous) or a different allele (heterozygous). What blood testing attempts to avoid is the potential breeding of animals that may pass on deleterious genes to the next generation. The more common outcome from immoderate inbreeding among animals is infertility; but there are other physical deformations and afflictions that geneticists identify as inbreeding depressions that can occur.

It is also similarly possible that mating of two very closely related animals with superior characteristics could produce offspring of unusual vigor and vitality, or as Darwin expressed, "hybrid vigour." Close breeding, such as sire to daughter, son to mother, or full brother to sister, is said to occasionally produce extremely high-quality animals, but is inherently more risky. Although a consistent practice of line breeding, that is, the mating of animals more distantly related, should eventually lead to the genetic base of a herd becoming consistent or homozygous, it also increases the opportunity for the matching of deleterious recessive genes. Both the American Bison Association and the National Buffalo Association had earlier urged producers to exercise caution regarding inbreeding practices. This is also the position currently taken by the National Bison Association, but in spite of these concerns it is recognized that certain selective processes, such as meatiness and animal disposition, may tempt a certain amount of inbreeding. Thus, it would appear that if we did not have the public herds (and a few of the larger private herds) that customarily rely upon the natural mate selection process, there is a risk that some of the species characteristics that are currently common to the bison could be lost.

The industry must arrive at an acceptable balance among selective breeding, natural selection, and exchanges of breeding animals that would optimize genetic variation. The objective should not be the creation of an animal that the industry believes a bison ought to look like but rather maintenance of what the species once was and, hopefully, now is. In other words, not breed solely for meat production but also consider the aesthetics of the founder animals. The Bison Industry cannot gain or endure if subspecies or hybrids of what is now the plains bison, *Bison bison bison*, are subsequently developed to enhance their meat marketing potential.

When reaching for terms to describe the American bison, the first Europeans attempted to describe its features in terms of certain familiar physical attributes associated with other animals: bunch on its back like a camel, neck covered with hair like a lion, head armed like that of a bull, and so on. Today, it is not so much its appearance as its presence that we find difficult to describe. It has been somewhat flatteringly referred to as a noble, magnificent, or heroic animal; but also occasionally labelled stupid, stubborn, and unmanageable. Native Americans find religious significance and solace in its existence, and more than a few of the past bison chroniclers have elected to view the bison with a scholarly but perhaps effete and antiseptic detachment. But what do we really know about the bison? Research has been minimal; significant bison health problems are usually treated by veterinarians whose initial medical training and experience have been with cattle; and they are also obliged to use medicines and drugs authorized for cattle since specific bison pharmaceuticals are nonexistent.

Bison cannot be considered to be just another breed or form of cattle. Although both cattle and bison are in the order Artiodactyla (even-toed ungulates), family Bovidae (hollow-horned ruminants with cloven hooves), they are of a different genus and thus a different type of animal. We cannot learn about bison by studying cattle, yet the Bison Industry budgets little or nothing for research and, in comparison, according to the National Cattlemen's Association, the Beef Board through its checkoff system spends nearly four million dollars annually just on cattle research. Bison are said to be extremely resistant, if not immune, to cancer. Why? We still don't know. Ed Newquist, one of the original fourteen founders of the American Bison Association, devoted considerable personal time and all the funds he could reasonably spare toward solving this question, but he was unable to solicit any support from the scientific community or the Bison Industry. Some people also know that bison meat is non-allergenic, but this, unfortunately for a number of people that have this affliction, is not generally known. Bison meat is said to contain less fat, less cholesterol, fewer calories, and more protein than any other red meat. But research thus far has been insufficient to convince a cynical public and competitive meat industry skeptics.

It would be easy to simply conclude that the Bison Industry should intensify its efforts to promote preservation, research, and public education. The industry, however, not only lacks the necessary monetary resources, it has also found that government rules and regulatory processes tend to favor those industries that have established and continue to nurture their legislative contacts. In addition, notwithstanding the number of official nonprofit bison associations, they have little power or authority. With the exception of two, or perhaps three, wealthy and politically astute producers who have the ability, if they so desired, to unilaterally seek changes, most bison ranchers lack the political or monetary resources to effect change individually. In order to achieve desired objectives, the Bison Industry must accordingly adopt the same levels of unity and discipline common to the beef, pork, and lamb industries. The smallest bison producers would appear to be deserving of the same measure of support and assistance from their industry as small cattle ranchers routinely receive from the Cattle Industry through the efforts of their administrators.

One of the worst possible suggested outcomes for the bison as a species would be an eventual organizational absorption of commercial bison breeders by the Cattle Industry. For the moment, beef barons feign disinterest and borderline contempt for the bison, but they are nevertheless actively seeking to produce leaner cattle that will be more competitive in our current health-conscious society. The Cattle Industry is interested in promoting beef; its administrators have their own procedures and policies for accomplishing this — and they are very good at it. Those few bison producers who are seemingly frustrated by the lack of organizational leadership and progress within the Bison Industry, and yearn for the ultimate merger, would find that the future of bison within a cattle culture would not be as promising as it now is.

The bison is one of America's more treasured mammal species. To exist in a world that does not also contain bison is unthinkable today, but it was a distinct possibility not too many years ago. In his *History of Animals*, Aristotle observed: "In the great majority of animals there are traces of psychical qualities of attitudes, which qualities are more markedly differentiated in the case of human beings." The bison manifests a quality of presence that is not replicated by other Bovidae. Placing a bison in a feedlot may possibly be an inevitable consequence of species proliferation, but it unavoidably instills a process repugnance that is not necessarily felt for the cattle who share the same fate. Regardless of the varied degrees of emotionalism that the bison can kindle in human beings, to guarantee the bison's continuance as a specie, the best thing we can now do as custodians of this resource is to eat the surplus products and thus encourage continued private sector investment in bison.

History has taught us that larger animals and birds cannot compete successfully or share in the same environment with human beings unless they are able to demonstrate that they possess direct utilitarian or economic values. There are those individuals who maintain that an animal should not have to justify its existence based on its practicality, but for the species to grow and prosper it is a necessity. Even the large mammals in world national parks are limited in number because of park boundaries, and in the event of social unrest, as is now the case with respect to many of the African nations, their continued existence cannot be assured. In the United States, a number of species are considered to be either endangered or threatened, and they continuously face extinction in spite of the expenditures of millions of dollars and the bestowal of uncountable numbers of hours of scientific time. The bald eagle is certainly a magnificent bird, but lacking the economic value of the common chicken or unable to perform other than aesthetic functions, there is no private sector involvement and its future is left to the whims of nature and the protective activities of governmental scientists. Without the intervention of the private sector, bison would not be as numerous as they are today. We only need to look to Canada to confirm this observation. The wood bison (*Bison bison athabascae*), which is governmentally managed and controlled, is still endangered, but those bison herds that are managed by Canadian private sector owners are flourishing.

To encourage private sector entrepreneurs to continue investing in the bison business, the bison and the Bison Industry should be subject to the same agricultural policies as those applicable to other commercially marketed meat animals and associated industries. It is not appropriate to exclude bison producers from the receipt of free federal meat inspection services, and then subject bison meat to governmental restrictions and regulations while excluding other meats from such compliance. Bison producers are not looking for governmental handouts, nor are they necessarily deserving of any, but they are entitled to an equal competitive opportunity to market their product. The public, the consumers of bison meat products, is also entitled to the same assurance of quality that they would receive by purchasing beef, pork, lamb, or poultry products. To enable needed changes to occur we all will have to make an effort, but if this ensures a continued future for the bison in America, can we afford to do less?

> *If nature makes nothing incomplete, and nothing in vain, the inference must be that she has made all animals for the sake of man.*
>
> Aristotle, Politics, 1256 b 20

Bibliography

Adair, James. *History of the American Indians (1775).* Edited by Samuel Cole Williams under the auspices of the National Society of the Colonial Dames of America, Tennessee. Promontory Press, New York, 1930.

Allen, Joel Asaph. *The American Bisons, Living and Extinct.* Memoirs of the Geological Survey of Kentucky Vol. 1 pt. II. University Press, Cambridge (Welch, Bigelow & Co.), 1876.

Allen, Lewis F. "Improvement of Native Cattle." In Commissioner of Agriculture, *Report for the Year 1866*, 199–300, Washington, D.C., 1866.

Anderson, Bernice G. *Indian Sleep Man Tales.* Bramhall House, New York, 1940.

Bauer, Erwin. *Erwin Bauer's Bear in their World.* Outdoor Life Bookclub, New York, 1985.

Benoteau, Gael and Barbara Charles. "Marketing American Bison Meat in Europe." *Bison World*, January/February 1994, 40–41.

Boulding, Kenneth E. *The World as a Total System.* Sage Publications, Beverly Hills, CA, 1985.

Bradbury, John. *Travels in the Interior of America.* Reprinting of the 1817 publication *Travels in the Interior of America in the Years 1809, 1810, and 1811.* March of America Facsimile Series No. 59, University Microfilms, Inc., Ann Arbor, 1966.

Braidwood, Robert J. *Prehistoric Men.* Chicago Natural History Museum, Popular Series Anthropology, Number 37, Chicago, 1964.

Branch, E. Douglas. *The Hunting of the Buffalo.* D. Appleton and Company, New York, 1929.

Breland, Osmond P. *Animal Life and Lore.* Harper and Row, New York, 1963.

Brown, Dee. *Bury My Heart at Wounded Knee.* Holt, Rinehart & Winston, New York, 1970.

Carbyn, L. N. "Wolves and Bison, Wood Buffalo National Park — Past, Present and Future." In *The Buffalo,* edited by John E. Foster, Dick Harrison, and I. S. MacLaren, 167–178, The University of Alberta Press, 1992.

Catlin, George. *Letters and Notes on the Manners, Customs, and Conditions of the North American Indians* (Vols. 1 and 2). Ross & Haines, Inc., Minneapolis, 1965.

Chittenden, Hiram Martin. *The Yellowstone National Park.* The Robert Clarke Company, Cincinnati, 1904.

Chorlton, Winsor. *Planet Earth: Ice Ages.* Time-Life Books, Alexandria, VA, 1983.

Clawson, Marion. *The Bureau of Land Management.* Praeger Publishers, New York, 1971.

Cleland, Robert Glass. *This Reckless Breed of Men.* Alfred A. Knopf, New York, 1963.

Cody, William F. *The Adventures of Buffalo Bill.* Harper and Brothers, New York, 1904.

———. *Buffalo Bill's Life Story: An Autobiography.* Time-Life Books, Alexandria, VA, 1982. Reprinting of the 1879 publication, F. E. Bliss, Hartford. Also Cosmopolitan Book Corporation, New York, 1920.

Cook, John R. *The Border and the Buffalo.* [Crane and Company, 1907] Citadel Press, New York, 1967.

Collinson, Frank. *Life in the Saddle.* University of Oklahoma Press, Norman, 1963.

Coulter, John Lee. *Co-operation Among Farmers.* Sturgis & Walton Company, New York, 1911.

Cushman, Dan. *The Great North Trail.* McGraw Hill, New York, 1966.

Danz, Harold P., ed. *Bison Breeder's Handbook.* 3rd ed. Jostens, Topeka, KS, 1993.

Dary, David A. *The Buffalo Book: The Full Saga of the American Animal.* Swallow Press/Ohio University Press, Chicago, 1989.

Davis, Donald S. "Summary of Bison/Brucellosis Research Conducted at Texas A&M University 1985–1993." In the published proceedings of the North

American Public Bison Herds Symposium, July 27–29, 1993, Lacrosse, WI, assembled and compiled by Ronald E. Walker, 347–361, Custer State Park, SD, 1993.

Davis, Simon J. M. *The Archaeology of Animals.* Yale University Press, New Haven, CT, 1987.

Day, Michael H. *Guide to Fossil Man.* 4th ed. University of Chicago Press, Chicago, 1986.

DeLiberto, Thomas J. and Philip J. Urness. "Comparative Digestive Physiology of American Bison and Hereford Cattle." In the published proceedings of the North American Public Bison Herds Symposium, July 27–29, 1993, Lacrosse, WI, assembled and compiled by Ronald E. Walker, 53–71, Custer State Park, SD, 1993.

DeVoto, Bernard. *Across the Wide Missouri.* Bonanza Books, New York, 1947.

Dodge, Natt N. "Wild Life of the American West." In *The Book of the American West,* edited by Jay Monaghan, 427–500. Simon & Schuster, New York, 1963.

Dodge, Colonel Richard Irving. *The Plains of the Great West and Their Inhabitants.* Archer House, Inc., New York, 1959.

Dowling, Kim, ed. *Buffalo Producer's Guide to Management & Marketing.* R.R. Donnelley & Sons, Chicago, 1990.

Drannan, Captain William F. *Thirty-One Years on the Plains and in the Mountains.* Rhodes and McClure Publishing Company, 1909.

Duval, John Crittenden. *The Adventures of Big-Foot Wallace.* Time-Life Books, Inc., Alexandria, VA, 1983. Reprinting of the 1871 publication, Claxton, Remsen & Haffelfinger, Philadelphia.

Easton, Robert and MacKenzie Brown. *Lord of Beasts — The Biography of Buffalo Jones.* Andre Deitsch, London, 1964.

Edmonds, Margot and Ella F. Clark. *Voices of the Winds.* Facts on File, Inc., New York, 1989.

Endangered Wildlife of the World, Vol. 1. Michael Cavendish Corporation, North Bellmore, NY, 1993.

Erdoes, Richard and Alfonso Ortiz. *American Indian Myths and Legends.* Pantheon Books, New York, 1980.

Erickson, Jon. *Ice Ages — Past and Future.* Tab Books, Blue Ridge Summit, PA, 1990.

Flerow, C. C. "On the Origin of the Mammalian Fauna of Canada." Paleontological Institute, Academy of Sciences of the USSR. In *The Bering Land Bridge*, edited by David M. Hopkins, 271–280. Stanford University Press, Stanford, CA, 1967.

Flores, Dan. "Bison Ecology and Bison Diplomacy: The Southern Plains from 1800 to 1850." *The Journal of American History*, No. 78, September, 1991, 465–485.

Force, Roland W. and Maryanne Tefft Force. *The American Indians*. Chelsea House Publishers, New York, 1991.

Foster, John E. "The Metis and the End of the Plains Buffalo in Alberta." In *The Buffalo*, edited by John E. Foster, Dick Harrison, and I. S. MacLaren, 61–77. The University of Alberta Press, 1992.

Froncek, Thomas, ed. *Voices from the Wilderness — The Frontiersman's Own Story*. McGraw-Hill, New York, 1974.

Gard, Wayne. *The Great Buffalo Hunt*. Alfred A. Knopf, New York, 1960.

Garretson, Martin S. *The American Bison*. New York Zoological Society, New York, 1938.

Gates, C., T. Chowns, and H. Reynolds. "Wood Buffalo at the Crossroads." In *The Buffalo*, edited by John E. Foster, Dick Harrison, and I. S. MacLaren, 139–165. The University of Alberta Press, 1992.

Gregg, Josiah. *Commerce of the Prairies, Volumes I and II*. Reprint of the 1844 publication *Commerce of the Prairies: or the Journal of a Santa Fe Trader*. Volume I, Great Americana, Readex Microprint. Volume II, March of America Facsimile Series No. 71, Ann Arbor, 1966. Reprint of the 1844 publication, edited by Milo Milton Quaife, The Citadel Press, NY, 1968.

Grinnell, George Bird. "The Last of the Buffalo." *Scribner's Magazine*, Vol. 12, No. 3, September 1892, 267–286.

Guthrie, Russell Dale. *Frozen Fauna of the Mammoth Steppe — The Story of Blue Babe*. University of Chicago Press, Chicago, 1990.

Haines, Francis. *The Buffalo*. Thomas Y. Crowell Company, New York, 1970.

Halloran, Arthur F. "The American Bison, or Buffalo." In *Alive in the Wild*, edited by Victor H. Cahalane, 472–477. Prentice-Hall, Inc., Englewood Cliffs, NJ, 1970.

Hamilton, William Thomas. *My Sixty Years on the Plains*. Time-Life Books, Inc., Alexandria, VA, 1982. Reprinting of the 1905 publication, edited by E. T. Sieber, Forest and Stream Publishing Co., New York.

Harmon, George Dewey. *Sixty Years of Indian Affairs.* University of North Carolina Press, Chapel Hill, 1941.

Harris, Marvin. *The Sacred Cow and the Abominable Pig.* Simon and Schuster, New York, 1985.

Heckert, Mark. "The International Bison Cooperative." In the published proceedings of the North American Public Bison Herds Symposium, July 27–29, 1993, Lacrosse, WI, assembled and compiled by Ronald E. Walker, 181–186, Custer State Park, SD, 1993.

Hennepin, Louis. *A Description of Louisiana.* Translation of the Hennepin edition of 1683 by John Gilmary Shea. John G. Shea, New York, 1880.

Hill, J. L. *The Passing of the Indian and Buffalo.* George W. Moyle, Long Beach, CA, 1917.

Hopkins, David M. Hopkins. "The Cenozoic History of Beringia — A Synthesis." U.S. Geological Survey, Menlo Park, California. In *The Bering Land Bridge,* edited by David M. Hopkins, 451–484. Stanford University Press, Stanford, CA, 1967.

Hornaday, William T. "The Extermination of the American Bison, with a Sketch of Its Discovery and Life History." *Report of the U.S. National Museum,* 1887, 367–548.

Hoyle, Fred. *Ice — The Ultimate Human Catastrophe.* The Continuum Publishing Company, New York, 1981.

Hunter, John Dunn. *Memoirs of a Captivity Among the Indians of North America (1824).* Edited by Richard Drinnon. Schocken Books, New York, 1973.

Inman, Colonel Henry. *Buffalo Jones' Adventures on the Plains.* [Crane and Co., 1899] University of Nebraska Press, Lincoln, 1970.

———, with "Buffalo Bill" Cody. *The Old Santa Fe Trail: The Story of a Great Highway.* 1898. Reprint of chapter on "The Buffalo," Outbooks, Olympic Valley, CA, 1977.

Irving, Washington. *A Tour on the Prairies.* Time-Life Books, Inc., Alexandria, VA, 1983. Reprinting of the 1835 edition, John Murray, London.

———. *Astoria.* Carey Lea and Blanchard, Philadelphia, 1836.

———. *Adventures of Captain Bonneville, U.S.A. in the Rocky Mountains and the Far West.* Carey Lea & Blanchard, Philadelphia, 1837. Also Richard Bently, London, 1837.

James, Edwin. *Account of an Expedition from Pittsburgh to the Rocky Mountains, Volumes I and II.* Reprinting of the 1823 publication. March of America Facsimile Series No 65, University Microfilms, Inc., Ann Arbor, 1966. Also Fulcrum, Inc., editor Maxine Benson, Golden, CO, 1988.

Johnson, Dorothy M. *The Bloody Bozeman.* McGraw Hill, New York, 1971.

Josephy, Alvin M., Jr. *Now That the Buffalo's Gone.* Alfred A. Knopf, New York, 1982.

Joutel, Henri. *The Last Voyage Performed by de la Sale.* Reprinting of the 1713 English translation of the French publication *A Journal of the Last Voyage Perform'd by Monsr. de la Sale, To the Gulph of Mexico, To find out the Mouth of the Mississippi River.* March of America Facsimile Series No. 31, University Microfilms, Inc., Ann Arbor, 1966.

Keith, Elmer. *Elmer Keith's Big Game Hunting.* Little Brown and Company, Boston, 1948.

Kreyche, Gerald F. *Visions of the American West.* The University Press of Kentucky, Lexington, 1989.

Kurten, Bjorn. *The Ice Age.* G.P. Putnam's Sons, New York, 1972.

———. *Before the Indians.* Columbia University Press, New York, 1988.

Laughlin, W. S. "Human Migration and Permanent Occupation in the Bering Sea Area." University of Wisconsin. In *The Bering Land Bridge,* edited by David M. Hopkins, 409–450. Stanford University Press, Stanford, CA, 1967.

Lee, Raymond. "History and Management of Arizona's Bison." In the published proceedings of the North American Public Bison Herds Symposium, July 27–29, 1993, Lacrosse, WI, assembled and compiled by Ronald E. Walker, 181–186, Custer State Park, SD, 1993.

Lee, Wayne C. *Scotty Philip, the Man Who Saved the Buffalo.* Caxton Printers, Ltd., Caldwell, ID, 1975.

Lewis, Meriwether and William Clarke (Clark). *History of the Expedition Under the Command of Captains Lewis & Clarke* (a complete reprint of the Nicholas Biddle, 1814 edition, 3 vols.). Allerton Book Company, New York, 1922.

Lopez, Barry Holstun. *Of Wolves and Men.* Charles Scribner's Sons, New York, 1978.

Mails, Thomas E. *The Mystic Warriors of the Plains*. Doubleday and Company, Garden City, New York, 1972.

Marquette, Jacques. *Voyages of Marguette*. Reprinting of the 1900 English translation of the 1681 French printing of the 1673 journals attributed to Marquette, and edited by Pere Dablon. March of America Facsimile Series No. 28, University Microfilms, Inc., Ann Arbor, 1966.

Marriott, Alice and Carol K. Rachlin. *American Indian Mythology*. Thomas Y. Crowell Company, New York, 1968.

Martin, Paul S. "Quaternary Extinctions, a Prehistoric Revolution." In *The Discovery of America*, edited by Paul S. Martin and R. G. Klein, 892–969. University of Arizona Press, Tucson, 1973.

Mattes, Merrill J. *The Great Platte River Road*. Nebraska State Historical Society, Lincoln, 1969.

Mayer, Frank H. and Charles B. Roth. *The Buffalo Harvest*. Sage Books, Denver, 1958.

McCreight, M. I. *Buffalo Bone Days*. Published by the author (Nupp Printing Co.), Dubois, PA, 1939.

McDonald, Jerry N. *North American Bison: Their Classification and Evolution*. University of California Press, Berkeley, 1981.

McHugh, Tom. *The Time of the Buffalo*. Alfred A. Knopf, New York, 1972.

Mead, James R. *Hunting and Trading on the Great Plains, 1859–1875*. Edited by Schuyler Jones. University of Oklahoma Press, Norman, 1986.

Meagher, Margaret Mary. *The Bison of Yellowstone National Park*. Government Printing Office, Washington, D.C., 1973.

———. "Bison in the Greater Yellowstone." In the published proceedings of the North American Public Bison Herds Symposium, July 27–29, 1993, Lacrosse, WI, assembled and compiled by Ronald E. Walker, 384–391, Custer State Park, SD, 1993.

Meriwether, David. *My Life in the Mountains and on the Plains*. University of Oklahoma Press, Norman, 1965.

Meyer, Margaret E. and Mary Meagher. "Brucella Abortus Infection in the Yellowstone National Park Free Ranging Bison Herd." In the published proceedings of the North American Public Bison Herds Symposium, July 27–29, 1993, Lacrosse, WI, assembled and compiled by Ronald E. Walker, 362–373, Custer State Park, SD, 1993.

Michelson, Truman. *Notes on the Buffalo-Head Dance of the Thunder Gens of the Fox Indians.* Smithsonian Institution, Bureau of American Ethnology, Bulletin 87. U.S. Government Printing Office, Washington, 1928.

Mooney, James. "The Ghost-Dance Religion and the Sioux Outbreak of 1890." *Fourteenth Annual Report of the United States Bureau of Ethnology,* 1892–1893, part 2, 641–1136. U.S. Government Printing Office, Washington D.C., 1896.

Muhlstein, Anka. *La Salle — Explorer of the North American Frontier.* Translated from the 1992 French edition by Willard Wood. Arcade Publishing, New York, 1994.

Muller-Beck, Hansjurgen. "On Migrations of Hunters Across the Bering Land Bridge in the Upper Pleistocene." University of Freiburg, Germany. In *The Bering Land Bridge,* edited by David M. Hopkins, 373–408. Stanford University Press, Stanford, CA, 1967.

Nowak, Ronald M. and John L. Paradiso. *Walker's Mammals of the World.* 4th ed. vol. II. Johns Hopkins University Press, 1983, Baltimore (previous editions 1964, 1968, 1975, 1983).

Palmer, Rose A. *The North American Indians.* The Smithsonian Series, Vol. 4, Editor-in-Chief, Charles Greely Abbot. New York, 1944.

Pielou, E. C. *After the Ice Age.* University of Chicago Press, Chicago, 1991.

Pike, Zebulon Montgomery. *Sources of the Mississippi and the Western Louisiana Territory.* Reprinting of the 1810 publication *An Account Of Expeditions To The Sources of the Mississippi, And Through The Western Parts of Louisiana, To The Sources of the Arkansaw, Kans, La Platte, and Pierre Jaun Rivers, and a Tour Through The Interior Parts Of New Spain.* March of America Facsimile Series No. 57, University Microfilms, Inc., Ann Arbor, 1966.

Popper, Deborah Epstein and Frank J. Popper. "The Great Plains: From Dust to Dust," *Planning* 53, December 1987, 12–18.

Reed, Erik K. "Bison Beyond the Pecos." *Texas Journal of Science,* June 1955, 130–135.

Repenning, Charles A. "Paleartic-Neartic Mammalian Dispersal in the Late Cenozoic." U.S. Geological Survey, Menlo Park, California. In *The Bering Land Bridge,* edited by David M. Hopkins, 288–311. Stanford University Press, Stanford, CA, 1967.

Roe, Frank Gilbert. *The North American Buffalo: A Critical Study of the Species in Its Wild State.* University of Toronto Press, Toronto, Canada, 1972.

Rorabacher, J. Albert. *The American Buffalo in Transition: A Historical and Economic Survey of the Bison in America.* North Star Press, Saint Cloud, MN, 1970.

Sandoz, Mari. *The Buffalo Hunters — The Story of the Hide Men.* Hastings House, New York, 1954.

———. *Old Jules Country.* Hastings House, New York, 1965.

Schneider, Stephen H. and Randi Londer. *The Coevolution of Climate and Life.* Sierra Book Clubs, San Francisco, 1984.

Schullery, Paul, ed., *American Bears — Selections from the Writings of Theodore Roosevelt.* Colorado Associated University Press, Boulder, CO, 1983.

Seton, Ernest Thompson. *Lives of Game Animals.* 4 vols. Doubleday, Doran & Co., Garden City, NY, 1926–1929.

Shaw, James H. "American Bison: A Case Study in Conservation Genetics." In the published proceedings of the North American Public Bison Herds Symposium, July 27–29, 1993, Lacrosse, WI, assembled and compiled by Ronald E. Walker, 3–14, Custer State Park, SD, 1993.

Shields, G. O., ed. *The Big Game of North America.* Rand, McNally and Company, New York, 1890.

Shoemaker, H. W. *A Pennsylvania Bison Hunt.* Middleburg Post Press, Middleburg, PA, 1915.

———. *Extinct Pennsylvania Animals, Part II.* Altoona Tribune Company, Altoona, PA, 1919.

Spencer, Oliver M. *Indian Captivity.* Reprinting of the 1835 publication *Indian Captivity: A True Narrative of the Capture of the Rev. O. M. Spencer.* March of America Facsimile Series No. 53, University Microfilms, Inc., Ann Arbor, 1966.

Sutcliffe, Anthony J. *On the Track of Ice Age Mammals.* Harvard University Press, Cambridge, MA, 1985.

Thwaites, Reuben Gold., ed. *Early Western Travels.* Vols. I–XXX. AMS Press, Inc., New York, 1966.

Townsend, John K. *Journey Across the Rocky Mountains to the Columbia River.* Henry Perkins, Philadelphia, 1839. *Early Western Travels, 1748–1846,*

Vol. 21, "Townsend's Narrative (1833–1834)," edited by Reuben Gold Thwaites. AMS Press, Inc., New York, 1966.

Tudge, Colin. *Last Animals at the Zoo.* Island Press, Washington, D.C., 1992.

Van Every, Dale. *The Final Challenge — The American Frontier, 1804–1845.* William Morrow and Company, New York, 1964.

Vangengeim, E. A. "The Effect of the Bering Land Bridge on the Quaternary Mammalian Faunas of Siberia and North America." Geological Institute, Academy of Sciences of the USSR. In *The Bering Land Bridge,* edited by David M. Hopkins, 281–287. Stanford University Press, Stanford, CA, 1967.

Wagner, Frederick H., Ronald Foresta, R. Bruce Gill, Dale R. McCullough, Michael R. Pelton, William F. Porter, Hal Salwasser, and Joseph L. Sax. *Wildlife Policies in the National Parks.* Island Press, Washington, D.C., 1995.

Webb, Walter Prescott. *The Great Plains.* Grosset & Dunlap, New York, 1931.

Whittlesey, Lee H. *Death in Yellowstone — Accidents and Foolhardiness in the First National Park.* Roberts Rinehart, Boulder, CO, 1995.

Wissler, Clark. *Indians of the United States.* Doubleday, Doran & Co., Inc., New York, 1940.

Wuerthner, George. "The Battle over Bison." *National Parks,* November/December 1995, 36–40.

Young, Stanley P., and Edward A. Goldman. *The Puma: Mysterious American Cat.* The American Wildlife Institute, Washington D.C., 1946.

Index

Pages with photos appear in italics.